Gift of
Jason Zweig

HENRY CLAY FRICK

THE MAN

© *Portrait by Elizabeth Shoumatoff*

HENRY CLAY FRICK

Henry Clay Frick

THE MAN

BY

GEORGE HARVEY

PRIVATELY PRINTED

1936

COPYRIGHT, 1928, BY CHARLES SCRIBNER'S SONS

Contents

		PAGE
I.	ANCESTRY	1
II.	BOYHOOD	12
III.	BEGINNING BUSINESS IN COKE	29
IV.	A TRIUMPH OF FAITH AND COURAGE	44
V.	INTERLUDE	67
VI.	ENTER THE CARNEGIES	76
VII.	"THE MAN" IN STEEL	93
VIII.	HOMESTEAD	106
IX.	THE STATE INTERVENES	124
X.	ATTEMPTED ASSASSINATION	136
XI.	POLITICS	146
XII.	"THE LAIRD" AND "THE MAN"	160
XIII.	VICTORY'S COST AND GAIN	175
XIV.	OLIVER AND FRICK	187
XV.	NEGOTIATIONS	200
XVI.	MR. FRICK RECEIVES HIS RESIGNATION	218
XVII.	THE FINAL DRAMATIC BREAK	227
XVIII.	MR. FRICK WINS HIS FIGHT	237
XIX.	THE UNITED STATES STEEL CORPORATION	258
XX.	A CAPITALIST	269
XXI.	PUBLIC AFFAIRS	289
XXII.	THE PATRIOT	313
XXIII.	AN ART COLLECTOR	331
XXIV.	BENEFACTIONS AND BEQUESTS	344
XXV.	PERSONALITY	356

HENRY CLAY FRICK

THE MAN

HENRY CLAY FRICK
THE MAN

I
Ancestry

THE American progenitors of Henry Clay Frick were JOHANN NICHOLAS FRICK and MARTIN OVERHOLT who followed William Penn from the continent of Europe in search of religious freedom and personal opportunity. Frick came from Switzerland and Overholt from the Palatinate on the Rhine. Both sailed from Rotterdam and landed in Philadelphia but they were only nominally contemporaneous. Martin arrived about 1732 and died in 1744. Johann came in 1767 and lived till 1786. Henry Clay was of the fourth generation succeeding his two great-great-grandfathers.

The Swiss family Frick, of Celtic-Burgundian origin, is very old; that is to say, it sprang into prominence and gave name to a village in the Sisseln-Thal nearly four hundred years before Columbus discovered America and it holds authenticated records of unbroken lineage from 1113 to the present day.

Among the adventurous members of the family who immigrated to America, following Conrad who led the van in 1732, was JOHANN NICHOLAS, who proceeded forthwith to Germantown, the rallying point of colonists from Switzerland and the Palatinate, where he found descend-

Frick the Man

ants of Conrad, and of nine others of the name who had arrived between the years 1732 and 1755.

The pioneering spirit naturally dominated newcomers from the old world bent upon acquisition of fertile lands in fresh territory and the trend necessarily was to the West. Already John, the eldest son of Conrad, had pushed on as far as the Susquehanna valley and established a prolific branch of the family in Lancaster. Others were gazing longingly toward the Alleghenies and avid for information concerning the vast country beyond when the patriots of Philadelphia and all the country round were thrilled by the sound of the big bell proclaiming the Declaration of Independence.

One of the first orders issued by the Continental Congress was addressed to the Scotch and Irish settlers of Western Pennsylvania to prepare immediately to protect the region from attacks anticipated by way of Lake Erie from the British and the Iroquois. The frontiersmen of the Youghiogheny and Monongahela valleys were not only willing but ready. They had been fighting Indians and Virginians all their lives and "every cabin contained a Bible, a rifle and a whiskey jug."

The famous Eighth Pennsylvania regiment, comprising seven companies from Old Westmoreland and one from Bedford County, was the first organized, with Colonel Aeneas Mackay in command, and was encamped at Kittanning arranging, under orders from Headquarters, to proceed up the Allegheny and build forts at Leboeuf and Erie, when a cry for help came from the East. The British were chasing General Washington across New

Ancestry

Jersey, Philadelphia was imperilled, the American cause seemed to be doomed and urgent calls for aid were issued to all the colonies. Of the commands summoned the Eighth Pennsylvania was the most distant and confronted by the greatest obstacles. Neither officers nor men had tents or uniforms or heavy clothing of any kind, flour alone was available for food, and cooking utensils comprised only pots and pans from farmhouses.

But there was no hesitation on the part of the men of Westmoreland and Bedford. Leaving their families virtually unprotected from impending attacks by savages and facing three hundred miles of mountain roads and trails, of which more than one-third were hidden by deep snows, they set forth upon a march unequalled in severity, except possibly by that of Benedict Arnold through the Maine woods, in the seven years of warfare.

At the end of nearly two months of toil and sufferings, worn to their very bones, footsore and starving, the survivors limped into a wretched camp near Philadelphia, only to learn that the battles of Trenton and Princeton had been fought and won and that they must hasten forward to join General Wayne's division in New Jersey.

One-third of the entire command, of whom fifty died in a few days, were so ill that they were left behind in Philadelphia and Germantown, and it was from these strange visitors that the sympathetic colonists from Switzerland and the Palatinate heard glowing descriptions of the fertile Youghiogheny valley.

Among the first to seek the promising land was JOHANN NICHOLAS FRICK who crossed the mountains with his

Frick the Man

family in a covered wagon as soon as peace was assured by the surrender of Cornwallis at Yorktown and settled at Port Royal, Westmoreland County, where he died in 1786. He was succeeded by his son GEORGE who remained on the farm until 1804, when he took a boatload of flour and whiskey down the Ohio and Mississippi rivers to New Orleans where he died of malarial fever. Of the nine children whom he left behind DANIEL was born in 1796, lived successively on farms near Port Royal, Adamsburg and Irwin, moving finally in 1849 to Van Buren, Ohio, where he died in 1855 and was buried first in Van Buren, then in Wooster, nearby. He married Catherine Miller, a smart, redhaired Irish girl, in 1818 and, following her death in 1838, Matilda J. Martin, each of whom presented him with nine children.

JOHN W. FRICK, Daniel's eldest son, born in Adamsburg in 1822, married ELIZABETH, daughter of Abraham Overholt of West Overton, Westmoreland County, in 1847, resided in that vicinity till 1880, when he moved to Wooster, where he died eight years later.

MARTIN OVERHOLT, born in the Rhenish Palatinate in 1709, was one of the thousands who were compelled by religious persecutions and the virulence of Franco-German warfare to forsake their native land in the early part of the 18th century. The exact date of his arrival is not known but it must have occurred soon after he attained his majority, in 1730. That he accompanied his fellow refugees to the recognized meeting place at Germantown may safely be assumed, but presently he passed on to Bucks County on the Delaware, acquired a farm appar-

Ancestry

ently by lease in Bedminster township, married in 1736, died in 1744 in his thirty-sixth year and was buried in the Mennonite graveyard, leaving a son, HENRY, born in 1739.

Subsequently Martin's widow was induced to become the third and last wife of William Nash, a pioneer, who made a will on November 18th, 1760, bequeathing to her "the stone end of my dwelling house for her to live in, as also 2 cows, and a young horse, with a sufficiency of hay yearly to fodder said creatures, with four sheep and sufficiency of hay yearly to fodder said sheep, as also my Sd wife's saddle she is to possess and enjoy."

The pioneer died the very next month and the cows gave so much milk and the sheep furnished so much wool, and both increased so greatly in numbers that only two years later "Augnis," as her second husband designated her in his will, was able to acquire the entire farm of 175 acres and 4 perches adjoining the graveyard for conveyance to her son, before she died in 1786, in consideration of "£357, 17 shillings and 2 pense."

Meanwhile, i.e., in 1765, Henry brought to the fine "Overholt Homestead" as his bride ANNA BEITLER, who kept the cradle rocking till 1789, when Susanna, the twelfth and last occupant, was born.

The Mennonites, like the Quakers, were pacifists by religion but patriots by nature, and were untroubled by conscientious scruples when it became necessary to fight for the freedom which they had crossed the ocean to win. Immediately upon the outbreak of the Revolution they organized the Bucks County militia and Henry

Frick the Man

Overholt was one of the first to join. He served throughout the war and, like his friends in Germantown, listened eagerly to the tales of the gallant soldiers from the West as they paused for rest and refreshment in Bedminster on their way to and from New Jersey. That he was no less keen than Johann Nicholas Frick to seek the wide spaces beyond the mountains upon the cessation of hostilities may well be believed, in the light of his subsequent adventure, but in 1783 his mother was too old and his eight children were too young to justify so hazardous an enterprise.

When the new century dawned Henry Overholt and his good wife Anna, aged respectively sixty-one and fifty-five, were rich in spirit and in health, in lands and in buildings, in cattle and in sheep and most joyously in sons and daughters, of whom six were already mated and four were single, including Henry, aged 21; Abraham, 16; Christian, 14; and little Susanna, 11. Only one, Sarah, who died in infancy, was missing.

Then it was that Henry Overholt, yielding to the increasing urge of the time and his long repressed inclination, sold the famous "homestead" for the handsome sum of "£1500, gold and silver money" and, loading his entire family, comprising his wife, five sons, six daughters, five sons-in-law, two daughters-in-law and thirteen grandchildren, thirty-three in all, along with a great quantity of goods and chattels, upon a string of covered wagons, set forth upon his long journey. The roads were uniformly bad, the mountains high and steep, the fords deep from swollen streams, the oxen slow and the dis-

Ancestry

tance quite three hundred miles, but the days were so sunny and the nights so cool that the hardy party reached its destination, "all safe and sound," in the Summer of 1800.

They found a rolling country surpassing their most hopeful expectations, well wooded and watered, suitably apportioned between rich meadows and green pastures and, best of all, so sparsely populated that desirable tracts of land could be acquired for small sums. The father of the flock bought several hundred acres in East Huntingdon township and built upon a hill in what afterwards became the village of West Overton a second "Overholt Homestead," even larger and more imposing than that which he had left. The married sons and daughters "colonized" roundaboutly on farms of their own.

ABRAHAM, then in his seventeenth year, was one of the three sons who remained at home. He had learned the weavers' craft in Bedminster and, while his brothers were clearing the land, he worked at the loom fabricating cloth for the clan until 1809. He then married MARIA, daughter of the Rev. Abraham Stauffer and granddaughter of the Rev. John Stauffer, both of whom had served in the Revolutionary War as members of the Lancaster militia, and purchased in partnership with his brother Christian, who had married his wife's sister Elizabeth, an interest in the homestead farm.

When the pioneer Henry Overholt died in 1813, Abraham came into possession of the entire farm and his mother continued her residence in the big house until her death in 1835.

Frick the Man

The portion of the farm which Abraham bought from Christian, one hundred and fifty acres at fifty dollars an acre, then considered a high price, included, in common with nearly all similar properties in the region, a small log distillery, which became the basis of the largest fortune in that section of the country. Promptly increasing the capacity of the still from three bushels to fifty bushels of grain a day, the new proprietor developed and expanded the business until, in 1859, the daily grain capacity of a big new factory, one hundred by sixty-three feet and six stories in height, reached two hundred bushels and the daily output of flour exceeded fifty barrels. The "Overholt" brand of whiskey became famous for its strength and purity and it is said that for years before he died, leaving a fortune of half a million dollars, the chief business pride of its originator, second only to the quality of his product, lay in the fact that the supply never equalled the demand.

But Abraham Overholt did not submerge himself in manufacturing. He discovered the coal whose subsequent mining and baking by his grandson produced directly one, and indirectly through application to steel fabrication many, of the greatest fortunes of America. His distinguishing traits in business were absolute integrity, straightforwardness, fairness, liberality, order, punctuality and consideration for the welfare of his employés. He never held public office but he took a deep interest in affairs and rendered signal service in helping to establish a common school system of the best type.

Originally a strong supporter of Jackson in national

Ancestry

politics, he balked at Van Buren and acted with the Whigs until the Republican party was organized, when he became an ardent supporter of Lincoln. Although nearly eighty years old during the Civil War, he strove incessantly to encourage enlistments and frequently visited the soldiers from Westmoreland County in the field.

A staunch Mennonite in religion, he attended church regularly on horseback with his devout wife and frequently permitted divine services to be held in his house, although he was prevented by diffidence and reticence from performing his allotted task as lay preacher, and it is recorded that he risked the penalty of excommunication by flatly refusing to observe the feet-washing regulation of the sect.

His personal appearance was impressive. Tall, straight, courtly and benign, clad invariably except when at work in broadcloth and a black tie relieved by a pearl stud, with a glossy wide-brimmed silk hat on his head and a gold-headed cane in his hand, he must have looked a somewhat austere figure, and yet his true nature was so well understood that, greatly to his own satisfaction, he was addressed by men, women and children alike as "Grandpap Overholt," truly an authentic type of the democratic lords to the manner born of his day and generation in the United States.

Abraham was well mated. All contemporaries agree that MARIA STAUFFER OVERHOLT was an admirable representative of the fine womanhood of her time, naturally intelligent, well educated, kindly but firm in her domestic relations, a helpful neighbor, a faithful friend

Frick the Man

and "the best housekeeper in the world." Her costumes befitted her position and, like her husband's, conformed strictly to the fashions of the time, black or "ashes of the rose" cashmere with white lace at the neck, caps of exquisite bobbinet lace tied with white linen strings, and for church a black debage bonnet and a silk cape trimmed with velvet.

The bearing of each to the other was invariably most respectful and if ever a disagreement marked the entire sixty years of their married life, no indication of the circumstance reached the attention of any one of their eight children.

ELIZABETH, the fifth child, was born in 1819 and remained at home until she was twenty-eight years old, when she accepted a proposal of marriage from JOHN W. FRICK. It was a common surmise in the community at the time that Elizabeth's parents would have preferred a more sedate and better established suitor than the impetuous, red-headed scion of the Celts and Burgundians, but as there was no withstanding her calm inflexibility, the wedding took place at the homestead on October 9th, 1847, and presently the little Spring House at the foot of the lawn, denuded of its pans of milk, jars of butter and preserves, crates of cheese, apples and plums, was assigned to the couple for temporary occupancy.

It was a unique abode, solidly built of stone, comprising three snug rooms; protected from gales in Winter by walls eighteen inches thick, and warmed by a huge fireplace containing serviceable ovens; cooled in Summer by pipes of running water, and furnished with bright red

Ancestry

carpets for the floors, blue china and steel knives and forks for the table; a small book case for the living room, a grandfather's clock, with works of wood, from Connecticut, and other paraphernalia of the period.

Here, following a girl baby born in the big house and called Maria for her Grandmother Overholt, a son was born on December 19th, 1849, and named, for the leader of the Whig Party to which all the Fricks and all the Overholts then adhered, HENRY CLAY FRICK.

II

Boyhood

CLAY FRICK, as he was called by his schoolmates and the neighbors, was an attractive lad. Slight and frail from his birth, his physical growth in childhood was slow and intermittently painful. While during this period there seems to have been no doubt in the minds of his parents and grandparents that he would attain manhood, they realized that his first few years would require most tender care, and he was seldom out of the sight of his watchful mother or grandmother while toddling back and forth between the tiny Spring House and the mansion towering above it across the lawn.

They regarded him as "delicate" rather than "sickly" and, although occasional manifestations of suffering impelled his mother to cover his stomach with foolscap paper, they felt no real apprehension until his father took him, at the age of six, on his first long journey to see his Grandfather Frick in Van Buren, Ohio, where he succumbed to the hardships of travel and developed a fever which compelled his retention for more than two months.

From the organic ailment, then first clearly revealed and subsequently diagnosed as "chronic indigestion" or as "inflammatory rheumatism," he was never thereafter

Boyhood

wholly free. During the period of his most strenuous activities it was not unusual for him, upon returning home from his office, to drop upon a sofa and suffer grievously until the prescribed restoratives, always at hand to be administered promptly, could bring relief. It was such an attack of exceptional virulence, involving deadly pressure upon a weakened heart, that immediately preceded his fatal illness.

Clay passed perceptibly from childhood into boyhood at the age of eight when, having regained his normal strength, he began to do chores on his father's farm and to attend the Independent School near West Overton during the winter months, when only he could be spared.

It was a memorable day in the records of the Frick family when the eager-eyed lad set forth from the Bixler farm, owned by his grandfather and then occupied by his parents, to seek an education. No more than acquaintance with the custom of the time is required to visualize accurately the pretty picture, typical of American pastoral life, when, scrubbed and brushed, in a brand new suit of store clothes and brass knobbed shoes, holding fast to his mother's hand, he awaited impatiently in the doorway the arrival of his cousin Isaac Overholt to escort him to school. And no less clearly can the mind's eye dwell with smiling sympathy upon the fair countenance of the proud daughter of Abraham Overholt as with hands folded, following a final pat upon his head, she watched her man-child march primly forward to take his place in the busy world.

Schoolmaster Voight greeted the little chap with a

Frick the Man

low bow and, taking him by the hand, led him upon the stage and announced impressively to the boys and girls:

"I present to you Mr. Henry Clay Frick."

The abashed recipient of this unusual honor, manfully overcoming an inclination to burst into tears, finally contrived to make a bow so like the schoolmaster's own that his quick movement to a bench was made to the music of loud cheers and gales of friendly laughter.

Recalling the episode years afterward, Mr. Voight said that he could account for his own unpremeditated and unprecedented act only as purely intuitive recognition of one who was to become his most illustrious pupil.

The school room was typical of the period, bare and cheerless but fairly well lighted and usually overheated from a woodburning stove. The pupils sat at desks upon benches without backs and the teacher watched them from a platform, surmounted in the rear by a blackboard whose glossy surface was relieved by an ominous ornament in the shape of a hickory stick showing signs of frequent usage. The curriculum comprised the familiar three R's, slightly amplified, the books allotted being McGuffey's reader, Pinneo's grammar, Mitchell's geography and Ray's arithmetic.

Clay attended the Independent School two terms, in 1857 and 1858; the Alverton, originally a Mennonite, School one term in 1859; the West Overton School "on the hill" two terms in 1860 and 1861; the "Western Pennsylvania Classical and Scientific Institute," Westmoreland College for short, in Mt. Pleasant, two terms in the Winter of 1864 and the Spring of 1865; and Otter-

Boyhood

bein College in Westerville, Ohio, ten weeks in the Autumn of 1866; thus acquiring his entire stock of educational training from five terms in primary schools and less than three terms in those of higher grades; comprising altogether approximately thirty months of tuition; and ending, happily for his ambitious and impatient spirit at the age of seventeen, in 1866.

The vividness with which his schoolmates, now well past the period of human existence allotted by the Scriptures, and generally maintained as a basis of calculation until recently extended by Science, recall circumstances and trivial episodes of sixty years ago clearly evidences that there was nothing commonplace in the youth's composition. Distinctive individual traits, whose subsequent development through his own endeavors marked his career, found early expression.

Chief among these was a veritable passion for concentration in the attainment of a specific purpose.

Apparently he was not averse to acquirement of the "general education" which those primitive schools were designed to provide; but his interest seems to have been only sufficient to avoid black marks for enforced exhibition at home, his attention was correspondingly casual, and he is remembered as no more than "an average scholar," except in one respect: He was "splendid in arithmetic," he "excelled us all, older or younger, in mathematics," he was determined to get "a good business training;" and time for diversion from that definite aim could not be spared.

That this rigid exclusion was attributable to the rea-

Frick the Man

soning of a lad not yet in his teens is hardly imaginable; inherited instinct may have exerted some influence, but environment undoubtedly played the controlling part. Born and reared in the long shadow of his distinguished grandfather, he could see but one glowing example worthy of emulation, and while very young he confided to his mates a determination to achieve success even greater than that won by the notable progenitor whose blood coursed through his own veins. If a fortune of half a million could be acquired by an Overholt of the preceding generation, there was "no reason" why, with wider opportunities, one of a million should not be gained by that Overholt's grandson, "and I propose to be worth that before I die," not only bespoke his own full faith in his ability to realize his ambition but was so convincing to the minds of his boy companions that half a century later they separately recalled his very words.

It is not surprising that the impressions still retained by the hair-braided pupils who, conformably to custom, sat on the other side of the aisle, are equally distinct, as he was a familiar figure in the village streets while still the brown curls nestled about his head or glistened in the breezes incited by the rapid movement of his grandfather's light-stepping span and glossy buggy.

"They made a very pretty pair when they came to town, the one so fresh and young, the other old and gray and very dignified, with little Clay always driving the team of one bay and one gray, except just after he had typhoid fever when of course he wasn't strong enough to guide them."

Boyhood

One can readily believe that when, even at the relatively advanced age of eight, the boy first faced a battery of girlish glances, following his teacher's overpowering introduction, and later broke down completely when he made a desperate effort to recite "Twinkle, twinkle, little star," the hot blood flew to his face. But it is not recorded that the girls laughed derisively even when the little star abruptly rejected the beseeching appeal. Here was the scion of Quality and Family, the pride of their own recognized magnate, prospective heir to wealth and position, born to the manner, bred by gentlewomen, and himself "the most perfect little gentleman I ever met," surely one not to be ignored or held unkindly by girlish fancies.

Nor was the lad's attractiveness merely superficial. Upon acquaintance he was found to be "pure in thought as well as in speech, never uttering a coarse word, never guilty of a rude act and always as polite to little girls as to older people," chivalrous, too, and notably protective of his own. "I remember that one time his distant cousin Susan was not getting along very well in her studies. The teacher was provoked at her, and he warned her that if she didn't do better he would have to give her a dose of 'hickory oil,' as a whipping was called in those days. When Clay heard this he was angry clear through. He was hardly more than a boy, but he served notice on the teacher that if he whipped his cousin Susan he would whip the teacher. And Susan didn't get whipped."

It is not surprising that so thrilling an episode should have stamped an indelible impression upon the sensitive

Frick the Man

mind of the narrator. Nor is there occasion to question the accuracy of her recollection. One's imagination can readily portray the impetuous young descendant of the fiery Fricks and the stern Overholts, with eyes flashing and fists clenched, hurling defiance and menace at the most burly of pedagogues in a crisis such as that depicted. Nevertheless, without minimizing in the slightest degree the fearlessness and gallantry of the young knight, it is highly improbable that the teacher was really deterred by his threatened reprisal. Hints at terrifying possibilities may have been permissible, but even in those days of salutary physical penalties there is no tradition of a custom justifying the actual whipping of girls by schoolmasters; so it is a fair assumption that Susan's danger was more apparent to the pupils than real to the mind of the teacher, who alone in this instance seems to have been humiliated.

Young Clay was less fortunate. Solomon's famous admonition was held to apply to boys in school even more rigorously than at home, where maternal intervention was feasible and not uncommon. "The teachers, who were always men, were very strict and would stand no monkey business. Most of us got lickings occasionally and, as I remember, Clay had his share, though I cannot recall the reasons, probably just mischief or maybe because he wouldn't study what he didn't like, though I never knew a fellow so eager to get on, and when he set out to do a thing he always did it, which I think was the secret of his success all through life."

Finally, we are told, he was "full of antics but never

Boyhood

a rowdy, though his quick temper got him into many a fight and he would tackle anybody who he thought wasn't playing fair with him."

Very early in life he began to demand for himself "the best there is," and would be satisfied with nothing less. Frankly disdaining the part-shoddy and ill-fitting garments commonly allotted to farmers' sons, he declared at the age of fifteen that thereafter he would clothe himself, and he kept his word despite the difficulty of earning enough money to buy "the best." Appearing one morning "in a pair of black boots, with yellow stitching, that had cost sixteen dollars," his extravagance was duly noted, but he smiled contentedly and "every morning they shone like new and at the end of six months the yellow stitching was as bright and spotless as when new." Years afterwards he confided with a twinkle that "by going barefooted during the summers" he "made them last three winters in the pink of condition."

Clay remained on his father's farm during the long intervals between school terms until 1863 when he secured a place in his Uncle Christian's store in West Overton and worked for his board and the privilege of sleeping on the counter. Thus for two years he obtained his keep and seems to have earned it since, at the expiration of that period, his Uncle Christian took him to Mt. Pleasant and recommended him so highly to his Uncle Martin that the latter hired him with money to clerk in his "general emporium."

Tradition has it that his wage was no less than three dollars a week but the evidence on this point is not con-

Frick the Man

clusive. In any case, his step upon the lowest rung of the financial ladder inspired the confidence which then evoked the avowal of his determination to "make a million."

He was an ardent salesman, "more aggressive"—meaning probably more ingratiating—according to their own testimony, than the older clerks, and winner of the only severe competitive test recalled extending through an entire year. His chief interest, however, was in bookkeeping and his assiduity in perfecting the somewhat ornate, though strikingly legible, chirography then in vogue for "accounts rendered" no less than for autograph albums, was limitless. Primarily, no doubt, the appeal most enticing to his nature in this painstaking endeavor was his inherent love of artistry, but hardly less impelling, one may reasonably surmise, was the development of rare workmanship which would open the way from the counter to the counting-room; but, whether foreseen or not, this did prove to be the effect, greatly to his advantage, in the attainment of his first partnership.

Clay's social life began in Mt. Pleasant at the age of sixteen under favorable conditions. Making friends readily among the hundred or more students at the Classical and Scientific Institute, he was welcomed to membership in the various college associations and quickly assumed, by common assent, responsibilities befitting his vocation as a potential man of business and trustworthy financier. The most distinguished and exclusive Literary Society, comprising barely twenty members, was the Philo Union, of which he became Business Manager immediately following his initiation. His chief official tasks consisted

Boyhood

of keeping the accounts, safeguarding the treasury, seeing to it that the cost of entertainments should never exceed the proceeds, "counting the money and paying the band."

It is not recorded that he participated in the Literary Exercises presented for parental and public approbation, but it is recalled distinctly that he inaugurated a movement to expand the meager library and trudged faithfully from house to house in search of segregated books, which invariably he bore in his own arms to add to the common hoard. He was "a great reader" himself and, though his selective privileges were necessarily limited, his tastes were notably catholic. His prime favorite naturally and irresistibly, as of his generation and years, was John S. C. Abbott's enthusiastical Life of Napoleon Bonaparte; second only to that were Walter Scott's tales and poems, most particularly the Lay of the Last Minstrel, "Breathes there a man with soul so dead," which he stood ready always to declaim; and third, Thomas Jefferson's Life and Morals of Jesus Christ, of which in later years he presented many copies to friends, with never a word in explanation of his enigmatical choice.

The Independent Order of Good Templars of Mt. Pleasant was organized in the Methodist meeting-house on May 1st, 1866, under the guidance of the pastor, the Rev. J. C. High, by whose invitation Clay became a charter member and, although only seventeen, he was appointed promptly on the important Committee on Admissions and soon thereafter on the Committee on Care of the Sick, Worthy Scribe, one of the editors of the Lodge pub-

Frick the Man

lication called the "Eastern Star" and, seemingly as a matter of course, on the Committee on Finance and, at the expiration of a year, treasurer of the association. The minutes contain no record of attendance but his steady official advancement leaves no room for doubt of the youth's diligence and exactness in performance of allotted tasks or of the subsequent value to himself of his first perception of the effectiveness of organized endeavor. That even at that early age, according to the recollections of his associates, his manifest pride was of achievement rather than of distinction may well be believed.

Round ball, a simple precursor of the intricate baseball of the present, was the most important of outdoor sports in those days, but a contest required so much time that play was restricted to Saturday afternoons and holidays and Clay, lacking strength and endurance to "bat and run," participated merely as umpire or scorer. The game most constantly employed for relaxation was that crude successor of the ancient exercise of throwing the discus called quoits but played with horse shoes and requiring skill and accuracy rather than physical strength. In this pastime the keen-eyed and painstaking young clerk excelled and "could make more ringers than any other boy in town."

The decorous and educational game of Authors afforded the chief evening diversion, "cards" being so universally condemned as an enticement of the Devil that "nobody ever saw a deck in town." But there was an occasional dance, to the music of a single fiddle, and the accommodating performer records sympathetic recollection of the

Boyhood

occasions when he "used to carry notes back and forth between the boys and girls when dates were being arranged for a walk."

The pleasurable and mildly adventurous experience of sleeping on a counter came to an end for Clay at West Overton. At Mt. Pleasant he boarded with his Uncle Christian and Aunt Katherine and, after working a few months for his Uncle Martin, was transferred, greatly to his satisfaction, to the new corner store of the "Mt. Pleasant Partnership," comprising his favorite Uncle Christian and Mr. Lloyd (Barney) Schallenberger. With the exception of three months' leave, which he obtained for the purpose of finishing his education at Otterbein College, whose records reveal that he scored eight out of nine attainable points in both Essays and Orations, he continued his clerkship in the Mt. Pleasant store for three full years.

This period, which he always remembered as one of the happiest in his life, reached an abrupt ending in 1868, when he was eighteen years old. On a very hot day in August, while sedulously mopping his brow and watering his horse at the trough opposite Peter Sherrick's house, John Frick was amazed to perceive his son trudging up the road from Mt. Pleasant. Waiting patiently until the young man had laved his perspiring face and head under the spout, he inquired somewhat caustically:

"What do you mean by walking three miles on a day like this? What's the matter?"

"Barney [Schallenberger] discharged me," was the laconic response.

Frick the Man

"Does Grandmother Overholt know about it?"

"No."

"Well, you had better go and tell her right away."

Aside from an amusing illustration of the taciturnity common in those days between father and son, this trifling episode affords convincing corroboration of contemporary testimony that Clay "was brought up mostly" by his maternal grandparents—a circumstance, in consideration of their exceptional characteristics, of no slight significance.

What occasioned the rupture at the store that morning further than "a difference of opinion" or what happened in the big house that evening is not recorded even by tradition. All that is known is that on the following day a very serious grandmother, standing in the doorway, watched a very solemn grandfather escort a very sober grandson on horseback to the Overholt distillery at Broadford for engagement in manual labor.

But it quickly proved to be, as doubtless it had been expected by his grandparents to become, a mere avocation, after all. Even though a reconciliation might be effected, Clay had no wish to return to Mt. Pleasant; his wings were beginning to spread; so after a few weeks he persuaded his devoted Uncle Christian to take him to Pittsburgh, fifty miles away, to recommend him for a position, which he readily obtained, and to lend him the fifty dollars required for the purchase of a "best" suit of clothes.

The situation procured for him by his uncle in Eaton's store yielded six dollars a week and seems to have been

Boyhood

agreeable and satisfying in all respects but one; it did not afford the wider opportunities which he desired; consequently, after prudently studying the mercantile conditions for a few weeks, he struck out for himself for the first time, boldly applied, with no recommendation other than his own statement and his pleasing appearance, for a position in the big store of Macrum and Carlisle, and was engaged forthwith at a salary of eight, presently increased to twelve, dollars a week.

Twenty clerks were employed and the firm strongly encouraged competition. Although not designated as Chief Clerk, William G. Blair had for long been recognized as the leading salesman and claimed the privilege of serving the best customers. This prerogative was conceded by all of the other clerks, but the latest recruit promptly challenged it as a violation of the principle of fair rivalry openly espoused by the proprietors and destructive of its intent.

"All young Frick asked," notes the only salesman who dared uphold him, "in the interest of the firm no less than of himself, was fair play, but that he would have and, without making any fuss about it, he calmly ignored all protestations and made himself so popular, especially with the ladies, that it wasn't long before his name began to appear at the head of the Sales List almost as often as Blair's."

Naturally the management perceived no cause for complaint or reason for interference and, although "it was gall and wormwood to Blair" and "general unpleasantness" ensued for a time, "Clay was so considerate of

Frick the Man

Blair's feelings and so tactful and goodnatured that after a while he won them all over and made them like him in spite of themselves."

That his previous experience, supplemented by his indefatigability and buoyancy, stood him in good stead, is clearly evidenced by his receipt of an offer from the firm of twenty dollars a week if he would return to their employ, less than a year later, when his feet had found at Broadford another round of the ladder to that avowed goal of no less than "a million dollars."

Convinced by quick observation that "H. Clay" savored of boyish affectation and seemed likely to be regarded as unbusinesslike, and detrimental to his progress, he saw to it that his name should appear in the Pittsburgh Directory as "FRICK, Henry C., clerk, Anderson St., Allegheny" and ever thereafter, except when at home, where he could not lose the "H. Clay," he signed his name simply "H. C. Frick."

He wasted no time. Rising and dressing for breakfast at seven o'clock on every week-day—there were no half-holidays then—he crossed the river and walked to the store, arriving promptly at eight and remaining till six, returned to his boarding-house for supper, recrossed the river to a business college, where he applied his mind sedulously to study of accountancy and methods of banking till nine-thirty; then finally "home" to his hall bedroom and sleep. His acquaintances were few and his only associate seems to have been the clerk who had "backed him up" in the store, with whom every Sunday morning he went to hear the eloquent young pastor,

Boyhood

Rev. Dr. Pearson, preach in the Fourth Avenue Baptist Church. Occasional attendance with his congenial comrade at a lecture, a concert or a play constituted his sole diversion.

Five months of this arduous routine, supplemented doubtless by imperfect sanitation and dubious drinking water, incited a severe attack of typhoid fever, and it was a greatly emaciated and very ill boy that was brought back to the big red house on the hill in West Overton. But the nursing of his devoted grandmother and sister Maria finally triumphed and, when September brought the cool, fresh breezes, again, old Abraham Overholt, this time in a buggy behind the span, took his favorite grandson to the enlarged distillery at Broadford and proudly installed him in the place he had fairly earned as chief bookkeeper at one thousand dollars a year.

The firm's name was "A. Overholt & Co., Manufacturers of Flour and Youghiogheny Whiskey," the "Co." comprising the founder's eldest son, Henry S. Overholt, and his grandson, Abraham O. Tinstman, one of his daughter Anna's nine children. Henry exercised a general supervision of the business and the sturdy patriarch Abraham, then in his eighty-sixth year, "drove over once in a while to see that everything was going all right," but the active manager was Mr. Tinstman, an alert and exceptionally capable man of thirty-six. Thus at last brought into close business relationship, upon a satisfactory basis, with his venerated grandfather, his uncle and his cousin, Clay found his association not only most congenial but highly favorable to furtherance of his own ambition.

Frick the Man

He needed no spur. Despite the continuing effects of his enfeebling illness, within a month, in addition to keeping the books and making out the bills with absolute precision and Spencerian flourish, he was measuring lumber, weighing grain and selling flour. Often, "as early as two or three o'clock in the morning," somewhat to the annoyance of others who wished to sleep, "he would get out the mules and hitch them up and drive all over the country," but that was later when he was prospecting for coal in lands whose hidden wealth was undiscovered.

On January 15th, 1870, Grandfather Abraham died suddenly from a stroke of apoplexy at the age of eighty-six and was laid to rest in the presence of a great gathering of the clans and neighbors and friends assembled from all the country round, to pay final tribute to the strong, kind man whom for so many years they had tacitly recognized as Squire of Westmoreland County.

III

Beginning Business in Coke

THE chief topic of conversation between the two cousins, Abraham Tinstman and Clay Frick, following the death of their grandfather, was the potentiality of coke manufacture from coal obtainable in the vicinity of Broadford. Often a discussion of some phase of the subject, begun at the ending of the evening game of chess, would run far into the night. Their views never clashed for the simple reason that they approached the general proposition from quite different angles. The elder spoke from experience; the younger possessed the vision.

So early as 1859, Mr. Tinstman, in partnership with Joseph Rist, had bought six hundred acres of coal lands and in 1868 had joined Colonel A. S. M. Morgan in opening the so-called Morgan mines for the manufacture exclusively of coke. Demand for the product, however, was slight and the prospect was far from alluring to a sense of mere realities. Back in 1842, loaded barges had been floated down the Ohio River in a vain attempt to find a market for the despised "cinders"; in 1860 the total number of coking plants in the country had increased to twenty-one from four in 1850; but in 1870 only four more had been added. As an industry, "mining and coking" seemed not merely doomed but already to have perished.

Frick the Man

But Mr. Tinstman had so much money invested that he could not afford to abandon hope and young Frick's odd compound of prudence and daring succumbed to two considerations: one, of his judgment convinced by thorough investigation that coke was the cheapest, if not indeed an essential, fuel for furnaces; the other, of his imagination which had been fired by contemplation of the huge requirements of the steel factories whose quick and tremendous expansion in Pittsburgh he had foreseen while not wholly engrossed in selling ribbons and trimmings.

The outcome of the deliberations of the cousins was a decision to take the plunge if two or three satisfactory partners could be obtained. Mr. Tinstman proposed Mr. Joseph Rist, his associate in previous purchases, and young Frick suggested his distant cousin, Mr. John S. R. Overholt, who was then courting and a year later married his sister, Miss Maria Overholt Frick. Both accepted and the interests were divided into fifths, Mr. Rist taking two-fifths and the others one each.

The first purchase was of one hundred and twenty-three acres of land at Broadford, carefully selected, from Mr. John Rist for the sum of $52,995. Just how Clay financed his first business undertaking, involving $10,599, is not known. His salary in Pittsburgh, averaging seven dollars a week, could hardly have exceeded his high cost of living, and his saving from compensation at Broadford at $1,000 a year for only a year and five months could have been no more than a few hundreds at most. Clearly, his initial venture was made on borrowed money,

Beginning Business in Coke

but that circumstance makes for no surprise because to his dying day Mr. Frick always stood ready to back his judgment to the extreme limit of both his cash and his credit.

Two deeds, dated March 3, 1871, were recorded—one conveying a three-fifths interest in the property to Abraham O. Tinstman and Joseph Rist in consideration of $31,797 and the other a two-fifths interest to John S. R. Overholt and Henry C. Frick in consideration of $21,-198. No purchase money mortgage was recorded and no promissory notes were recited, but in fact the vendor, John Rist, did accept from the four purchasers personal notes in payment, in full or in part, for their respective shares. It is known that Clay borrowed a legacy from her grandfather, amounting to $2,000, from his sister Maria as soon as she received it, but as the distribution was not made by the executors until December 1st, the probability is that either he obtained a loan from the trustees of his mother's residuary share, amounting to $58,000, of which ultimately he was to inherit one-sixth, or his partner, Mr. John S. R. Overholt, advanced whatever, if any, cash was required on their joint obligation.

In any case, the making of this relatively heavy commitment of ten thousand dollars less than three months after he attained his majority on December 19th, 1870, clearly evidences not only the young man's eagerness to strike out for himself but the implicit faith of his family, no less than of himself, in his capacity to succeed.

From time to time thereafter the trustees of his mother's estate, Martin S. Overholt and faithful Christian S.

Frick the Man

Overholt, his two uncles, and Jacob O. Tinstman, his cousin, loaned trust funds to the young man upon his promissory notes and when, in 1874, they received from the executors $37,000, they loaned him the entire amount, payable three years after date. Before his note fell due, however, the trustees became involved in the panic and, at their own instigation, the Court discharged them and paid eloquent testimony to Clay Frick's reputation for integrity by appointing him, the only debtor of the estate, its sole trustee.

While exhausting the available resources of the maternal side, moreover, Clay did not overlook parental potentialities. John W. Frick was only a struggling farmer, but with the aid of his capable and thrifty Overholt wife he "managed," in the proud phrase uttered frequently in after years by his highly successful son, "to bring up six children without running into debt"—a circumstance of utmost importance, as it subsequently developed, to the young man himself in his time of need.

Although father and son, owing partly to their natural reticence and partly to the overshadowing Overholt association, were never on terms of close intimacy, their relationship was always friendly and their spirits were akin in dash and daring. One may readily believe that the relatively unlettered farmer contemplated with admiration approaching awe the recognized proficiency of the youthful accountant while yet in his teens and the readiness with which older men of experience not only took him into full partnership but constituted him head of the firm when he was barely twenty-one. That the

Beginning Business in Coke

explicit confidence of the entire Overholt clan in the promise of the young man was shared by his father, no less than by his mother, is certain; else he would hardly have consented to the placing of his wife's entire inheritance at the boy's disposal.

But John Frick went further. He did unhesitatingly for Clay what he had steadfastly refrained from doing for himself; he pledged his credit without stint, risking bankruptcy and the loss of his eight-thousand-dollar farm by endorsing notes, which the budding financier peddled to all the farmers around, "often hitching up at dawn and driving all over the country and coming back at night with pockets full of greenbacks." The sums thus gathered, though small as units, were considerable in the aggregate at a time when fright was inducing the hoarding at home of moneys which ordinarily would have reached the banks.

Occasionally, too, the amounts involved were far from negligible, and renewals, even in part, were far from certain. One instance indicating the peril of the time and the hazard of the undertaking is distinctly recalled. On a critical evening in 1873 Clay returned from his quest throughout the country with unexpectedly meager pickings. On the following day a note for $10,000 was payable to Joseph Myers, a framer by trade, a portion of the anticipated proceeds being needed in his business and the total constituting his entire savings—facts of which the debtor was only too painfully aware.

Disappointed beyond measure, and wearied to the verge of exhaustion, the young man could not fail to realize

Frick the Man

that for the first time even his extraordinary fertility of resource had failed utterly; sleep would not come; he must have it out. One o'clock in the morning found him pounding the door of his creditor, whom he knew but slightly and who had been magnified by his imagination to the figure of an ogre. Mr. Myers raised the window of his bedroom.

"Who's there? What do you want?"

"Clay Frick. My note is due tomorrow and I can't pay it."

"Well, it's endorsed."

"I know, but B. F. O. (Benjamin Overholt) is busted and A. O. T. (Abraham O. Tinstman) is busted and I don't want you to close me out."

Silence—and then:

"John Frick is still on the back of that note and he ain't busted; he'll pay some time. I won't close you out."

Slam!

Presently Clay was able to pay enough to relieve his creditor of embarrassment in carrying on his business and when, two years later, he took the last instalment to Mr. Myers, he said simply:

"That was the best investment I ever made"—and he added quietly:

"It may prove to be the same for you."

Not only on this occasion but much earlier, in the course of his family financing, Clay had utilized his father's credit to even greater subsequent advantage in carrying through his ambitious projects. On December 1st, 1871, only nine months after he bought one-fifth interest in

Beginning Business in Coke

the firm "on a shoestring," John Frick joined him in the purchase from the executors of Abraham Overholt's estate the Alexander Miller farm, comprising 189 acres and 34 perches, in East Huntingdon township.

This transaction called for skilful manoeuvering. The executors were willing to accept joint notes of father and son for two-thirds of the purchase price of $37,842.50, payable respectively one and two years thereafter, but they demanded $12,514.16 in cash, and neither Frick père nor Frick fils had any money. Nevertheless the requirement was met on the date fixed from the proceeds of the following note:

$12514 16100   Mt. Pleasant, Penna.

   One day after date we promise to pay M. S. Overholt, C. S. Overholt and J. O. Tinstman, Trustees of Elizabeth Frick's portion of A. Overholt's decd estate, or order, Twelve thousand five hundred and fourteen dollars and sixteen cents, without defalcation, value received with interest from December 1st, 1871.

                                  JOHN W. FRICK
                                  H. CLAY FRICK

That is to say, the farm was acquired from the executors of Abraham Overholt's estate with money provided in part by the trustees of Elizabeth Overholt Frick's share in that estate. Three years later Clay completed the operation on his own account by purchasing his father's undivided interest at an advance of several thousand dollars and, his estimate of the value of the land for mining purposes having then been verified, he was enabled to obtain his first mortgage loan from T. Mellon & Sons, the foremost bankers of Pittsburgh, upon the farm as sole security, and thus not only escaped the bankruptcy

Frick the Man

which engulfed his partners but paved the way for the purchase of many other properties at panic prices.

This, however, was not his first financial transaction with the bankers. The selection of a name for the firm confronted the partners at the outset and called for serious deliberation. Mr. Tinstman and Mr. Rist were men of affairs and standing in the community but their identification with other enterprises of like nature seemed likely to prove confusing if heralded in connection with a new concern whose complete independence, it was thought, would constitute an asset. Overholt was, of course, a name to conjure with, but John S. R. did not wish to assume the responsibility. The process of elimination clearly pointed to the most youthful partner, and the appearance of "Frick & Co," as miners of coal and manufacturers of coke was thus signalized to the industrial world.

The designation was both fitting and shrewd, affording the recognition which the elders considered the just due of the initiator of the enterprise and also assuring unremitting application of the zeal and resourcefulness which he had already displayed. Young Frick neither sought nor shirked the responsibility, conditioning only that he should have full authority under the nominal direction, for a time at least, of an Overholt, namely his Cousin John, as the head of the firm, and that in lieu of drawing a salary as manager, he himself should be free to continue his bookkeeping for A. Overholt & Co. for the twenty dollars a week which he needed for his living expenses and was loath, in any case, to forego. Natu-

Beginning Business in Coke

rally Mr. Tinstman and Mr. Rist found this arrangement wholly to their liking and Mr. Overholt accepted his assignment for one year, at the expiration of which he withdrew from the business entirely, chiefly as a consequence of apprehensiveness caused by an excavation which nearly resulted in the burial alive of thirty miners.

The young manager adopted a bold policy at the outset. Determined that the firm should profit to the full extent of its means in whatever enhancement of values might result from its operations, he invested its entire capital in low-priced land. This left no money whatever for development but the purchases had been so shrewdly made that additional funds were readily obtainable upon the original basis and, though not regarding the method as altogether prudent, his partners raised no objections. Indeed it is quite conceivable that they would have been willing to increase their own contributions.

But there was nothing further from the manager's contemplation than an enlargement of partnership which would reduce automatically his own percentage of interest in the business. Why not finance the firm, as he had financed his own fifth, on credit? True, the firm, unlike himself in the first instance, had no family resources to draw upon, but it had a considerable acreage of promising coal lands which he had insisted upon keeping free and clear of purchase-mortgages with this very purpose in view. The difficulty lay in inducing local investors to make straight loans without participation in ownership or future profits. Clearly, his first step was to establish the credit of the firm by demonstrating its ability to bor-

Frick the Man

row money elsewhere and, if possible, from the most cautious and conservative of lenders. He decided to make the attempt and, while about it, to fly high.

Among the Scotch-Irish settlers in Westmoreland county was Andrew Mellon, who followed his father from the county Tyrone in 1818 and brought with him his son Thomas, aged five. He acquired a farm in Franklin Township and remained there until 1833, when he moved to Allegheny County, where ultimately he died. One of the first to make his acquaintance was Abraham Overholt, who was of the same age, thirty-four, and of like disposition and tastes. The two became excellent friends and young Thomas was a frequent caller, with his father, at the big brick house in which Elizabeth Overholt was born six years later than himself and became a big girl of fourteen before he went away with his father, at the age of twenty, fully cognizant of the intrinsic worth and high standing of Mr. Overholt.

To doubt that this interesting bit of local history loomed large in the mind's eye of Elizabeth Overholt's son while he was groping for financial succor would be to question the activities of resourceful intelligence. During the thirty-eight years that had elapsed Thomas Mellon had never missed a step on the high road to success. Endowed with a remarkable blend of Scotch and Irish traits, studious, thoughtful, philosophical, indefatigable, prudent and thrifty, he easily acquired a substantial fortune, chiefly from sagacious speculations in real estate, while simultaneously gaining such pre-eminence at the Pittsburgh bar that the leaders of the Republican party

Beginning Business in Coke

virtually demanded that he become a candidate for assistant Judge of the Common Pleas.

Professional pride having triumphed over the satisfaction of making money and the requirement of a personal outlay of $150 for campaign expenditures, he was duly elected and served with marked distinction for ten years when he declined a renomination in order that he might "engage in plans and projects for Thomas and James while watching over the development of my younger boys, Andrew, Dick and George," aged respectively fourteen, eleven and nine.

Not caring to resume the practice of law, "having now too many pecuniary and other interests of my own to make it profitable to attend to the affairs of other people," Judge Mellon "began to cast about for a new vocation" and finally "concluded to open a banking house." His two elder sons having already founded a prosperous joint stock savings bank at East Liberty, the father established an institution of his own for the prospective use of the "boys" and opened the doors of a building on Smithfield Street on January 1st, 1870. The venture proved successful from the start. General business was flourishing, speculation was rife, money was abundant, rates of interest to borrowers were high and satisfactory deposits were obtained without solicitation. Within a year the "Mellon bank," operating in conjunction with the savings institution at East Liberty, was recognized as one of the most important in Western Pennsylvania.

This was the situation when, one morning, late in 1871, H. Clay Frick, aged twenty-one, without announc-

Frick the Man

ing his purpose to anybody, quietly boarded a train at the village station for Pittsburgh to negotiate a loan designed to serve for the time being as working capital for the budding firm of Frick & Co. Proceeding straightway to the new building then in process of construction for the use of the bank, he announced that he had come from Broadford "to see Judge Mellon on a matter of business" and was admitted promptly.

What actually happened at this momentous meeting, the eventual fruits of which garnered by each comprised many millions, has never been revealed but can readily be imagined. A more courtly old gentleman never received a politer young one. One can almost see him, in his long frock coat, gleaming shirt front and black bow, rising with judicial dignity, and motioning his boyish-looking, brown-haired visitor, equally handsome as of a later generation and no less immaculately attired, to a chair. And nobody who ever met the latter can fail to picture with assured accuracy the wholly deferential, though anything but obsequious, manner in which he introduced himself as the grandson of Abraham Overholt, the son of John W. Frick and Elizabeth Overholt and the partner of John S. R. Overholt, Abraham O. Tinstman and Joseph Rist and set forth in precise terms the purpose of his mission, to wit:

Frick & Co. wished to borrow $10,000 for six months at 10 per cent, with which to build fifty coke ovens, upon security consisting of undeveloped but unmortgaged coal lands and of his strong conviction, based upon results of personal investigation which he outlined in

Beginning Business in Coke

painstaking detail, that the coking process was an essential factor in the fabrication of steel.

It is more than doubtful that any other banker in Pittsburgh would have entertained the proposal for a moment, but Judge Mellon, the most cautious and conservative of them all, made the loan at once, without requiring endorsements, authorization or corroboration of the young man's statements from his partners.

"He just got it on his nerve," was the common interpretation when he returned to Broadford on the first train with the money in his pocket.

But did he? Judge Mellon was not impulsive; he was notably cautious. That he was favorably impressed by the terse representations, direct methods and engaging manners of his confident young customer may well be believed, but his trust reposed in Overholt integrity and, though wholly devoid of sentimentality, there lay deep in his nature a grain of fine sentiment that might have been touched by recollection of his father's friend of his own boyhood days. But the interesting circumstance cannot be ignored that, while arranging to go on the bench, he had invested all of his "loose means" in coal lands which might be enhanced in value immensely if some zealous and intelligent young man should devise at his own expense "a coking process" that should prove indispensable to the steel industry. One might almost suspect that Clay had not failed, before attempting to plough the hardest ground in sight, to acquaint himself with the peculiarities of the soil and to select with care the seed best adapted to its tillage.

Frick the Man

But Frick & Co. were both active and impatient. Before the first fifty ovens were finished, while the construction force was still intact, the manager sought an additional loan of $10,000 for the building of fifty more. This time Judge Mellon's prudence asserted itself and a representative of the bank was sent to Broadford to investigate and report. The representations respecting both the property and the construction were found correct in every detail, but the attendant features were far from satisfactory.

It was, to begin with, a very small enterprise and evidences of prosperity were not visible. Not only was the sole responsible director hardly more than a boy, but he was giving part of his time to keeping books for a big store and another portion to "prints and sketches," some made by himself, and all quite out of place in his "half-office and half-living room in a clapboard shack." The application should be denied.

But the wise Judge was unconvinced. In point of fact, nothing could have appealed more strongly to his own thrifty soul than the information that the young man was saving the firm's money by working overtime outside to earn his own frugal living. More interested than ever, he sent his mining partner, Mr. James B. Corey, to make an independent examination. The report of that experienced observer was terse and decisive:

"Lands good, ovens well built; manager on job all day, keeps books evenings, may be a little too enthusiastic about pictures but not enough to hurt; knows his business down to the ground; advise making the loan."

Beginning Business in Coke

Judge Mellon accepted Mr. Corey's recommendation; the additional fifty ovens were built and put into operation; business was good from the start; the Mellon loans were paid from earnings; steadily increasing profits were invested in more lands and more ovens and, within two years after the partnership was formed, Frick & Co. were close upon the heels of A. S. M. Morgan & Co., who were supposed to be making large profits.

Then out of a clear sky came the financial collapse and industrial crash of a nation which brought to Henry Clay Frick, in his twenty-fourth year, the supreme ordeal, with one exception, of his remarkable career.

IV

A Triumph of Faith and Courage

THE panic of 1873 was not foreseen. Beginning with the completion of the Union Pacific railway in 1869, the opening up of the Middle West, long delayed by the Civil War, gained tremendous momentum. During the preceding three years less than six thousand miles of additional track had been laid but in the four years following new construction leaped to twenty-four thousand. Demand for rails so far exceeded the domestic supply that recourse was had to England to make up the deficiency and "the vilest trash that could be dignified by the name of iron" was greedily accepted by the eager promoters. Prices responded inevitably, profits increased accordingly, expansion of mills was limited only by possibilities of construction, employment at high wages awaited every laborer, settlers rushed by lake and land to the fresh fields, immigration increased rapidly and prosperity was universal.

Although specie payments had not been resumed, public credit endangered by the greenback movement was restored and the confidence of the world was regained immediately following the second inauguration of President Grant by the Act of March 18, 1869, pledging payment in coin of all obligations not specifically redeemable

A Triumph of Faith and Courage

otherwise and promising redemption of the legal tenders in coin as soon as practicable.

Money, though hardly plentiful, became easy forthwith and the bourses of Europe vied with one another in bidding for American securities. Railway bonds in particular sold abroad like hot cakes and the New York and Philadelphia bankers were not backward in supplying the markets and raking off big commissions from enterprises of doubtful merit. So great a bull movement in foreign securities had never been known on the European exchanges and speculation in all kinds of schemes was correspondingly rife at home. All lessons from experience were forgotten, all precedents were ignored; a new era initiated by a new country seemed to have been ushered into the old world.

The certainty, which should have been patent, if not glaring, that there must be a bottom even of Europe's well of opulence was manifested clearly enough in the autumn of 1872, when the demand began to slacken and the New York bankers found themselves obliged to strain their own credit to carry their latest undertakings, but nothing beyond a general tightening of money really happened until a panic on the Vienna bourse in May, 1873, sent shivers of apprehension down the spines of Continental investors and virtually closed the doors upon new offerings from the States.

But, even so, American bankers and brokers, unconsciously perhaps screening the thought with the wish, and yet with sincerity unquestioned by history, scoffed at the obvious warning as a false alarm and proved their

Frick the Man

faith by continuing and increasing their commitments. A few failures early in September caused "an unsettled feeling" but were not considered seriously significant and when, on September 18th, announcement was made that the great and goodly House of Jay Cooke and Co., financiers not only of the Northern Pacific railway but also, throughout the war, of the Government itself, and custodians of the funds of millions of the most pious folk in the land, had failed, "it was received with almost derisive incredulity on the part of the mercantile public."

The panic that followed confirmation of the report was instantaneous and unprecedented in manifestations of frenzy and terror. Stocks on the Exchange, following New York Central and Western Union, the two least vulnerable, fell to inconceivable levels in a few hours; within the next few days a score of firms were avowedly unable to keep their contracts; bids were not forthcoming for shares at any prices and the Exchange was closed; the old Union Trust Company suspended; the National Bank of the Commonwealth failed; Fisk & Hatch, Howes and Macy, Henry Clews & Co., and many lesser banking houses put up their shutters; deposits were withdrawn from national banks; runs began on savings banks; money was unobtainable; Clearing-House certificates were issued for the first time; President Grant and the Secretary of the Treasury went to New York and pledged all aid the Government could give under the laws.

And yet it is not surprising that the far-reaching and demoralizing effects bound to ensue from such a shock to the financial center of the country found slight comprehension

A Triumph of Faith and Courage

beyond the Alleghenies. A mere "Wall Street panic," presumably involving only gamblers in money, stocks and bonds, was no concern of those actively engaged in legitimate industry and wholly engrossed in their own affairs. They had no interest in the cut-throat games of kid-gloved and silk-stockinged parasites who, producing nothing themselves, fought over the fruits of the toilsome enterprises of honest men and were regarded as natural enemies. What mattered it if ruin should overtake the rascals? Good enough for them! The upset might teach them a lesson. It would be all over in a month anyway. The United States had struck its gait at last and was too big to be stopped or retarded. On with the work! Full steam ahead!

Even Judge Mellon, who recalled distinctly the precisely analogous panic of 1819, following the war of 1812, and the widespread adversity that ensued for ten years, imposing a most desperate struggle for very existence upon his own parents, perceived no serious significance for Pittsburgh in the failure of Jay Cooke & Co.

"While I was seated at my desk on the afternoon of September 18th," he wrote long afterward, "our notary public, Mr. Whitney, looked in and asked if I had heard of it. I replied no. He said it had caused a good deal of excitement in New York and Philadelphia. The news did not disturb me, indeed it scarce attracted my attention, as we had no relations with Cooke or his railroad projects; and I supposed the flurry caused by it would blow over without any serious effect, as it had done after similar failures of others."

Frick the Man

This pleasurable anticipation naturally was not realized. Not only did the strain become more severe daily in the large money centers; it spread rapidly over the country and reached Pittsburgh within a week. T. Mellon & Sons had substantial balances in New York and Philadelphia but "unfortunately our depositories in both these cities failed before we could secure our funds" and the Judge awoke to the disagreeable fact that they had in their two banks barely sixty thousand dollars with which to meet deposits of ten times that amount, "Our customers, however, were not aware of our predicament and no one entertained the slightest apprehension of our solvency as I was always looked on as impregnable."

But the consternation caused throughout the entire region by several bank failures can readily be imagined, and nowhere within the Pittsburgh orbit was it felt more deeply than in the humming little village of Broadford and by the members of the firm of Frick & Co. Mr. Tinstman and Mr. Rist required all of their resources to safeguard their other investments and could not be relied upon to render any assistance whatever to their latest speculation. More definitely and comprehensively than ever, the entire burden devolved upon the manager. Having taken over unhesitatingly—on credit, as usual—his cousin's share, he now held a two-fifths interest, and was giving his undivided attention to the conduct of the business for the same modest remuneration that he had received for keeping the books of Overholt & Co. He still owed money right and left but having always paid full interest promptly, and never defaulted, renewals

A Triumph of Faith and Courage

were obtained easily and profitable expansion upon a large scale seemed to be well within the range of financial possibilities in the near future.

Meanwhile, the Wall Street panic had run its course, the stock exchange had reopened and the machinery of finance had begun to function as smoothly as ever. Upon the whole, the prospect, though far from reassuring, was less dismal than it had appeared at first and Manager Frick returned from a hurried visit to Pittsburgh fairly well convinced that he had only to postpone his more ambitious projects for a time in order to keep his head above water and weather the storm. In any case, gritting his teeth, he would not let go of anything he had and would continue unwaveringly to assume any kind or form of obligation required to obtain whatever in addition might seem worth having.

It was more than double or quits; it was a hundredfold or less than nothing; either a tremendous success or an overwhelming collapse even of hope.

This grim determination was not unnatural to a redoubtable spirit, uplifted by the buoyancy of youth, which thus far had overcome all obstacles, but it is incredible that Clay Frick, at twenty-four, foresaw either the severity or the duration of his undertaking. What he, in common with all experienced observers and learned economists, failed to perceive was that the real disaster did not end, but only began, in Wall Street and that the money panic was but a prelude and a bagatelle to the industrial crisis that was bound to follow.

Revelation of the bitter truth came quickly and no-

Frick the Man

where more poignantly than to western Pennsylvania. As early as November 1st several railway companies of high repute defaulted in payment of interest on their bonds; soon thereafter the Pennsylvania Railroad paid its dividend in scrip; the paper of a construction company bearing the endorsements of Vice-President Thomas A. Scott and his associates went to protest; new construction practically ceased and even ordinary maintenance contracts were cancelled; iron mills were shut down and "reduced to the value of a scrap heap"; coal mines were abandoned; laborers began to walk the streets in vain search of employment; strikes and lockouts presaged the great railway riots to come; "a veritable paralysis," in the words of Rhodes, possessed Pittsburgh.

Inevitably the demand for coke began to dwindle and as early as the Spring of 1874 seemed likely to disappear altogether. Theretofore marketing of the superior products of the Connellsville mines had been a simple matter; commission merchants in Pittsburgh had eagerly accepted and readily disposed of all that was offered; the manufacturers had only to load the cars and await remittances at fixed rates. A few orders continued to trickle through but at prices which did not equal the bare cost of production and diminished so greatly in volume that many dealers could no longer afford to maintain their offices and abandoned business entirely. Disposal of their coke upon any terms soon became a problem for the manufacturers even more serious than producing it at a loss and, gradually, one after another, the mines were shut down.

A Triumph of Faith and Courage

"It was," said Mr. Frick nearly half a century later, "an awful time."

Frick & Co., practically alone, stubbornly persisted. Calculating with his usual precision that deterioration from disuse of a new plant would far exceed the difference between cost and revenue, at even as low as ninety cents a ton, and that readiness to meet demands promptly upon resumption of a profitable basis would give the firm an enormous advantage over its competitors, the manager decided to become his own sales agent and, going to Pittsburgh, hired an office, on his promise to pay.

Thereafter, through the Spring and torrid Summer, he "got up at six, looked over the ovens and set things going, took the train for Pittsburgh at seven, reached his office at ten, 'legged it' from factory to factory soliciting orders till three, reached home at about six, and attended to the details of mining till bedtime."

But his training behind the counter stood him in good stead and whatever market there was for Connellsville coke he soon obtained for Frick & Co., and although it was said that he always held his customers, changes were frequent as mills opened or closed, and unremitting attention was essential to the disposal of his product. Occasionally he was obliged to remain at home to scurry around among the farmers for savings, which then had become most meager, with which to make up the deficit from operation. The $37,000 which he borrowed from the trustees of his mother's portion constituted an excellent backlog but was waning rapidly in partial payments

Frick the Man

for additional lands when his fertile mind evolved a truly dashing stroke.

A year or two before, the community had furnished money for the building of a ten-mile railroad from Broadford to Mt. Pleasant to connect with the Baltimore and Ohio and facilitate the marketing of coke. The investment brought satisfactory returns while business was good, but dividends had ceased and bankruptcy was threatening when the traffic was reduced practically to the Frick shipments. The stockholders, moreover, were in desperate straits and eager to sell their shares, not merely to avert complete loss, but to save their mortgaged homes. Conditions were approaching a crisis and stoppage of the little railway's operation, which might in turn enforce closing of the mines, seemed imminent. What to do, what could be done, to avert this peril, was the question perplexing the manager on his way home from Pittsburgh one afternoon when suddenly, after having discarded every conceivable solution, he hit upon an outside chance and decided to take it while there was yet time for successful negotiation.

During the evening he obtained a list of the stockholders, who were widely scattered, and prepared options for the signatures; then very early in the morning, he borrowed Captain Markle's fast gray single-footer, which subsequently he purchased, and set forth, returning late at night worn and weary but hopefully happy, with the options in his pockets.

On the next day but one, the management of the Baltimore and Ohio railroad were notified that there was a

A Triumph of Faith and Courage

young man outside who was in a position to sell them a railroad which he thought they would want to acquire promptly upon terms, for the moment, most favorable. The very audacity of such a proposal, at a time when even the biggest railroads were not buying even the littlest ones, probably won an audience. Whereupon Mr. H. Clay Frick, of Broadford, Penn., accomplished salesman, calmly exhibited his goods in the form of options upon a property of marked strategic importance, frankly conceded its present undesirability from the standpoint of earning capacity but expatiated at length upon vast development plans of the coking industry which could not fail to enhance its value enormously, both intrinsically and as a feeder, which might otherwise be diverted to another trunk line, dwelt briefly upon the extraordinarily low price at which, owing to temporarily distressful conditions, it could be obtained, and confidently awaited their acceptance at actual cost plus a commission for himself as negotiator and intermediary of fifty thousand dollars.

No alternative proposition could be entertained and he should consider himself free to withdraw the offer at the expiration of forty-eight hours. His address was H. C. Frick of Frick & Co., Broadford, Pennsylvania, the only firm in the Connellsville region then producing coke in quantity. If they should wish for anything in his line in the near future, he should be happy to meet their agents with a guaranty of full supply at satisfactory prices.

The transaction was consummated within the specified time; the stockholders were duly compensated greatly

Frick the Man

to their relief; the feeder surpassed all expectations in earning capacity for the purchasing company within three years; Frick & Co. were assured adequate transportation; and Clay received a check for $50,000, a large part of which he promptly invested in more lands and more ovens while holding the remainder in reserve for possible contingencies.

Not least among the helpful effects of this successful negotiation was the strengthening of the favorable opinion already held by Judge Mellon of the capabilities of his youthful customer. That it helped to facilitate the making of his first mortgage loan, from the proceeds of which he was enabled not only to purchase freight cars, costing fifteen thousand dollars, for coke shipments over the railroad which he had just sold, but also to obtain "a line of discount not exceeding twenty-five thousand dollars for said Frick or Frick & Co." appears from the recital of his bond.

Although this was probably the only mortgage purchased by T. Mellon & Sons during 1874, when the firm was striving energetically to sell a portion of its own holdings, the circumstance is less noteworthy than it would appear, owing to the fact that real estate still commanded a market at fair prices. The slump came later.

"Our sales books," the Judge records, "show this with great exactness. In the first year after the collapse we sold more real estate, and at higher prices, than we did in the second; more in the second than in the third; and so on until 1877, when real estate was unsalable at any price, and business of all kinds was equally depressed."

A Triumph of Faith and Courage

Nevertheless, as late as December 4th, 1876, Clay Frick induced the bankers to accept a fresh mortgage as security for $76,000 advanced and an agreement to discount business paper not exceeding $24,000, thus fixing the sum total of Mellon credits during the bad years at $100,000, resting upon 471 acres of land, coal underlying 143 acres and two town lots in Broadford.

How much additional acreage he acquired from other sources during this period of enforced liquidation cannot be ascertained definitely but it must have been considerable, as he was the sole purchaser in a community which had become convinced that the coke industry was dead, if not for all time, at least for many years. But his own appetite was insatiable and his supply of promissory notes was inexhaustible. Partial payments in cash, however, were often required and he quickly perceived that the expansion which he craved must soon come to an end unless he could devise some method of providing for current operating costs. While credit might and did furnish materials in large part, it could not be utilized by workmen to procure the necessaries of life for themselves and their families.

To meet this requirement young Frick literally made his own money.

Soon after beginning business, following the custom of the times, he opened a store, for the convenience chiefly of the employés of the firm, and utilized his experience to make modest profits in competition with others. Having practically no capital available for the enterprise, he bought goods from wholesale merchants in Pittsburgh

Frick the Man

and, selling for cash, had no difficulty in making payments at stated intervals. Consequently, when the money became scarce in 1874, and the supply houses were obliged to meet the changed conditions in order to keep their concerns going, his reputation for prudence and trustworthiness was so well established that continuance of his custom upon any reasonable terms was not only welcomed but sought.

This gratifying situation gave rise to an opportunity of which he promptly, ingeniously and somewhat audaciously availed himself by constituting his store a virtual clearing house and issuing his firm's certificates in substitution for the United States currency which had practically disappeared from circulation. His shrewdly designed bills were baldly imitative of those which the Federal Government had made familiar during and following the Civil War, of the same size, shape and color, and so like, even typographically, that the difference in labels, though necessarily distinguishable, was not glaringly noticeable. The wording was simple, to wit:

NO.	FRICK & CO'S MINES	3
DUE BEARER		IN MERCHANDISE
AT OUR		STORE AT
	ONE DOLLAR	
	BROADFORD, PA. 1874	

At the left side of the face of the due bill appeared an emblematical figure of an attractive female gleaner in the fields and in the center a picture of husky laborers wielding pickaxes in a mine, both admirably engraved in

A Triumph of Faith and Courage

the style affected by the Bureau of the Treasury Department. The reverse side was a plain greenback of the light official shade.

These bills were used primarily in payment of wages; then by the workmen, at first in purchases at home, but soon elsewhere for other purposes, until presently they constituted the common currency of the entire community; with the result that business increased materially at the store, greatly to the satisfaction of the wholesalers, and Frick & Co. had the use of all of the proceeds received in legal tender from sale of their products, barring only the small portion required from time to time to extend or to expand their credits in Pittsburgh, and the mere cost of printing the good-looking bills.

A bitter blow fell toward the end of the trying year. From the day when he first saw light in the little Spring House, beginning with the anxious periods of childhood and boyhood and continuing through his aspiring young manhood, there can be no doubt that Grandmother Overholt served as his chief guide and sympathizer and when his grandfather passed away in the critical year of his majority, she succeeded naturally to a position of main reliance in his daring adventure. She was in her eighty-fourth year when his cousin and partner, Abraham Overholt Tinstman, made these entries in his diary:

Oct. 11.—Clay and I went to Overton on horseback. Took dinner with Uncle Jacob. Spent part of afternoon with Aunt Abbie. Grandmother was very poorly. Fear she cannot live very long.

Oct. 19.—Came from Uniontown on train. Clay and I went to Overton to see Grandma.

Frick the Man

Oct. 25.—Clay and I went to see Grandmother. Found her very sick with little prospect of living many days.

Nov. 1.—At Mill Grove, then West Newton. Rode from Connellsville on horseback. Went to church. Grandma died at 5 p.m.

Nov. 4.—Was all night at Aunt Abbie's. Attended Grandmother's funeral. It was very large. Thus ended the life of a great and good woman.

Clay took his loss grievously. "He wasn't the brooding kind and never showed much of what he felt but he couldn't seem to smile and his eyes were very sad." He was ill equipped at the time to bear the blow. Torn mentally by anxiety over his affairs, strained to utmost capacity by constant need of finding expedients, physically wearied by five hours daily on trains and incessant trudging of the streets of Pittsburgh, and worn to a shadow, his power of resisting the malady of his youth waned with the passing of his mainstay, and further ominous entries began to appear in Mr. Tinstman's diary.

Jan. 25, 1875.—Clay came home from Williamsport, sick.

Jan. 26.—Clay is very sick with Inflammatory Rheumatism. Dr. Phillips called to see him.

Jan. 27.—Clay still very sick.

Jan. 28.—Clay no better. Uncle C. S. Overholt here again.

Jan. 29.—Clay is a little better, but very sick and restless.

Jan. 30.—Clay not so well today as yesterday. He is very sick.

Feb. 2.—I wrote Dr. Phillips (Connellsville) to get Dr. Fuller (of Uniontown). He did. They had a consultation. They say Clay is in a critical condition.

Feb. 3.—Clay no better. Was with him most of the day.

Feb. 4.—Clay not any better. Think he is not as well as he was. I telegraphed for Dr. Dixon, Fuller and Phillips again this afternoon. Dixon came in the evening. Frank came in the evening. Clay is very low. They don't think he can get well.

A Triumph of Faith and Courage

Feb. 5.—Dixon, Fuller and Phillips were all here in the morning. They all agreed that he was some better, think he may get well. I was home all day and up with Clay last night.

Feb. 6.—Clay still improving slowly.

Feb. 7.—Was with Clay all night; is still improving but very weak.

Feb. 8.—Clay better but not able to sit up yet.

Feb. 9.—Clay not doing very well. Is getting a little troublesome, wants to eat.

Feb. 14.—Washed and dressed Clay and left him feeling better.

Feb. 17.—Came over from Philadelphia last night. Arrived Pittsburgh 8 A.M. Spent day there. Home in evening—found Clay better.

Feb. 19.—Clay still improving.

March 9.—Clay was at the office for the first time in six weeks.

March 10.—Clay and I walked up to Morgan's mines.

March 12.—Clay and I went to Pittsburgh. C. S. O. was with us. This was Clay's first trip for seven weeks. We talked of consolidating Frick and Company and Morgan and Company.

March 14.—Clay came to Connellsville on horseback, and I walked home with him (he on horseback).

March 21.—Clay did not get up until after 11 A.M. He got quite sick and had to stay in his chair all day.

March 25.—Clay and I went to Pittsburgh on accommodation train. Met Cassius C. Markle with Morgan and Company offer to organize stock company.

The proposed consolidation of the Morgan and Frick companies did not take place. Clay discovered quickly that while, during his seven weeks of illness, his own small organization had functioned satisfactorily, the friendly rival concern had become so widely extended and so deeply involved that he could not see his way clear to shoulder the additional burden without gravely imperilling the property which he had built up and now deemed fairly secure.

Frick the Man

Doubtless his enfeebled condition was a factor in consideration but in any case the decision soon proved to have been a wise one. Morgan & Co. went steadily from bad to worse and the partners were soon driven to last resorts. Clay helped to the extent of his ability by purchasing the interests of Mr. Tinstman and Mr. Rist in Frick & Co. and paying all he could raise in cash, but Colonel Morgan was unable to produce his larger share and the utter collapse that followed showed unmistakably that, if Clay had made the combination, his resources would have been wholly inadequate and Frick & Co. also would have been engulfed in bankruptcy.

But Mr. Tinstman, a true Overholt, was so far from being dismayed by even the loss of all he had in the world that he recorded sententiously in his diary:

> July 1.—Married Cornelia Markle.
> Sept. 27.—Went to West Overton. Party at Clay's house.

The two cousins remained firm friends and continued to be mutually helpful through the lean years following, with the result that early in the eighties Mr. Tinstman, operating in other fields and profiting from his knowledge and prescience, not only retrieved his losses but acquired a handsome fortune from the very industry which seemed to have dragged him to irretrievable ruin.

It was four years almost to a day, after he began business for himself, when Clay Frick emerged from his sickroom and feebly made his way to the familiar office of Frick & Co. Somewhat possibly to his surprise and much surely to his gratification, he quickly discovered that he had builded better than he had imagined. "Bills and

A Triumph of Faith and Courage

Accounts Payable" had not diminished, but neither had they increased materially; creditors had considerately refrained from pressing demands and had granted renewals willingly; business was proceeding peaceably and, of course, unprofitably, as usual; and everybody was unfeignedly glad to see him out and about again.

Congratulatory messages from Pittsburgh in particular were most reassuring. Not only was his chief and practically sole asset, credit, unimpaired, but apparently stronger than ever. He could not help feeling that he had won valuable confidence, which in turn promptly begot confidence in himself. While, of course, he had not fully established himself as a man of affairs, he was clearly on his way; after all, he was only twenty-five and—well, "he went home after a while a little tired, but looking pretty happy"; and the next day he "walked up to the Morgan mines."

But the illness which had proved so nearly fatal had conveyed a useful warning. Disdainful as he was then, and continued through life to be, of restrictions imposed by physicians, he recognized the necessity of giving Nature a chance to aid in restoration of his health. It was a favorable time, in any case, to abridge his activities. General trade conditions were still very bad and showed no signs of early improvement, national finances were chaotic as a consequence of continuing inflation, railway companies were either bankrupt or destitute of funds and iron and steel concerns, deprived of markets, had no use for coke.

Obviously Frick & Co. must bide their time and could

Frick the Man

well afford to do so while competitors were going to rack and ruin and coal lands were decreasing steadily in value. If conditions should remain static or grow worse, the firm's preservation would be easier without additional commitments and charges; and if they should take a quick turn for the better, the manager was not likely to forfeit opportunities through inattentiveness. In either event, the firm had only to retain the advantages already gained to control the situation. Already, "Connellsville coke," as a term for the best variety, had been supplanted by "Frick coke," a trade mark of distinct commercial value which still, at the end of half a century, holds its supremacy. Presently, moreover, as doubtless he foresaw to be inevitable, Clay was to reap in part the rewards of four years of incessant toil and desperate struggle, by becoming the sole owner of the one really "going" concern in the district which, unaided, he had created out of relatively nothing and held fully prepared to meet instantaneously the call for tremendous expansion which he never doubted was bound to come.

Content, in these circumstances, to seek physical recuperation and mental relaxation, Clay spent most of his daytime during the Summer of 1875 on the back of the horse which he had purchased from Captain Markle for twenty-five dollars, following his successful sortie for railway stock options, which had yielded his first ten-strike commission of fifty thousand dollars. If he made incidental observations of promising coal lands while he jogged over the hills, nobody else became the wiser, and he made no purchases or offers. After supper he "used

A Triumph of Faith and Courage

to go over to the office and take a look at the day's accounts and then generally dropped into the Tinstmans' to play a game of chess with A. O. and tease Cornelia," and then went home to read till time to go to bed.

The enforced respite proved highly beneficial. Before the year ended his health was fully restored, his weight had increased fifteen pounds and open-air exercise had contributed to his countenance the ruddy hue which never afterward, even while he was recovering from the shock of attempted assassination, wholly forsook it.

The beginning of 1876, signalizing his twenty-seventh year, brought a return of normal restiveness; he had "loafed" long enough; so presently, after somewhat prolonged negotiations, he opened a brand new "Store Day Book and Journal—H. Clay Frick" and made this initial entry:

Monday, March 20, 1876.
Commenced store business here this day. Bought out stock, fixtures, etc., from E. H. Reid at invoice price and 10% added. Amount in all, $5,418.95. Gave my personal note for same.

Although the store was conducted chiefly for the accommodation of the neighborhood and the handling of pay-rolls and petty accounts for the firm, the balance sheet at the end of the year showed holdings of more than three hundred thousand dollars in real estate and mortgages, representing apparently the proprietor's personal acquisitions in addition to those of the firm. Entries covering renewals, reductions and transfers of various promissory notes appear, but none of significance until December 14, 1877, when "the proceeds of a note for $8,400 made by me" were advanced to Daniel David-

Frick the Man

son and Alfred Patterson, "in order to start their business properly at Morgan mines." This apparently served to hold the property and to put the plant into working condition pending resumption of a policy of expansion. The plan was simple yet ingenious, namely, to keep in a position to complete the purchase and start the only competing ovens in the district, instantly upon a revival of business which would produce profits.

It seems altogether probable that he could have carried through this transaction, as usual, on credit but, partly no doubt as a second lesson from his protracted illness, he decided to enlist capital instead of borrowing money, hoping thereby to obtain the advantage of a useful and resourceful partnership.

With this purpose in view, he offered and sold an interest in the business to Mr. E. M. Ferguson, a Pittsburgh capitalist of high standing, completed the "Morgan investment" with the proceeds, supplemented by $5,000 on his own account, and on March 9th, 1878, rechristened the firm "H. C. Frick & Co." He was now, in his twenty-ninth year, fully equipped in experience, in physical vigor, in manufacturing capacity and in financial backing, to meet all comers in his chosen field at the very moment which, with accurate prevision, his judgment had foreseen as most propitious.

He had not long to wait. Financial conditions throughout the country had been improving steadily for some time and already manufacturers and business men were discounting the stabilizing effects of resumption of specie payments on the first of the year. New England was

A Triumph of Faith and Courage

peopling the Middle West, whose restive resident settlers, in turn, were filling up the vast grain territories beyond the Mississippi. Renewal upon a large scale of immigration which had been severely checked in 1873 reflected the resuscitation of common faith abroad in the future of the States. Austro-Hungary, Bohemia, Italy and Poland were sending the vanguard of the great army of laborers soon to fill the manufacturing plants. Pittsburgh and Cleveland were pushing Buffalo from tenth to thirteenth place in population.

Nearly five hundred railroads sold under foreclosure of mortgages during the preceding three years had been reorganized under plans which provided funds for reconstruction. Replacement of streaks of rust with new and heavy rails suddenly became an absolute necessity of the big combinations effected under the lead of the Pennsylvania and Vanderbilt systems.

Iron and steel factories could not resume operations rapidly enough to meet the demands. Furnaces yawned for fuel. Pittsburgh cried out to Connellsville for coke, coke, coke, only to find a single firm producing eighty per cent of the entire output and the only one capable of quick and tremendous expansion. Ironmasters, no less than purchasing agents, flocked in eager competition to little Broadford where, at a plain desk in his modest office, calmly sat a sturdy, alert, keen-eyed, soft-spoken young man of few words but of amazing activities, no less surely than unpretentiously conscious of his complete mastery of the situation.

He disclosed the condition and expectations of the

Frick the Man

firm with entire frankness to one and all alike. The previous week's output had been so many tons; the next week's would be so many more from additional ovens; further increases would follow steadily from rapid construction already under way; more than two thousand acres of land had been acquired; the plant would comprise nearly one thousand ovens within a year; there was no stock on hand for sale at the moment; he would make no discrimination between purchasers and no contracts for future delivery; he would sell all coke as produced "at the market." That was all. Clearly, the salesman, no less than the manufacturer, as reported five years previously by Mr. Corey to Judge Mellon, "knew his business."

Already the price had advanced materially from the unprofitable ninety cents a ton; it now leaped suddenly to two dollars; then to three, again somewhat hesitatingly to four; and finally to five dollars a ton, of which three-fifths was net profit.

Both production and construction were pushed to the very top notch of capacity; employés numbered nearly a thousand and car-loads shipped daily nearly a hundred before the year 1879 was ended.

On the evening of December 19th, his thirtieth birthday, Clay Frick dropped into the store on his way home from a prolonged game of chess following supper with his cousins, took a look at the books preliminary to the annual accounting, bought a fresh five-cent Havana cigar on credit, lighted it thoughtfully, strolled placidly around the corner to the Washabaugh House and went to bed.

He had made his million.

V

Interlude

THE year 1880 opened auspiciously for H. C. Frick & Co. Orders were plentiful and business was brisk; wages were satisfactory to the miners and profits were equally gratifying to the firm; the little village of Broadford resounded from daylight to dusk with the clanking of freight cars fetching building materials and carrying to market every ton of precious coke that could be produced; the whole country round, so recently sleepy and despondent, was stirred by unceasing activities of farmers and tradesmen; and, best of all, not a cloud could be discerned upon the sky of widening prosperity.

Free now for the first time from financial exigencies and strengthened in both resources and confidence by his partnership, the head of the firm concentrated his energies upon the art of organization whose mastery was destined to constitute the basis of his subsequent achievements. He had little to go upon. The potency of this mighty force, except in military undertakings and to a limited extent in railway operation, had never been recognized in commercial affairs although for centuries it had been fully appreciated by the Church of Rome. Great industries had flourished abroad, notably in England, but rather as segregated units profiting from arduous

Frick the Man

endeavors than as aggregations skillfully blended into integral agencies designed primarily to attain highest efficiency through eliminations of waste.

That the eye of this young man's mind should have been among the first, if not indeed the very first, to perceive the full efficacy of the methodic process whose development has given to America its present world supremacy must be attributed probably to sheer instinct. Observation surely contributed little and experience, at that early day, of course, nothing at all. We can only conclude that this was one of those rare instances of a correct theory being educed contrarily from experimental practice.

In any case, when Springtime came, the various factors of mining, manufacture, transportation and selling had been welded into a smoothly-working machine, whose essential attributes required only expansion to assure the ultimate success of the gigantic steel corporation, and the originator of the marvelous system saw his way clear to take his first holiday. He had become well acquainted with Baltimore and Philadelphia and had made fleeting excursions as far north as New York and south to Washington. The West possessing no lure for a diverting jaunt of pleasure, he determined to go to Europe if a congenial traveling companion could be found. Of those available within range of his acquaintance but one seemed to meet all requirements.

And so it came about that one morning early in May Clay Frick appeared at the Mellon banking house upon a quest quite different from that which had first drawn him to that financial haven. He was not now calling

Interlude

upon a stranger to solicit aid which he feared might be denied but upon a friend to proffer a suggestion which he hoped would be accepted. Judge Mellon had withdrawn from business in 1878 and had installed as his successor in the bank his son Andrew, who, even before attaining his majority, had evinced exceptional aptitude for financial management. Clay was twenty-six and Andrew twenty-two at the time of their first meeting in 1876. When the former had accomplished the purpose of his visit and had left for return to Broadford, the Judge turned to his son and said:

"That young man has great promise. He is very careful in making statements, always exact and wholly reliable. He is also able, energetic, industrious, resourceful, self-confident, somewhat impetuous and inclined to be daring on his own account, but so cautious in his dealings with others disposed to take chances that I doubt if he would make a successful banker. If he continues along his own line as he has begun, he will go far unless he over-reaches. That is his only danger."

Acquaintanceship, enhanced by mutual attraction of two somewhat similar, though more distinctively supplementary, personalities, ripened rapidly into a friendship and virtual partnership which continued, without break or rift, to mutual advantage of amazing proportions, for more than forty years. The four years' difference in age and experience received tacit recognition from the beginning, partly as the consequence of a slight incident which tended to fix the respective personal attitudes of each to the other.

Frick the Man

Very soon after the two young men had scrutinized each other inquiringly, Andrew accepted an invitation to "spend Saturday and Sunday"—the English term "weekend" being then unknown in Pittsburgh—at Mt. Pleasant and, arriving at his lodgings early in the afternoon, was surprised to find his host engrossed in study; surprised and somewhat dismayed for the excellent reason that "heavy reading" had not been comprised in his joys of anticipation. Some weeks previously the philosophic Judge had become deeply interested in the publication of Herbert Spencer's novel reflections and, owing to failing eye-sight, had drawn so heavily during the long evenings upon the dutiful patience and modulated voice of his son that Andrew had gleefully welcomed a respite.

What, then, must have been his emotions upon discovering his prospective playfellow confronting a table full of books, of which Addison's Essays and Macaulay's History of England were the most conspicuous, while closely perusing Chesterfield's Letters to his Son, may readily be imagined. Slightly awestruck by the spectacle and overwhelmingly appalled by the prospect, he gulpingly wished himself back to what had become largely a mechanical rendition of Spencerian ontology, but for a moment only. The admonitions of the master of mannerliness had not been absorbed in vain; instantly, the really charming courtesy, derived from instinct and perfected by cultivation, that became noteworthy in Henry Clay Frick, asserted its predominance, and Andrew Mellon breathed forthwith the atmosphere of frank friendliness untouched by affectation.

Interlude

It is nevertheless an interesting circumstance that, during the full two-score years of intimate relationship which ensued, the most distinguished financier of his time invariably addressed his comrade as "Mr. Frick," while the latter, with unfailing affectionate note, referred to his closest friend and his brother Richard, regardless of their years, as "the Mellon boys."

Naturally, after three years of close and continuous application at his desk, the young banker eagerly welcomed the suggestion of a trip abroad and, having his affairs in perfect order as usual, he readily arranged for an absence of four months. Presently Clay proposed to increase the party by inviting two acquaintances to join them. One of those suggested was a popular young man who wrote poetry, sang gleefully and told amusing stories. Andrew readily assented to this thoughtful provision of entertainment enhanced by the desirability of having "some one along to do the talking." The other was an older man, no more loquacious than themselves and commonly considered a dull companion. He could perceive no advantage from this addition and only acquiesced doubtfully upon a vague assurance that there was a "special reason" for the inclusion.

So the party of four sailed joyously in June and, landing at Queenstown in excellent form, reached the Blarney Stone on the Fourth of July, when the leader delighted his companions by producing an American flag from some hiding place and waving it over their heads while they performed the customary rite. Thence they jaunted, as boys on a lark, to Dublin, Belfast, Glasgow, Edin-

Frick the Man

burgh, London, seeing all the sights, and presently crossed to Paris for a brief sojourn, followed by "a dash across the continent" to Venice, their objective point. Meanwhile, incited by growing wanderlust, the older companion conceived the idea of extending his tour around the world, and the leader of the expedition graciously facilitated the execution of the bold project by purchasing his coal lands in the Connellsville region, greatly to the advantage of H. C. Frick & Co., and the amusement of the young banker who then comprehended the mysterious "special reason" for fetching the owner of the property along.

Clay and Andrew returned home in October, not only invigorated mentally and physically but so pleased with their experience and cemented attachment that they toured Europe together many times. One effect of the initial trip was arousal of the former's interest in the other sex as a consequence of his admiration of the attractive daughter of an American banker in Paris, resulting in an understanding which proved, however, upon his return, to have been only tentative and was soon tacitly ignored by mutual assent. But the inclination persisted; moreover, he was approaching thirty and the question of future domesticity called for grave attention, as his young friend was soon to learn.

The season of 1880-81 was noteworthy for social activities in the Iron City and the popularity of Andrew Mellon and the growing fame of Clay Frick brought invitations to many functions, of which the very first of importance proved to be a landmark in personal history. This

Interlude

was a reception attended by all of the elite and among the first to arrive, somewhat conscious but quite undismayed in their finest raiment, were the two friends who lost no time, after making their obeisances after the manner prescribed by the great Lord Chesterfield himself, in ensconcing themselves in an embrasure from which they could scan the brilliant assemblage. Presently the observant younger became conscious that his companion's penetrating eyes were fixed upon a most charming young woman, barely out of her teens, in the center of an animated group and, waiting patiently, he soon heard a whisper:

"There is the handsomest girl in the room. Do you know who she is?"

He did. She was Miss Adelaide Howard Childs.

"Daughter of Asa P.?"

She was,—the youngest.

"I want you to introduce me."

Andrew demurred; his acquaintanceship was slight; besides, an older person, better known, would be more impressive; he would try to find such a one and succeeded, with the result that in a few moments Clay, belying his reputation for reticence, found himself in an eager conversation which ended with a request for permission, which was graciously granted, to call on the following Sunday afternoon. The proverbial "first sight" had sufficed.

It was not quite clear that the permittance comprised another but, yielding finally to his friend's insistence and his own pardonable curiosity, Andrew consented to "stand by" and, at the appointed hour, the two young

Frick the Man

men, crossing the lawn of the Childs residence, perceived Miss Adelaide conversing placidly with her elder sister, with whom presently the youthful banker found himself chatting while the two most concerned strolled about the place. When the hour struck for departure Clay Frick realized that the delicate task confronting him was more difficult than any he had ever essayed, but this very fact enhanced his determination, and after three long months of patient and persistent wooing, he was rewarded by acceptance of an engagement ring, and three months later, on December 15th, 1881, a very pretty wedding took place. It was universally recognized as a highly suitable match of the most successful industrialist of his years in the community with the beautiful and accomplished daughter of a distinguished New England family, and all relatives on both sides were pleased.

Washington, Baltimore, Philadelphia and Boston were duly visited in leisurely fashion,—and finally New York, where the happy couple occupied an elegant suite in the famous Fifth Avenue Hotel, and were entertained at midday dinner at the exclusive Windsor Hotel by Mr. Andrew Carnegie and his revered mother, each of whom they met for the first time. It was a noteworthy occasion. The two gentlemen, one voluble and hilarious, the other reticent and courteous, eyed each other thoughtfully during the repast, at the end of which the host sprang a surprise upon the ladies by adding to an exuberant toast the announcement that Mr. Frick and himself had entered into partnership.

A moment of silence ensued and then the old Scots-

Interlude

woman, recovering from her amazement, remarked drily:

"Surely, Andrew, that will be a fine thing for Mr. Frick, but what will be the gain to us?"

Gaily her son reassured her while the guests quietly prepared for departure,—and thus casually and oddly was heralded the opening of a new chapter in their own and many other lives.

VI

Enter the Carnegies

WHILE Henry Clay Frick was lifting his coke company to a pre-eminent position, Thomas Morrison Carnegie was achieving like triumphs in the steel industry. Although his elder brother Andrew, his senior by eight years, still retained stock control of the Carnegie concerns, his directive interest became incidental to other activities when he moved from Pittsburgh to New York in 1867 and, opening an office downtown, engaged in construction work and the marketing of bonds, chiefly for the Pennsylvania Railroad, and Thomas conducted the iron manufacturing throughout the critical panic period.

But for the overshadowing effects of the elder's extraordinary fame and his own untimely decease, the younger would surely have shared the credit for placing the name Carnegie at the head of steel manufacture; indeed, but for his energy, resourcefulness, skill, tact, and popularity, there can be no doubt that the value of the Carnegie properties would have suffered severely from the financial stress of the time. In any case, with the aid of his sagacious partner, Henry Phipps, Jr., who had been his playmate as a schoolboy, he not only weathered the storm but, when only twenty-seven years old, disregarded the opposition of his brother and on his own account joined

Enter the Carnegies

with his father-in-law, William Coleman, in a speculative undertaking, out of which in 1874 sprang into being the big Edgar Thomson works, which soon surpassed those of the Carnegies in valuation and earning capacity and, by shrewd manipulation, were incorporated in 1881 in the new firm of Carnegie Brothers & Co., Limited, with $5,000,000 capital, of which, it transpired, when the deal had been consummated, Andrew Carnegie personally owned a clear majority.

Meanwhile, Mr. Thomas Carnegie and Mr. Frick, as buyer and seller respectively of coke, had formed an acquaintanceship affording mutual commercial advantage and personal gratification. The two had attained success along similar lines while still in the early thirties and each admired, respected and trusted the other. Although Mr. Carnegie was the older by four years, in experience their ages were approximately the same and they had many attributes, as well as aspirations, in common. It can scarcely be doubted that, in his remarkable history of the steel company, James Howard Bridge reflected the mature judgment of Mr. Frick in the following striking tribute to one who, for reasons already noted, was deprived of just recognition:

> Mr. T. M. Carnegie's abilities were too numerous and complex to be summed up in a sentence. He was a man of sterling integrity; and it was a common saying in Pittsburgh that his word was better than some men's bond. He had remarkable judgment; and his opinion on commercial questions was valued above that of much older and more experienced men. Quick and keen in his perceptions, cautious but progressive in his ideas, faithful to his engagements, and just in all his dealings, he gave to his company that which corporations are habitually lacking, a conscience. His death in

Frick the Man

1886, at the early age of forty-three, was a loss not only to his associates, but to the whole business world in Pittsburgh. To this day all who knew him, great and small, rich and poor, workman and master, revere his memory.

That young Carnegie's estimate of the younger Frick would have corresponded to this appraisal of himself there can be no doubt. It was but natural, therefore, that the two, as a consequence of harmonious cooperation in their business dealings, should have conceived the idea of a closer relationship. The amalgamation of the steel companies, resulting instantly in Carnegie Brothers & Co. becoming by far the largest purchaser of fuel simultaneously with the increasing need of additional capital for further expansion of coke-producing facilities, brought this project to a head and the terms of the "partnership" announced by Mr. Andrew Carnegie at the luncheon in the Windsor Hotel were finally agreed upon while Mr. Frick was on his wedding journey.

The "H. C. Frick Coke Company" was formed to take over the firm's assets and liabilities and to provide fresh capital through the sale of stock, of which $2,000,000 was issued in 40,000 shares of $50 par value to original holders, as recorded on May 5th, 1882, as follows:

Andrew Carnegie	1,000 shares
Thomas M. Carnegie	500
Henry Phipps, Jr.	500
H. C. Frick	680
E. M. Ferguson	660
Walton Ferguson	660
Carnegie Bros. & Co., Ltd.	2,500
H. C. Frick & Co.	33,500
	40,000 shares

Enter the Carnegies

After the 33,500 shares allotted to the old firm had been divided in thirds between the two Fergusons and Mr. Frick, the actual ownership of shares stood: Fergusons, 23,654; Frick, 11,846; Carnegie group, 4,500. Thus Mr. Frick had reduced his percentage of interest in the property from 33⅓ to 29½ per cent, but this he was willing to do in consideration of the $325,000 cash provided, assumption of the old firm's indebtedness by the stronger corporation, greatly enhanced credit for purposes of expansion, and association with his largest customer, which could not fail to assure a market and stabilize the business.

The wisdom of his course was demonstrated promptly. In the first fourteen months of operation, ending on February 28th, 1883, no less than 946,065 tons of coke were sold, the net profits exceeded $400,000, the equivalent of 20 per cent on the entire capital, liens assumed amounting to $214,000 were paid and $44,000 was invested in new properties. The month of March showed a further reduction of $44,000 liens and $20,000 applied to new purchases, leaving only $54,000 of indebtedness to be met during the succeeding ten months. In these circumstances Mr. Frick urged enlistment of additional capital to provide immediate expansion, and Thomas Carnegie, on the ground, approved, but Andrew, in New York, demurred. Whereupon Mr. Frick, in his first letter to the senior written by his own hand, set forth the situation succinctly and frankly in these words:

Aug. 13th 1883.
My dear Mr. Carnegie:
 By the end of this season there will be 10,100 ovens in the Connellsville region proper, of which as we now stand, we shall have

Frick the Man

but one-tenth, so that to keep our position we must do something towards securing new properties. Our trade is large and steadily growing. We do not have coke for our orders, neither can it be bought at present and handled at a profit—I do not think we will ever see the time when coke properties can be bought cheaper. There is no industry today wherein the demand so nearly equals the supply and the demand in new channels is increasing rapidly.

The C. G. C. Co. & Hutchinson properties are the best outside of what we have. They were not built to sell; are good in every respect—good coal—good improvements and, what is of no small importance, well located.

Together their producing capacity is equal to ours—not quite so many ovens, but larger, and owned and operated in common with ours about as cheaply operated.—So in fine, together equal to ours in production and with 1400 acres of more coal for $500,000 less than ours is capitalized at. Fourteen hundred acres of such coal cannot be bought for less than $250 per acre, or $350. In that view, you have a plant with as large producing capacity as ours costing $850,000 less money.

Taking it for granted that it is desirable to acquire these properties at the prices at which we have them optional, is it not wise to have a good strong party join us in increasing our capital to such an extent as will leave us comparatively free of debt? If we increase to $3,000,000, that will give us money sufficient to pay for C. G. C. Co. entire and about all we need pay on Hutchinson for five years.

Our office expense will be about the same in conducting the business as it now is, which is no inconsiderable item, and I do not see why we should not handle as large a proportion of outside coke.

I am free to say, I do not like the tone of your letter. Outside of my desire to follow and accept your views as the largest stockholder in our Company—I have great admiration for your acknowledged abilities and your general good judgment, and would much prefer to defer to your views—in the matter of the values of the properties in question and the propriety of increasing our stock I shall have to differ with you and I think the future will bear me out.

Everything that has been done so far, has been with the consent of your brother, and with his approval.

Yours very truly,
H. C. Frick.

Enter the Carnegies

Whatever annoyance Mr. Carnegie may have felt at the discovery that his new partner held tenaciously to his convictions seems to have been offset by the tribute to his own sagacity, and he finally assented to the increase in stock. But Mr. Frick's appetite for expansion and consolidation was insatiable and before the year ended he proposed that the company purchase the holdings of himself and associates in properties which had not been included in the original transaction.

"What I think you should do," he wrote on November 13th, "is to agree that the Frick Coke Company purchase our interests in those properties for $600,000,—thus enabling us to pay up that million of Frick & Co. increase—and buy from us $500,000 of Frick Coke Co. stock, giving us your paper at three, four and five years for the same. You will then be the owner of one-half of Frick Coke Co. which will have over eight thousand acres of coal and about three thousand ovens. It does seem to me that we should have all of our coke interests consolidated."

This was a shrewd appeal to Mr. Carnegie's avidity for actual stock control of every company in which he was interested. It seems strange, at first glance, that Mr. Frick should have made it, but Mr. Carnegie had already become the largest stockholder through purchase of shares from the Fergusons and could readily obtain more at a price whenever he should see fit to do so. To this Mr. Frick had no objection. Obviously the Carnegies could be more helpful as partners than outsiders if their good faith could be safely assumed and, upon this point, his transactions with the younger brother were convincing.

Frick the Man

The general advantage bound to accrue from such enormous expansion as he had now begun to visualize would benefit his unchanged percentage of interest proportionately in any case. What he most desired at the moment was immediate enlargement and consolidation of all his holdings in order to enable him to apply that complete concentration of energies which he had come to regard as the key of great success.

Mr. Carnegie, for his part, could imagine nothing more favorable to his concerns than the acquisition of two vital essentials—a virtual monopoly and an exceptional man.

"We found," he wrote many years later, with the slight inaccuracies peculiar to age and impaired memory, "that we could not get on without a supply of the fuel essential to the smelting of pig iron; and a very thorough investigation of the question led us to the conclusion that the Frick Coke Company had not only the best coal and coke property, but that it had in Mr. Frick himself a man with a positive genius for its management. He had proved his ability by starting as a poor railway clerk (?) and succeeding. In 1882 (3) we purchased one half of the stock of this company, and by subsequent purchases from other holders we became owners of the great bulk of the shares."

So the arrangement was made along the lines suggested and the company, under Mr. Frick's unquestioned control, both prospered and grew until 1887, when the number of ovens had increased five-fold from 1,000 to 5,000 and the output had leaped to six thousand tons per day.

Enter the Carnegies

Then came the trouble, not merely between owners and workers, but among both proprietors and wage-earners separately, which afforded the preliminary test of Henry Clay Frick's quality as a fighting champion of property rights.

Early in 1887 the coke operators of the entire Connellsville district proposed for the ensuing year a wage scale which the miners refused to accept and by agreement the whole matter was referred by the labor unions and the operators, acting in unison, to a Board of Arbitration which pronounced the workmen's demands excessive and upheld the owners. The labor unions, duly authorized, accepted the decision, but the local lodges refused to abide by the decision and called a strike which the officers of the Knights of Labor promptly proclaimed illegal. Nevertheless the men went out and the struggle began, with the operators standing their ground firmly and unanimously behind a small committee of which Mr. Frick was the leading spirit, and with the miners and their sympathizers brutally assaulting non-union men who wanted to work, destroying machinery and blowing up the works with dynamite.

Suddenly, to the dismay of the owners and the amazement of Mr. Frick, at the very moment when the men were in convention and showing signs of yielding, the directors of the Frick Company ordered complete surrender to the strikers and resumption of operation upon the terms demanded. Unfortunately for the management, Thomas Carnegie, whose sympathy at least would have been with his friend, had died in 1886, and Mr. Frick

Frick the Man

and the two Fergusons, constituting a small minority of the Board, were helpless.

The chief factors in control of the Board were Mr. Henry Phipps, Jr., and Mr. John Walker, chairmen of the two Carnegie companies. Whether, as commonly believed, they acted in pursuance of a peremptory order cabled by Mr. Carnegie, who was in Scotland at the time on his honeymoon, is immaterial. That the latter acquiesced in reversing the policy of Mr. Frick is certain, but the fact that both Mr. Phipps and Mr. Walker, who were men unaccustomed to yield their own convictions, personally favored the action taken cannot be ignored.

Their reasons were plain. Prolongation of the strike would be disastrous to the two steel companies, which had already banked seven blast furnaces and were menaced with complete stoppage of iron production from lack of fuel. They naturally held their obligation to their own companies of primary consideration and as outweighing their responsibility, as directors, to the coke company. Technically, they were within their rights in overriding their President and, morally, they did not feel bound by his engagements with other operators.

That Mr. Frick felt deeply humiliated by such repudiation and regretted for the moment that he had ever joined with or trusted the Carnegies, may safely be assumed. Even more distressing than the personal mortification, such as he had never before experienced, was his apprehension that surrender would serve only to invite vastly greater labor difficulties in the near future; but, having failed to convince his partners of the correctness

Enter the Carnegies

of his judgment, on May 13th he warned them, and through them Mr. Carnegie, of his personal determination, in a letter written by his own hand to the following effect:

May 13th, 1887.

Messrs. Henry Phipps, Jr., John Walker, and others.
Gentlemen:

I cannot honorably carry out your policy in regard to this company, and beg to tender my resignation as President.

Having temporized with our employés and made concession after concession to satisfy them and largely in your interest, and against the interest and judgment of all other coke producers, and finally prevailing on them to agree to arbitration and decision having been rendered in our favor, I think that, cost what it may, we should abide by it, and not start our works until our employés resume work at the old wages, but inasmuch as you have large interests depending on our works being operated I do not feel like standing in the way of you managing the property as your judgment and interests dictate.

Very respectfully,
H. C. Frick.

Both parties to the controversy then rested upon their oars, each earnestly hoping that the other would capitulate, until June 7th when, as in honor bound, after having outlined the situation to the other owners, to enable them to safeguard their interests as they might deem best, and having notified them of his own intention, Mr. Frick called a meeting of the Board and resigned peremptorily and simultaneously submitted the following communication addressed to Messrs. Phipps and Walker:

Messrs. Henry Phipps, Jr., John Walker, et al. June 7th, 1887.
Gentlemen:

As you hold a majority of the stock and are entitled to control in the Frick Coke Company, and in view of what has passed between us on the subject, I feel compelled to vacate my position as its President. I therefore enclose, herewith, my resignation.

Frick the Man

But I accompany it with this my serious protest against the course you propose to take regarding the pending strike. I am satisfied that it must occasion heavy loss to the Coke Company. Besides the loss occasioned by granting the men's present unreasonable demands, it will only lead to still more unreasonable demands in the near future. The loss to the Coke Company may be far more than made up, so far as you are concerned, by gains in your steel interests, but I object to so manifest a prostitution of the Coke Company's interests in order to promote your steel interests.

Whilst a majority of the stock entitles you to control, I deny that it confers the right to manage so as to benefit your interests in other concerns at the loss and injury of the Coke Company in which I am interested.

       Very respectfully yours
        H. C. FRICK.

"Matters," he wrote to Mr. Ferguson, "came to a crisis today. Things have been pointing that way for several days. I felt quite sure that the men, at their convention on Monday, would decide to resume work at the old wages, but they did not do so. The conventions, however, at this writing, are still in session and they may do so yet. The Carnegies, however, got restless and made up their minds that they would do anything to get the works started, so I insisted that they accept my resignation at once. This they did this afternoon, and elected Mr. Phipps as President in my place. I handed in the resignations of yourself and brother, which were accepted, and Mr. John Walker was elected to fill one of the vacancies; the other, they said would be filled in a day or two.

"Everything passed off pleasantly and I told the Carnegie crowd that I would do everything I could to clean the business up and put it in proper shape. I made them the enclosed proposition."

Enter the Carnegies

(ENCLOSURE)

June 7th, 1887.

Messrs. Carnegie Brothers & Co., Limited,
Gentlemen:

Regarding my interest in the Frick Coke Company and its kindred Companies, I will sell you the same at the same valuation we paid the Messrs. Ferguson, with interest from same date, as paid to them, payable as follows: Fifty thousand dollars ($50,000.00) cash, and fifty thousand dollars ($50,000.00) every six (6) months until paid, with interest payable semi-annually, and to be secured by the stocks hereby agreed to be sold. Or I will take such a proportion of the Frick Coke Company property as we may agree upon, with its share of the debt; for instance, the Standard Mines property, and its interest in the United Coal & Coke Company, and the Mount Pleasant Water Company.

If we cannot agree on valuations, I will leave it to three disinterested persons chosen in the usual way; and if that property is allotted to me I should like an assignment to me of the North Chicago Rolling Mill Company contract.

The propositions are open for your acceptance until June 15th next, and, if either is accepted, to be fully closed by July 1st, next.

Very respectfully yours,
H. C. FRICK.

Thus, with characteristic thoroughness and fairness, though surely not without a heartache, Henry Clay Frick did all within his power to make complete his severance from the splendid property, to the building of which he had given seventeen of his best creative years. The differences of opinion which resulted in a change of management fortunately produced no serious animosities. Dignity and restraint characterized the conduct of both parties throughout the controversy and no running sores were left to be healed.

But Mr. Frick's offer to sell his interest upon obviously low and easy terms was not accepted. Probably Mr. Car-

Frick the Man

negie had not expected the young man to burn all of his bridges; possibly he did not fancy the best equipped man in the business as a potential rival of the company which he had created; in any event, the dullest, not to mention one of the shrewdest, of minds could hardly have failed to perceive the merits of a Fabian policy. And when presently the other operators had won their battle, despite the Carnegie defection, and the Carnegie companies found themselves burdened with 12½ per cent higher wages than their competitors, thus wholly confirming Mr. Frick's anticipation, one can readily understand why Mr. Carnegie's attitude became distinctly propitiatory.

On July 22nd, Mr. Frick, accompanied by his wife, their two young children, and Mrs. and Miss Childs, the mother and sister of Mrs. Frick, sailed for Europe and, upon reaching London, found this cordial note awaiting him:

August 2, 1887.

Welcome to Britain's Isle,
    Of course you will all come and spend a week with us.
    It's superb—Come and see what one gets in Scotland these summer days.
    Just off this morning, ten in all, for three days coaching tour. Blaine the happiest man you ever saw. Let me hear your movements. Can take you all in any time.

                    Yours always
                    ANDREW CARNEGIE.

P.S.—Kind regards to Mrs. Frick and sister in which Louise [Mrs. Carnegie] heartily joins.   A.C.

Arrangements having been made, however, for immediate continuance of their journey, acceptance was not feasible and the party proceeded forthwith to the

Enter the Carnegies

continent. A second request of like tenor was made in September to the following effect:

September 9th, 1887.

My dear Mr. Frick:

H. P. [Mr Phipps] tells me you can spare a few days about 19th to visitors.

Come ahead. Shall be so glad to have Mrs. Frick and her sister and yourself and any others of your party.

We hope you will find Scotland in fine trim but we can't expect July weather in September so don't expect it to be *always* dry. Wire day and train.

We sail Fulda 9th Oct. Can't you come with us? Splendid ship and captain.

Yours always
A. C.

Regards to Mrs. Frick in which Louise joins, also sends same to you.

Mr. Carnegie seems to have been misinformed by Mr. Phipps respecting the movements of the travellers and it was forwarded from London reaching Mr. Frick in Hamburg. The inconvenience of changing plans made necessary another declination for the time, but the visit was finally paid before the families returned to America.

The way having been thus opened, overtures from Messrs. Phipps and Walker, authorized by Mr. Carnegie, found a ready response and early in January, 1888, Mr. Frick was duly re-elected President of the H. C. Frick Coke Co., to the great relief and gratification of all concerned, not excluding the competing operators who now felt confident that they would not suffer again from what they had regarded as a breach of faith.

Mr. Carnegie no longer questioned the wisdom of the Frick policy of expansion on a large scale and made the completeness of his conversion plain on February 18th,

Frick the Man

1889, when upon receipt of news of a fresh acquisition he cabled from Christiania:

> Frick hearty congratulations splendid must get options other properties promptly or too late, don't be afraid, want all.

An active correspondence quickly developed between the two men, Mr. Frick constantly making reports and outlining fresh projects, often by his own hand, and Mr. Carnegie responding with words of encouragement usually scribbled in pencil upon scraps of paper and the backs of envelopes. Nearly every communication closed with jottings like these:

> You can't justly estimate what a tremendously big man you are.
> Perhaps some day you will realize that you are a much bigger man than Prest of P. R. R.
> Take supreme care of that head of yours. It is wanted again. Expressing my thankfulness that I have found THE MAN, I am always Yours, A.C.
> "F is a marvel let's get all Fs."

Mr. Frick's prediction that the Carnegie settlement of the strike in 1887, made against his protest, would serve only to fetch fresh demands, was fulfilled unexpectedly early in August, 1889, when all of the Connellsville men stopped work. The miners not only allowed nothing for the 12½ per cent higher wages paid by the Frick Company but cleverly made that schedule the basis for further advances along the line gauged to put all workmen on the same plane. Frankly confessing that the strike came as a complete surprise and "led one to lose almost all faith" in the company's unappreciative employés, Mr. Frick, in his report to Mr. Carnegie, then abroad, could not resist the impulse to add significantly:

Enter the Carnegies

The men seemed to have made up their minds not to return to work under any circumstances nor at any wages until all of the men in the region returned to work at the same wages. They had before them the experience of the Frick Coke Company men getting an advance in 1887, the men of other operators having been kept out and having had to return at the old wages, thus creating a demoralization in their ranks and resulting in almost every operator paying different wages.

But the union had chosen shrewdly a time when stoppage of all furnaces for even so much as a fortnight would be disastrous; so there was nothing for it but to consent promptly to a 12 per cent increase continuing to February 1st, 1890, when a new general scale was to be agreed upon for a year.

Mr. Frick was not caught napping a second time, as the miners quickly discovered upon repeating their tactics pending a renewal of this contract. The coke bins were well filled and the steel business was so dull that the Carnegie companies had only to raise prices slightly to reduce orders to suit their convenience. The Frick Company was fully prepared for a siege and, accepting the issue forced upon it, calmly proceeded to fetch non-union workers into service. The enraged strikers and their sympathizers adopted a policy of terrorism and "the whole region was given over to rioting, arson and murder,"—but to no avail.

There was no interference with the President this time and no effective pressure could be brought to bear upon him. Gradually, under the compelling force of public opinion, the County authorities intervened sternly on behalf of law and order, shooting to kill and actually

Frick the Man

killing, until at the end of three months the rioters had been driven out of the region, and mining was resumed peaceably, without recognition of the union, upon the company's own terms, which incidentally proved to be eminently satisfactory to the miners.

VII

"The Man" in Steel

CONVINCED by the happenings in 1887 and 1888 of the "genius for management" of Mr. Frick, Mr. Carnegie concluded that he was "THE MAN" whom he had been seeking in vain to effect a sadly needed reorganization of the steel forces, and offered him a partnership, with the result that in January, 1889, the "coke king" acquired, with money loaned to him by Mr. Carnegie personally, a two per cent interest in Carnegie Brothers & Co., and became Chairman of the firm. This interest was increased by the same process at various times during the next three years, at the expiration of which it amounted to 11 per cent, equalling the holdings of Mr. Phipps and second only to Mr. Carnegie's majority of $55\frac{1}{3}$ per cent.

The new Chairman made haste slowly but surely. He had never anticipated engaging in steel manufacture and was ignorant of its details. What and practically all he did realize, as a consequence of casual observation, was that the business had outgrown the management to such an extent that conditions had become chaotic. Obviously the pressing necessity was, first, consolidation of the many segregated units into an effective, harmonious whole and, secondly, immense enlargement along safe lines upon a sound basis.

Frick the Man

No other kind of work could have appealed so strongly to his imaginative ambition. But the task was so great and the ramifications so many that painstaking acquirement of accurate knowledge of all phases was absolutely essential and, profiting from his invaluable experience, he began an intensive study of the entire problem as a requisite preliminary to any single move toward development.

The financial condition of the properties revealed by the balance sheet was not encouraging. An unsuspected slump in net profits from $2,900,000 in 1886 and $3,441,000 in 1887 to $1,900,000 in 1888 was most disquieting to the chief partners. Foreseeing this outcome, Mr. Phipps had quietly sold nearly one-half of his holdings during the year and Mr. Carnegie would probably have done likewise but for the necessity of retaining an actual majority for controlling and trading purposes. Both felt that the extreme limit of earning capacity might have been reached in 1887 and that the appalling break in 1888 only presaged a steady and irresistible shrinkage. All depended upon two factors,—higher prices from increased demand and lower costs from efficient management.

Fortunately these essentials came into play simultaneously and before the middle of the year 1889 had been reached profits were showing a marked advance. The time seemed propitious for sale of the properties and Mr. Carnegie, convinced that the rally was only temporary, determined to take advantage of it. Mr. Phipps acquiesced somewhat reluctantly and the elder partner sailed for England on a selling mission but for some reason,

"The Man" in Steel

possibly because his price seemed too high or because investors recalled that fifteen years before he had sold to them $6,000,000 of railroad bonds which subsequently proved to be worthless, or both, bankers manifested no interest and the project failed, greatly to his own disappointment and to the relief of Mr. Phipps, who wrote to him from Dresden on November 1st, 1889:

> With Mr. Frick at the head, I have no fear as to receiving a good return upon our capital. Being interested in manufacturing keeps us within touch of the world and its affairs instead of being on the shelf. Of course I am anxious that you should not be worried by the business—only pleasantly interested.

If a sale had been made for a sum reasonably based upon earnings and prospects, Mr. Carnegie could hardly have obtained for his share more than one-tenth of the amount which he received twelve years later from the Morgan syndicate.

Meanwhile the opening of new and delicate relations between Chief Stockholder and Chairman was not auspicious. Mr. Carnegie early in February evinced a desire to revive an old dispute over a matter of no great importance with the Pennsylvania Railroad, despite his own certainty that "the narrow legal minds that led it into a mess at first will no doubt assure Mr. Roberts that there is no legal liability,"—an anticipated opinion in which he did not concur.

But Mr. Frick demurred at asking the firm's lawyers to interpose if certain conditions should arise in Mr.

Frick the Man

Carnegie's absence, and won from him an admission that "our interests lie in future with the P. R. R."

But the concession, even though addressed to "My Dear Pard," was made with obvious reluctance and Mr. Carnegie became distinctly querulous as soon as he reached Europe in May.

"I very much fear," he wrote on June 1st from Paris, "that your coke matter will be allowed to fall through. It will be a sad ending to all, this fight. I believe you will fail and am disposed to be like the Frenchman this morning: 'Just filled with one grand disgust' at the whole affair." And then, somewhat incongruously:

> Busy visiting the various republics (Southern) but shall return to London by 13th to give that dinner to Mr. & Mrs. Lincoln Gladstone, etc.—All well. Take care of yourself—dont work too hard and dont grieve as I do over that $50,000 *per annum*—gone on ore rate—*I just hate compromises* after we have won a victory. They are so gratuitously needless. Now lets see if we can do the coke rate, straight cut, clear and once for all, 40¢ Pgh 30 E. T.

"Costs," he wrote from Christiania, "are the most alarming change I have known in our history. Jones must have made some radical change for sake of product. Now one or two thousand tons more per month is nothing if we are to be fleeced so in cost. Am awfully sorry you failed in your coke matter—wish now I had persisted and fired another gun at the monopoly,"—etc.

This letter arrived while the Chairman was wrestling with the coke strike and evoked the following response, written on the morning after the settlement at midnight of August 8th:

"The Man" in Steel

August 9th, 1889.

My dear Mr. Carnegie:

I have read with interest yours from Christiania.

It is very much pleasanter to agree than differ with you and in most things I would and will always defer to your judgment because there is no one whose attitude I hold in as high esteem, but I always hold to the opinion that your attack on P. R. R. was wrong and I should deprecate its renewal—You cannot expect me to succeed in carrying everything through that is wished for or undertaken.

I could not and would not remain the official head of any concern that was not well managed. If a concern is to be mismanaged, the official head's policy must have due consideration.

I cannot stand fault-finding and I must feel that I have the entire confidence of the power that put me where I am, in a place I did not seek.

With all that, I know I can manage both C. B. & Co., and Frick Coke Co., successfully.

Sincerely yours
H. C. FRICK.

Apparently this letter did not reach Mr. Carnegie before he sailed for home and was forwarded to Bar Harbor, where he had gone for a visit to James G. Blaine. In lieu of a specific reply, on September 2nd he addressed a long communication to "My Dear Mr. Frick and Boys in general," in the course of which he admonished "Our Chairman" to "remember that no buyer comes to him except because he can do better with him than with others" and closed with these words:

I will give you all my views freely. It is evident a new leaf must be turned over in C. P. & Co., perhaps you will find me at fault about the remedy and can devise a better policy. So be it. It rests with you—only don't give me any more surprises. Let us all know month after month, promptly, where we are going. I can stand losses with you but object to be deluded.

Yours A.C.

Frick the Man

But on the following day he wrote to "My Dear Mr. Frick" saying:

> Let me express the relief I feel in knowing that the important departments of our extended business are in the hands of a competent manager. Phipps and I exchanged congratulations upon this point. Now I only want to know how your hands can be strengthened. I am most anxious to carry out the work I told you about but you can well understand that neither Phipps nor I feel sure that C. P. & Co. is fairly off our hands.

Having succinctly defined his own attitude, Mr. Frick continued about his business, duly reported progress, was duly congratulated and closed the year's correspondence with an invitation to Mr. Carnegie to pay him a visit and inspect the recent acquisitions in the coke region constituting "a great property."

The first year of the new manager's direction of the chief Carnegie concern showed for the combined properties an increase in steel ingots produced from 332,111 to 536,838 gross tons and a net profit of $3,540,000, as against $1,991,555 for 1888.

This highly gratifying result served to modify the few irritations that had begun somewhat ominously to tincture the correspondence of two naturally, controlling spirits. Letters passed with increasing frequency to and from "My dear Mr. Carnegie" and "My dear Pard," to distinct mutual advantage; fault-finding ceased entirely, giving way to helpful and welcome suggestions, which might or might not be heeded without inciting resentment; opinions were exchanged with complete frankness from what seemed to be perfect understanding and a true cooperative spirit; and the way was cleared for full exer-

"The Man" in Steel

cise of the talents and energy of THE MAN, without let or hindrance, for more than two years.

Great progress was made. The various segregated plants, until then operated by dissociated and independent managements, jealous of and actually competing with one another, were assembled in masterly fashion; connecting railways were built; possession of yards which had been secured by the railroad companies was regained; waste was reduced to a minimum; and young, active and ambitious men headed by Schwab and Morrison were installed in authority and, while encouraged in every conceivable way, were held to strict accounting.

None was expected to work harder or longer than the Chairman himself, who rose methodically at 6 a.m., walked two miles to his office to keep fit, was at his desk invariably at eight o'clock ready for business, conferred at luncheon with one or more of his lieutenants, returned home when he had finished the day's work, joked with his seven-year-old son, played with his two little daughters, dined almost always alone with his wife quietly and quickly, studied business problems till early bed-time, and slept soundly till the whistle blew for the beginning of another identical day.

There can be little doubt that 1890 was the happiest year in the life of Henry Clay Frick. He revelled in doing and gloried in achieving big things. No project conceived by his own growing imagination or suggested by another's mind fazed him for a moment, provided only that it tended to concentration of effort and expansion of business. And he not only kept close hold of all the

Frick the Man

reins of operation, but he did practically all of the financing of all the companies for whose direction he was responsible.

The most striking instance of his application of ingenuity and patience was afforded by his acquisition of the Carnegie group's only rival. The Duquesne Steel Company was incorporated in 1886 by William G. and D. E. Park, and E. L. Clark, competent and successful manufacturers, and its plant, three years in building, was the best equipped in the country, with new and improved machinery adapted to superior methods which could not fail to produce first-quality rails at a far lower cost than could be attained by Carnegie machinery.

Mr. Frick was awake to the menace and made a tentative offer of $600,000 for the works in 1889 before they had been put into full operation, but the price was not satisfactory and he bided his time. At the end of a year Mr. Park, harassed by strikes and handicapped by refusal of his partners to furnish additional capital to meet the cost of expensive construction, evinced a desire to sell and Mr. Frick promptly raised his offer to $1,000,000 in bonds of Carnegie Brothers & Co., which had then become, as a consequence of the first year's showing under his management, gilt-edged. He probably could have obtained the property for less money, as the company was on the verge of bankruptcy, but, having thoughtfully procured a market for the next year's product in the event of being able to supply it, he perceived no possibility of loss or occasion for haggling, and his offer was accepted.

On October 30th, 1890, his thoroughly trained organi-

"The Man" in Steel

zation took over the splendid plant, with young Thomas Morrison, a relative of Mr. Carnegie, already cocked and primed to take full charge and with arrangements made in advance for connecting up by rail with the Carnegie plants in record time. Results were amazing. The net profits for the first year exceeded the purchase price of $1,000,000; when the bonds fell due, the plant had paid for itself six times over; and surplus earnings were "ploughed back" into the property to so vast an extent that ten years later the plant had attained the enormous capacity per year of 750,000 tons of pig-iron and 600,000 tons of raw steel, with adequate facilities within its own area for turning the entire huge quantity of raw material into finished products.

Few, if any, achievements surpassing this in magnitude and celerity combined are recorded in industrial history.

But further consolidation was required to perfect the organization. The firm of Carnegie, Phipps & Co., which had been formed in 1886 to take over the plant at Homestead, was still a separate concern. Its ownership was identical with that of Carnegie Brothers & Co., and Mr. Frick was elected a manager in 1889 but took no part in administration. There was no antagonism between the two companies but the fact was evident that actual consolidation was highly desirable for economy's sake. The real obstacle was financial. Working capital had been obtained by discounting notes given by one company to another, as buyer and seller respectively, thus providing the "two-name paper" required by banks and inciden-

Frick the Man

tally funds for whichever concern stood in need. In these circumstances, it seemed hazardous to extinguish Carnegie, Phipps & Co., but happily the H. C. Frick Coke Company's credit was responding so strongly to steadily increasing earnings that Mr. Frick felt justified in writing to Mr. Carnegie:

(OWN HAND)

My dear Mr. Carnegie: February 10th., 1890.

Referring to the condition of our finances, and looking towards consolidating C. B. & C. P. & Co., I find there is outstanding $1,185,000.00 of paper made by Carnegie Phipps & Co., to the order of Carnegie Bros. & Co., $860,000.00 of paper made by Carnegie Bros. & Co., to the order of Frick Coke Co., the proceeds of which was paid to Carnegie Bros & Co., $590,000.00 of paper made by Carnegie Bros. & Co., to the order of Frick Coke Co., for the accommodation of the Frick Coke Co.

So you see a few months of such earnings as we are now having will enable us to get along without the necessity of taking paper from C. P. & Co. If anything of the kind is needed, the Frick Coke Co. can be used. Had a talk with Abbott who favors making one company.

Yours very truly
H. C. FRICK.

Upon these confident expectations which were abundantly realized during the period allotted by Mr. Frick, the merger was agreed to by all of the twenty-two partners, to go into effect on July 1st, 1892, through the sale of the physical properties to a new company called The Carnegie Steel Company, Limited, capitalized at $25,000,000. It was duly stipulated in the Articles of Association that the entire amount should be "paid in cash" by the subscribers, i.e., the partners in proportion to their holdings, and so indeed it was,—from the treasuries of the absorbed companies and the proceeds of the sale of

"The Man" in Steel

the properties at valuations made to match. No new money was contributed. The transaction, in effect, was a mere increase in capital from the original $5,000,000 to $25,000,000 through what amounted to a 400 per cent share dividend.

And it was a modest capitalization at that, for the simple reason that the second year of Frick management, 1890, showed net profits of $5,350,000, an increase of $1,810,000 and more than 20 per cent upon the entire $25,000,000.

The "subscribers," as of July 1st, 1892, were:

	CAPITAL		
NAME	ORIGINAL	INCREASE	TOTAL
Andrew Carnegie	$2,766,666.67	$11,066,666.66	$13,833,333.33
Henry Phipps, Jr.	550,000.00	2,200,000.00	2,750,000.00
Henry Clay Frick	550,000.00	2,200,000.00	2,750,000.00
George Lauder	200,000.00	800,000.00	1,000,000.00
William H. Singer	100,000.00	400,000.00	500,000.00
Henry M. Curry	100,000.00	400,000.00	500,000.00
Henry W. Borntraeger	100,000.00	400,000.00	500,000.00
John G. A. Leishman	100,000.00	400,000.00	500,000.00
William L. Abbott	50,000.00	200,000.00	250,000.00
Otis H. Childs	50,000.00	200,000.00	250,000.00
John W. Vandevort	40,000.00	160,000.00	200,000.00
Charles L. Strobel	33,333.33	133,333.34	166,666.67
Francis T. F. Lovejoy	33,333.33	133,333.34	166,666.67
Patrick R. Dillon	25,000.00	100,000.00	125,000.00
William W. Blackburn	16,666.67	66,666.66	83,333.33
William P. Palmer	16,666.67	66,666.66	83,333.33
Lawrence C. Phipps	16,666.67	66,666.66	83,333.33
Alexander R. Peacock	16,666.67	66,666.66	83,333.33
J. Ogden Hoffman	16,666.67	66,666.66	83,333.33
John C. Fleming	16,666.67	66,666.66	83,333.33
James H. Simpson	12,500.00	50,000.00	62,500.00
Henry B. Bope	5,555.55	22,222.23	27,777.78
F. T. F. Lovejoy, Trustee	183,611.10	734,444.47	918,055.57
Total	$5,000,000.00	$20,000,000.00	$25,000,000.00

Only Messrs. Carnegie, Phipps and Frick were really independent shareholders. The others were "debtor part-

Frick the Man

ners," owing the Company for the holdings allotted to them, which were expected to be and, in fact, were eventually paid for out of earnings and other revenues.

Mr. Frick's interest had been increased from his original 2 per cent to 11 per cent, partly through purchase of a deceased partner's share and partly at the instance and with the cooperation of Mr. Carnegie, who obviously wanted to hold fast to THE MAN who was coining money for him.

"I wish we could get H. P. (Mr. Phipps) satisfied," he wrote in February, 1890—"Never had a difference before with him—He has sold and is sorry. I'm quite sure he feels that your interest is too small just as I do, but it was you who said 'decide (or 'divide') even', and I did so. Should you like to merge or do something to get more (?) for really it is to be wonderfully profitable. I don't understand why you owe (me) so little—You must have been paying up from outside fortune. Think over all this and suggest best plan—any plan that's good and fair will suit me."

But a full year elapsed before Mr. Frick, with his annoying experiences of 1889 still fresh in mind, became convinced that he could go along with Mr. Carnegie and signified his willingness to incur further obligations, evoking the following cheery response:

Sunday, March 29th, 1891.
My dear Mr. Frick:
   I am delighted to think you can now go in and increase your interest—You ought to—for theres no business in this world that I know of which will make more money or give your talents greater scope.

"The Man" in Steel

The "margin" idea is satisfactory—highly approved for I do not wish you to be anxious about the future.

My hope is you will then "concentrate" upon the business and make it the greatest ever seen—even Chicago would rank second—

I'll fix it all with you next week when I go to Pittsburgh.

Yours A.C.

The arrangement was soon made along the lines proposed, to the satisfaction of all interested in the future welfare of the company, and Mr. Frick, as Chairman of Carnegie Brothers & Co., assumed full charge of plans preliminary to the fateful negotiations with the Labor Union spokesmen of nearly four thousand workmen at Homestead. Simultaneously, following the formal retirement of Messrs. Carnegie and Phipps, officers of the new Carnegie Steel Company, Limited, scheduled to begin operation on July 1st, were unanimously agreed upon as follows:

CHAIRMAN, Henry Clay Frick; TREASURER, Henry M. Curry; SECRETARY, Francis T. F. Lovejoy; MANAGERS, Henry Clay Frick, George Lauder, William H. Singer, Henry M. Curry, John G. A. Leishman, Lawrence C. Phipps, Francis T. F. Lovejoy.

The reorganization was complete and absolute control of the greatest steel company, including the largest coke company, in the world, employing thirty thousand men, was vested for one year in Henry Clay Frick at the promising age of forty-one.

VIII

Homestead

THE seeds of the most famous of all strikes, at Homestead in 1892, were planted in the wage settlement imposed upon Carnegie, Phipps & Co. by the Amalgamated Association of Iron & Steel Workers in 1889. Prior to that time there had been no standards of compensation, and no provision had been made for readjustment to conform to the increase in the output of individual workmen arising from new methods and improved machinery applicable particularly to the fabrication of Bessemer and open-hearth steel. As a consequence, earnings based upon tonnage had not only advanced to grossly excessive figures but were distributed most inequitably, unskilled laborers in many instances getting from five to ten times as much as highly trained mechanics.

To rectify these inequalities, Chairman Abbott proposed, with the approval of Mr. Carnegie, a general reduction in wages of about 25 per cent and automatic regulation of future compensation by a scale which should follow, from month to month, the prices received by the firm for steel sold. This so-called "sliding-scale" basis had already been adopted at Braddock and Duquesne and had proved so satisfactory to all concerned that the union felt constrained to accept it. But the leaders flatly rejected

Homestead

the other proposals and imposed so many operating conditions, including participation in determining selling prices, that a strike or a lock-out seemed inevitable when, after adjuring the Chairman to stand firm, Mr. Carnegie sailed for Scotland.

Mr. Abbott, left to interpret his instructions, private as well as public, as best he might, refused to accept the stringent terms prescribed by the union and, reluctantly deciding to continue operations, called upon the county authorities for protection of property and new employés. The Sheriff assured him that he need have no apprehension on this score and promptly steamed up the river with a posse of a hundred men to fulfil his pledge. A great preponderance of workmen, fully equipped for battle, awaited them at the dock and dared them to try to land. Retreat obviously was the better part of valor and the Sheriff escorted his henchmen back to their firesides.

Intimidated by threats of violence and destruction of property, Mr. Abbott accepted a summons to parley with the officers of the union and signed an agreement for three years which in effect constituted a complete surrender.

Results were disastrous. The price of rails declined steadily from $36 at the close of 1889 to $25.75 in 1890, and so on to $22.50 in May, 1892, when the firm was losing money on its chief products and was heading straight, in Mr. Frick's opinion expressed convincingly to the Congressional Committee, to "eventual bankruptcy."

Obviously when the time approached for renewing or revising the agreement the financial prospect was bad

Frick the Man

enough, but the actual situation was worse. Of the thirty-eight hundred men employed at Homestead only about eleven hundred were native-born, more than eight hundred could not speak English and the remaining two thousand were incapable of perceiving the futility of requiring a strangled goose to continue to lay golden eggs. A more fallow field for ambitious labor agitators could not be imagined. The Amalgamated Association, moreover, had demonstrated its power three years before and in consequence had strengthened its position, with the widespread Knights of Labor in sympathetic accord in a Presidential year.

Mr. Carnegie had promulgated his famous dictum to individual laborers, "Thou shalt not seek thy neighbor's job" and was still controlling owner of the property. That he would uphold his own adage and repudiate any manager who should propose to fill the places of striking workmen was considered a certainty. The fact that he had once, in precisely similar circumstances, in the coke strike, overridden and forced the resignation of Mr. Frick seemed conclusive; and yet—

Why had Mr. Abbott been supplanted? What did the accession of Mr. Frick portend?

Here, of all managers, was THE MAN who had never truckled, never yielded, and who seemed impervious to either threats or danger of assaults. He appeared to the officials of both the miners' union and of the potentially forceful Knights as the most formidable lion in their path to industrial control. Never could they hope for a more favorable opportunity to break his rapidly growing

Homestead

authoritativeness among employers. Then, if ever, was the time to subject him, single handed and alone, to the ordeal of battle for supremacy.

Mr. Frick did not welcome the test; he stood ready to concede much for a peace that would enable the other plants to forge ahead at the unprecedented pace they had struck; "the magnitude of our business," he wrote to the chief stockholder, "is such that there are plenty of important matters to take up without being troubled with strikes."

It was to avoid being caught in the meshes of unpreparedness which had placed the firm at the mercy of the union that Mr. Frick invited the Amalgamated Association to take up the matter in January, but to no purpose. The union leaders neither accepted nor rejected the suggestion; they simply ignored it; and two months passed before unceasing insistence evoked a response in the form of a proposed new scale providing a general advance in wages all along the line.

As the most that had been expected was maintenance of the old rates, this demand was gravely disconcerting, but conferences ensued in good temper until the last of May, when the firm submitted a counter scale reducing the wages of 325 of the most highly paid employés from 15 to 18 per cent and continuing the compensation of 2,475 lower paid men at the old rates.

"The scales," wrote Mr. Frick to Superintendent Potter under date of May 30th, 1892, "have had most careful consideration, with a desire to act toward our employés in the most liberal manner. A number of rates have been

Frick the Man

advanced upon your recommendation, and the wages which will be earned thereunder are considerably in advance of those received by the employés of any of our competitors in the same lines. You can say to the committee that these scales are in all respects the most liberal that can be offered. We do not care whether a man belongs to a union or not, nor do we wish to interfere. He may belong to as many unions or organizations as he chooses, but we think our employés at Homestead Steel Works would fare much better working under the system in vogue at Edgar Thomson and Duquesne."

The schedules were submitted immediately to the Joint Committee, accompanied by this communication and by a request from the Chairman for a response not later than June 24th, pending the expiration of the existing agreement on June 30th.

On June 23rd the union leaders sought a conference and Chairman Frick and Superintendent Potter met them. Three questions were raised:

1. Should the minimum selling price of steel determining the wage-scale remain at $25 per ton as required by the men or be reduced to $22 as asked by the firm? After full discussion the union offered to reduce the amount to $24 and the firm conceded an increase to $23.

2. Should the date of operation of the scale be changed from June 30th to December 31st, as desired by the firm to facilitate the making of annual contracts with consumers, or be retained, by wish of the union, to avert any disadvantage from negotiating during the slack period of manufacturing?

Homestead

3. Should a reduction in tonnage rates be made in three departments to compensate in part for the large sums expended for improvements and new machinery which greatly increased the output of every workman without requiring additional exertion?

These differences were not vital; the first indeed was trivial and the other two could have been adjusted readily but for extrinsic considerations of prestige bearing upon general rolling-mill scales then under discussion throughout the country. So no further concession was offered by either side and the issue of dominance, if not of actual control, between capital and labor, personified by owners and unions, was squarely joined and Mr. Frick, relying upon the inviolability of "property," no less than of "life and liberty," guaranteed by the Constitution, decided to close the mills on July 1st and to reopen them, unless prevented by force, on July 6th.

There ensued a week of mildly ominous calm as viewed by the public and the Press, but under the surface active preparations were being made for the struggle which had then become imminent and unavoidable. The workmen quietly elected an Advisory Committee of five members from each of their eight lodges, with Mr. Hugh O'Donnell, one of the skilled employés earning $144 per month on an eight-hour shift, as Chairman, and vested it with full authority.

Action was prompt and decisive. On July 1st, the day following cessation of operations, the Committee adopted resolutions whose tenor was indicated by the following announcement by the Chairman:

Frick the Man

> The Committee has, after mature deliberation, decided to organize their forces on a truly military basis. The force of four thousand men has been divided into three divisions or watches, each of these divisions is to devote eight hours of the twenty-four to the task of watching the plant. The Commanders of these divisions are to have as assistants eight captains composed of one trusted man from each of the eight local lodges. These Captains will report to the division Commanders, who in turn will receive the orders from the Advisory Committee. During their hours of duty these Captains will have personal charge of the most important posts, i.e., the river front, the water gates and pumps, the railway stations, and the main gates of the plant. The girdle of pickets will file reports to the main headquarters every half-hour, and so complete and detailed is the plan of campaign that in ten minutes' time the Committee can communicate with the men at any given point within a radius of five miles. In addition to all this, there will be held in reserve a force of 800 Slavs and Hungarians. The brigade of foreigners will be under the command of two Hungarians and two interpreters.

So audacious a manifesto as this had never before and, to our knowledge, has never since been put forth. It heralded much more than a renewal of the policy of terrorism which had proved successful three years previous. It was an avowal of a right to possession of property belonging undeniably to others and of determination to retain occupancy by "forces organized on a truly military basis" to repel invasion from whatever source.

The plan was put into effect forthwith. First the foremen representing the owners were "stopped and intimidated" at the gate, prevented from entering the mill and "turned back." Then the Sheriff, acting for the County, visited the scene and "tried to make an arrangement" with Chairman O'Donnell and other members of the Advisory Committee, "to allow me to put watchmen in for the protection of the works."

Homestead

"What did they say to that?" asked Chairman Oates of the Congressional Committee, later on.

"They said there was no necessity for watchmen there," the Sheriff replied, "that it was not required, that there was no danger of that property being destroyed. I explained to them that I was not the judge of that and that this firm had notified me to that effect and that under the law I was compelled to protect their property."

"So you came away. What did you do next?"

"Then I came back to town."

"What did you do next?"

"I sent up twelve deputies from my office force. They were not permitted to enter the works. They were driven away."

When they reached the station, the Deputy Sheriff in charge of the posse testified, "Some of the men came up to us and the spokesman said 'What are you fellows doing here?' I said 'I am a special officer representing the Sheriff of Allegheny County to put deputies in the mill to act as a guard and to protect the property for the Company.' He said, 'No deputy will ever go in there alive.' There was one gentleman, the doctor up there, who had been suggested as a possible deputy and who knew nearly every man connected with the lockout, and he said, 'I would not go there because I know they would kill me as quickly as anybody else; I should be afraid for my life to go near that mill.' I returned to the city and reported to the Sheriff."

Meanwhile, Mr. Frick, having anticipated these very

Frick the Man

happenings, was making his own arrangements for the recovery of the firm's property. On June 25th, the day following the breakdown of negotiations, having already been assured by the Pinkerton agency that an adequate number of men could be supplied for protective service at short notice, he sent the following letter:

> The Carnegie Steel Company, Limited,
> Pittsburgh, Pa., June 25th, 1892.
>
> DEAR SIR: I am in receipt of your favor of the 22nd.
>
> We will want 300 guards for service at our Homestead mills as a measure of precaution against interference with our plan to start operation of the works on July 6th, 1892.
>
> The only trouble we anticipate is that an attempt will be made to prevent such of our men with whom we will by that time have made satisfactory arrangements from going to work, and possibly some demonstration of violence upon the part of those whose places have been filled, or most likely by an element which usually is attracted to such scenes for the purpose of stirring up trouble.
>
> We are not desirous that the men you send shall be armed unless the occasion properly calls for such a measure later on for the protection of our employés or property. We shall wish these guards to be placed upon our property and there to remain unless called into other service by the civil authorities to meet an emergency that is not likely to arise.
>
> These guards should be assembled at Ashtabula, Ohio, not later than the morning of July 5th, when they may be taken by train to McKee's Rocks, or some other point upon the Ohio River below Pittsburgh, where they can be transferred to boats and landed within the inclosures of our premises at Homestead. We think absolute secrecy essential in the movement of these men so that no demonstration can be made while they are en route.
>
> Specific arrangements for movement of trains and connection with boats will be made as soon as we hear from you as to the certainty of having the men at Ashtabula at the time indicated.
>
> As soon as your men are upon the premises we will notify the

Homestead

Sheriff and ask that they be deputized either at once or immediately upon an outbreak of such a character as to render such a step desirable.

Yours very truly
H. C. FRICK,
Chairman.

Robert A. Pinkerton, Esq.
New York City, N.Y.

"Why," Mr. Frick was asked later in connection with the Congressional inquiry, "did the company call upon the Pinkertons for watchmen to protect their property?"

"Because," he replied, "we did not see how else we could get protection. We only wanted them for watchmen to protect our property and see that workmen we would take to Homestead—and we had had applications from many men to go there to work—were not interfered with."

"Did you doubt the ability of the Sheriff to enforce order at Homestead and protect your property?"

"Yes, sir; with local deputies."

"Why?"

"For the reason that three years ago our concern had an experience similar to this. We felt the necessity of a change at the works; that a scale should be adopted based on the sliding price of billets, and we asked the county authorities for protection. The workmen began tactics similar to those employed in the present troubles. Under that stress, in fear of the Amalgamated Association, an agreement was made and work was resumed. We did not propose this time to be placed in that position."

"The Pinkerton men, as generally understood, had been summoned and all arrangements made with them to be

Frick the Man

on hand in case of failure by the Sheriff to afford protection. Is that a fact or not?"

"The facts concerning the engagement of the Pinkerton men are these: From past experience, not only with the present Sheriff but with all others, we have found that he has been unable to furnish us with a sufficient number of deputies to guard our property and protect the men who were anxious to work on our terms. As the Amalgamated men from the 1st of July had surrounded our works, placed guards at all the entrances, and at all avenues or roads leading to our establishment and for miles distant therefrom, we felt that for the safety of our property, and in order to protect our workmen, it was necessary for us to secure our own watchmen to assist the Sheriff, and we knew of no other source from which to obtain them than from Pinkerton agencies, and to them we applied.

"We brought the watchmen here as quietly as possible; and had them taken to Homestead at an hour of the night when we hoped to have them enter our works without any interference whatever and without meeting anybody. We proposed to land them on our own property, and all our efforts were to prevent the possibilities of a collision between our former workmen and our watchmen."

The plans were carefully laid and shrewdly executed. On the morning of July 5th the Pinkerton guards numbering three hundred were assembled at Ashtabula, Ohio, conveyed by train to Bellevue, transferred to two barges and towed by tugboats up the river after dark to Pittsburgh, where boxes containing arms had already been placed upon the barges.

Homestead

Scrupulous care was taken to comply with all provisions of law. Superintendent Potter, by suggestion of the firm's counsel, Messrs. Knox and Reed, was warned by Chairman Frick that "no matter what indignities he may be subjected to, neither he nor any of the Company's employés should do any act of aggression nor under any circumstances resort to the use of arms unless for the protection of their lives," and Captains Heinde and Kline, in charge of the watchmen, were ordered by the Pinkertons not to open the boxes until they were placed in the mills and even then to do nothing until regularly sworn in as deputies by the Sheriff and compelled by their oaths to obey his orders.

All promised well when, shrouded in darkness, the tugboat LITTLE BILL set forth towing the two barges toward Homestead. Aboard the boat were Captain Rodgers and crew, Superintendent Potter and several of his superintendents, Captains Heinde and Kline and finally ex-Sheriff Joseph H. Gray, who had been deputized by Sheriff McCleary to act as his representative and was supposed by the others to be in command of the expedition by virtue of the following communication which he presented to Superintendent Potter at the dock:

June 5th, 1892.
John A. Potter:
Dear Sir: This will introduce Col. Joseph H. Gray, deputy sheriff.
Yours truly,
KNOX & REED.

You will understand that Col. Gray, as the representative of the sheriff, is to have control of all action in case of trouble.
KNOX & REED.

Frick the Man

Although subsequently the Sheriff admitted that this authorization was added to the line of introduction by his own "direction and sanction," he testified further that Deputy Gray was not actually empowered to take control in case of trouble but was merely "sent along to preserve the peace" and "if there was liable to be a collision" over landing, to instruct the guards to "back out and leave"; but the Deputy did not reveal the limitations of his personal authority and the little fleet set forth under a nominal commander bereft of powers either to act himself or to deputize others to act for him.

The military organization created by the Advisory Committee to prevent either the owners or the State authorities from regaining possession of the six-million-dollar plant proved far more efficient than anybody had supposed it to be. No sooner had the LITTLE BILL got under way, with the two barges in tow, about midnight, than word of its departure was flashed by an alert spy to Chairman O'Donnell in Homestead, and the moment the report was confirmed from Lock No. 1, three miles below the town, the steam whistles shrieked the alarm and the entire population scrambled out of their beds into the streets and rushed to the river banks.

Rifle fire was opened on the tugboat and barges about a mile below Homestead and was continued eagerly but wildly, scoring many hits but finding no human targets, while the LITTLE BILL puffed doggedly along past the town to the landing place on the firm's property and the crew threw out a stage plank. The mob of a thousand or more at this point were clambering down the bank when

Homestead

a young man leaped forward and threw himself flat upon the stage and, as Captain Heinde stepped forward to push him off, he fired the first bullet that reached its mark and brought the Captain to the deck with a bullet in his thigh.

Instantly the crowds along the river and on the bank pelted the boat and barges with bullets and rushed forward to board them, but the Pinkerton men, firing then for the first time, repelled the assault and drove the assailants back to their intrenchments protected by pig iron and iron plates. Firing then practically ceased for a time while both sides attended to their wounded.

The lack of a responsible commander then became even more serious than at any previous time. Twice Captain Heinde had urged Deputy Sheriff Gray to deputize the watchmen and twice the Sheriff's representative had refused, saying that it would be time enough to do that when they had obtained possession of the mills. This imposed upon him the necessity of disregarding his own orders or abandoning his men to certain death. He finally authorized distribution of twelve rifles to men whom he sent below in the hope that others armed only with night sticks would suffice to resist invasion successfully. This project naturally failed when he fell unconscious at the first fire and the use of guns was required to repel the boarding crowd.

While this fighting was taking place at the landing several watchmen on the first barge were wounded and Superintendent Potter, discovering that their comrades were retaliating and beginning to unpack the boxes, ordered them to stop, and was obeyed.

Frick the Man

This was the anomalous condition of affairs when, following the tacit armistice, a consultation participated in by Deputy Sheriff Gray, Superintendent Potter, Captain Nordrum, in place of Captain Heinde, and Captain Rodgers, shipmaster, was held on the boat.

"It was a question," testified Mr. Potter, "whether we could get into the works by force or whether we should let the thing take its course. Mr. Gray did not feel like taking the responsibility upon himself, and I would not. He refused to take any action and I felt that my instructions had been carried out. It was decided that the wounded had to be taken care of and that we would leave the barges to remain where they were, as the crowd seemed to be going away, and we thought in an hour or two or three hours, there could be a peaceable landing made."

So the tugboat steamed away to Port Perry where Superintendent Potter and the six wounded men took a train for Pittsburgh. Two hours later the tugboat bearing Captain Rodgers, his crew of six men, Deputy Sheriff Gray and a Pinkerton man, returned to Homestead. The Captain testified:

> We went back with the intent to land with the barges and stay with them, or go on to town for further commissary supplies which had been left behind. In anticipation we would be fired on we determined to fight under the colors, and so ran up two flags, one at each end. When we attempted to land alongside the barge we were met with heavy volleys from both sides of the river, particularly the Homestead side, and from behind intrenchments. The firing was so heavy the pilot and engineer were compelled to leave their posts and we were compelled to stop the boat, which drifted around at the mercy of the mob, which continued firing. This lasted until

Homestead

we drifted away from the point and to some extent out of the range of the guns. The shore was lined with thousands on the Homestead side, and a good number on the opposite side, all of whom seemed bent on destroying our lives and our boat. Holes in the boat show missiles were fired from artillery. This firing gradually died away until we were 1½ miles from Homestead, when it ceased.

When we were drifting to the point, in point-blank range of the mob, and only 30 or 40 feet away, our destruction would have been inevitable had we not used means of defence we found on the boat. We did this with such effect that the mob scattered and we were enabled to put the pilot and engineer at their posts and so get away.

I can only say, in conclusion, that I have never heard or read of any such inhuman action as that of this mob, or a part of it, in shooting at wounded men, and doing it with fiendish delight.

The plight of the three hundred watchmen, confined in the stranded and deserted barges, was desperate indeed. Surrounded by thousands of bloodthirsty enemies bent solely upon their complete extinction and equipped with all diabolical agencies of destruction, they could not even fight for their lives. Any one who showed a head for an instant at a hatchway or porthole gasping for a breath of air was pelted with bullets by sharpshooters; oil was pumped upon the surface of the water and set on fire; natural gas, directed from a large main, was exploded by rockets; dynamite was hurled upon the barges to blow them to bits; burning rafts were floated down to set them on fire; cannon blazed at them from the opposite bank; —such was the inferno in which the prisoners barely existed until, without hope of succor and destitute even of food, they raised a white flag in token of surrender, only to see it riddled by bullets.

A second attempt to save their lives if possible, late in the afternoon, drew an answering signal from the Ad-

Frick the Man

visory Committee, and Chairman O'Donnell, having addressed the crowd who, in his own words, "pledged themselves to a man to let the watchmen go unharmed and in peace if they surrendered," went down to the boat and accepted the sole condition asked by the prisoners "that you will give us free passage from Homestead."

"When all was ready," continued Mr. O'Donnell in his testimony, "I gave the order and they marched out, and I remained on the boat until the last man. I will state by this time people were coming up, down, and across the river, and that the barges were in the hands of the rabble. I left the boat and they were marched to the rink, and the people formed on either side—men, women, and children—and I must say they were subjected to very inhuman treatment, which our men were powerless to protect them from, and I know that many of our men have received scars and bruises in their endeavor to protect the Pinkertons. We took them to the rink and that night we sent them off."

The "very inhuman treatment" noted by Mr. O'Donnell, who incidentally followed the procession, was depicted in his book by Mr. Bridge from information garnered from newspaper accounts, in these words:

> The doors of the barges were flung open and the victorious strikers crowded into the barges. The reporters who followed them found one dead and eleven wounded watchmen. The rest were disarmed and marched out, while the crowd swarmed over the boat for loot. Cases of provisions were broken open and the contents distributed among the women and children; bedding and every portable thing was taken away. Then the barges were set on fire; and the strikers turned to escort their prisoners to a public hall in

Homestead

town. One by one, with bared heads, the latter descended the gangplank, climbed up the incline to the mill yard, and across it to the public road; and never did captives suffer more in running a gauntlet of redskins. For nearly a mile the watchmen walked, ran, or crawled through a lane of infuriated men, women, and children; and at every step they were struck with fists, clubs, and stones. Their hats, satchels, and coats were snatched away from them; and in many cases they were robbed of their watches and money. Not a man escaped injury. One of them, Connors, unable to move and defend himself, was deliberately shot by one of the strikers and then clubbed. Another, named Edwards, also wounded and helpless, was clubbed by another striker with the butt end of a musket. Both of these men died; and another became insane and committed suicide as a result of the fearful beating received after surrender. About thirty others were afterwards taken to the hospital with broken arms and disjointed ankles, shattered noses, gouged eyes, bruised heads, and injured backs.

Sheriff McCleary, at the instigation of Mr. Frick, who provided a special train, went to Homestead at midnight accompanied by President Weihe of the Amalgamated Association and brought the watchmen back to Pittsburgh hospitals. The day's casualties were ten killed and more than sixty wounded.

The rout was complete; the triumph hardly less impressive than that which followed the first battle of Bull Run; the victory the most costly of its kind ever won.

IX

The State Intervenes

THE morning of July 7th dawned upon a wholly peaceful community, with the Advisory Committee of the Amalgamated Association in absolute possession of the properties owned by the Carnegie Steel Company and in full military control of the town of Homestead with its ten thousand inhabitants and all the approaches by land and water to both. A state of siege was declared. Strangers were excluded, citizens were arrested without warrant, telegrams to newspapers and individuals were censored and reporters suspected of writing unfavorable accounts were kicked out hatless and coatless to grope their way through the darkness of night to Pittsburgh as best they could.

"Mob law," a special correspondent who had been thus treated telegraphed to the NEW YORK TIMES, "is absolute. Never were rioters better armed. Not only have they in their possession the guns captured from the three hundred Pinkertons, with all the ammunition belonging to that fateful expedition, but they have also been supplied with rifles by three independent military organizations of Pittsburgh, known as the Hibernian Rifles, and by a Polish gun club. Today they received a box of ammunition from Philadelphia, and yesterday one of the strikers informed a reporter that enough dynamite was

The State Intervenes

at their disposal to blow all the Carnegie works out of sight—a remark which was exaggerated into a rumor that they would destroy the works before non-union men were permitted to enter them.

"Reinforcements are hourly pouring into Homestead from all quarters of the country—lawless, desperate, murderous characters. They all claim to be workmen, sympathetic and interested—sympathetic over the trouble which has fallen upon their brethren, interested in the final result.

"It is impossible to reach the Carnegie works. Today Mr. Frick's assistant, Mr. Childs, accompanied by Mr. Potter, the Superintendent of the works, walked toward the works. At the railway track they were stopped.

"'We desire to visit the works,' said Mr. Childs.

"'You cannot visit them,' was the reply.

"'You know who I am?' asked Mr. Potter.

"'Yes, but we have orders not to allow any one to enter the works.'"

There was no strike, no lockout; there had not been at any time; work had simply ceased automatically when the time fixed by the agreement expired and terms for continuance had not been arranged. It was no mere riot, it was organized rebellion as clearly as Shay's in the early history of the Republic.

"It was not" sternly declared Chief Justice Paxson later, "a cry of 'bread or blood' from famished lips or an ebullition of angry passions from a sudden outrage or provocation. It was a deliberate attempt of men without a grievance to wrest from others their lawfully acquired property and to control them in their use and enjoyment of it.

"A mere mob, collected upon the impulse of the moment, without any definite object beyond the gratification of its sudden passions, does not commit treason, although it destroys property and takes human life. But when a large number of men arm and organize themselves by divisions and companies, appoint officers, and engage in a common purpose to defy the law, to resist its officers, and to deprive any portion of their fellow-citizens of the rights to which they are entitled under the Constitution and laws of the Commonwealth of Pennsylvania, it is a levying of war against the State, and the offense is treason."

This phase of the situation, imperceptible to the exultant rioters, was one which could not fail to give rise to uneasiness in the minds of the leaders of the Amalgamated Association and their experienced advisers. After all, it was a matter, not of wages for ignorant workmen known to be fully paid, but of establishment of their own power as officials of the union, that constituted the chief stake in the contest. True, they still held fast the powerful factors which they had counted upon originally to ensure their success. Neither of the two great political organizations would dare antagonize the millions of workingmen whose votes could and probably would be massed by their various unions throughout the entire country in the forthcoming National election. Aggressive Democratic and timorous Republican newspapers would be equally solicitous for the "rights" of labor

The State Intervenes

as contrasted with the "privileges" of capital, and reason would be submerged in waves of public sympathy.

The wholly practical leaders of both parties would point to dreaded tariff reduction as suspended by a thread over the heads of steel manufacturers, extinction of "protection" would be certain in the event of Democratic success, and severance of the tacit alliance which had provided heavy duties would surely follow a Republican defeat which could be attributed to the selfish obduracy of a favored "infant industry."

The consequences to the Carnegie shareholders clearly would be disastrous if a settlement satisfactory to both unions and men should not be effected before election day, —and Mr. Carnegie, who owned a majority of the stock, had expressed his approval and pledged his support of unionism over and over again and in one signal instance had overridden the very manager who now blocked the way of the ambitious labor leaders. Surely not only the controlling owner but all other stockholders, every one of whom was a lifelong Republican, a high protectionist and an eager recipient of political favors, both past and to come, could be relied upon to temporize for permanent advantage.

All? Yes, all but one; only one of all the Company's shareholders, only one of all contributing Republicans, only one of all tenderly nurtured manufacturers, to beat! It looked easy. So the leaders argued. AND YET—

It might be the better part of valor to waive magnanimously the claims of the men, to allay conceivable public resentment at their shocking resort to brutality and

Frick the Man

murder and thereby, in any case and above all, to save the face of the union.

No time was lost in trying to appease public opinion. On the day following the battle Chairman O'Donnell, tacitly admitting that all other demands had lacked justification, singled out the insistence that the date of fixing the scale of wages should not be changed from June to December as the one unalterable resolve which "under no circumstances" would be modified, and declared that "the final adjustment must be made now." Another member of the Amalgamated Association who had the confidence of the Sheriff informed that official that mere acceptance by the company of a proposal to "confer with," i.e., to recognize, the union, would suffice to "stop the rioting."

Mr. Frick publicly rejoined that terms ceased to be an issue when the company was deprived of possession of its property by force, and murder of its employés began. The sole question was whether the Carnegie Company or the Amalgamated Association should have absolute control of the company's property, and this could be answered only by the State authorities.

"We today," he continued, "are turned out of our plant at Homestead and have been since the first of July. There is nobody in the mills up there now; there is simply a mass of idle machinery with nobody to look after it."

He refused to confer with the officers of the union whose followers were rioting and destroying property.

"I may say with the greatest emphasis," he concluded calmly, "that under no circumstances will we have any

The State Intervenes

further dealings with the Amalgamated Association as an organization. This is final."

"What of the future?" he was asked.

"That is in the hands of the authorities of Allegheny County. If they are unable to cope with the situation, it is clearly the duty of the Governor of the State to see that we are installed in our property and permitted to operate our plant unmolested."

On the evening of the day—July 8th, 1892—when this vitally important declaration was published, a second son, Henry Clay, junior, was born to Mr. and Mrs. Frick, and there were grave doubts of the survival of either mother or son for many days. The father, after a sleepless night, was at his desk as usual, recipient of hourly bulletins, from 8 a.m. to 6 p.m. on the following day.

Meanwhile, beginning on the day of the battle, Sheriff McCleary and Governor Robert E. Pattison were exchanging telegrams, as follows:

JULY 6.—SHERIFF TO GOVERNOR.—Situation at Homestead is very grave. My deputies were driven from the ground and watchmen sent by mill owners attacked. Shots were exchanged and some men killed and wounded. Unless prompt measures are taken to prevent it further bloodshed and great destruction of property may be expected.

The striking workmen and their friends on the ground number at least 5,000 and the civil authorities are utterly unable to cope with them. Wish you would send representative at once.

GOVERNOR TO SHERIFF.—Local authorities must exhaust every means at their command for the preservation of peace.

SAME DATE—SHERIFF.—The works at Homestead are in possession of an armed mob; they number thousands. The mill owners this morning attempted to land a number of watchmen, when an attack

Frick the Man

was made on boats and 6 men on boats were badly wounded, a number of men on shore were killed and wounded; how many can not say. The boat later came down and was fired on from the shore and pilot compelled to abandon pilot house. I have no means at my command to meet emergency; a large armed force will be required; any delay may lead to further bloodshed and great destruction of property. You are, therefore, urged to act at once.

Governor.—How many deputies have you sworn in and what measures have you taken to enforce order and protect property? The county authorities must exhaust every means to preserve peace.

Same Date—Sheriff.—After personal visit to Homestead works yesterday morning and careful inquiry as to surroundings, I endeavored to gather a force to guard works, but was unable to obtain any. I then sent twelve deputies (almost my entire regular force) to Homestead, but they were driven from the grounds. The mill owners early this morning sent an armed guard of 300 men by river. Boats containing this guard were fired on while on their way up the river, and when they attempted to land at company's ground were met by an armed mob, which had broken down company's fences and taken possession of the landing. An encounter ensued, in which a number were wounded on both sides; several are reported dead. The coroner has just informed me that one of the guards has just died. The guards have not been able to land, and the works are in possession of the mob, who are armed with rifles and pistols and are reported to have one cannon. The guards remain on the barges near landing, having been abandoned by the steamer which towed them there. The civil authorities here are powerless to meet the situation. An armed and disciplined force is needed at once to prevent further loss of life. I therefore urge immediate action on your part.

Governor.—Your telegram indicates that you have not made any effort to execute the law to enforce order, and I must insist upon you calling upon all citizens for an adequate number of deputies.

July 7.—Sheriff reports inability to secure adequate force; makes no request for military assistance.

July 10.—Sheriff.—The situation at Homestead has not improved, while all is quiet there. The strikers are in control, and openly express to me and to the public their determination that the works

The State Intervenes

shall not be operated unless by themselves. After making all efforts in my power I have failed to secure a posse respectable enough in numbers to accomplish anything, and I am satisfied that no posse raised by civil authority can do anything to change the condition of affairs, and that any attempt by an inadequate force to restore the right of law will only result in further armed resistance and consequent loss of life. Only a large military force will enable me to control matters. I believe if such force is sent the disorderly element will be overawed and order will be restored. I therefore call upon you to furnish me such assistance.

GOVERNOR.—Have ordered Maj. Gen. George R. Snowden with the division of the National Guards of Pennsylvania to your support at once. Put yourself in communication with him. Communicate further particulars.

Conformably to arrangements made in pursuance of this order, on July 12th the entire division of the Pennsylvania National Guard, comprising eight thousand men, headed by Major General Snowden and Sheriff McCleary, marched into Homestead and put the Carnegie officials in possession, under continuing guard, of the Company's property without encountering resistance.

Immediately upon issuing his order to General Snowden, Governor Pattison, smarting under criticism for alleged dilatoriness, made this statement:

The law is very explicit on this point and left me no other way to act. Besides, Sheriff McCleary had not demanded military aid as yet. He had only suggested it. The statutes expressly provide that military aid shall not be furnished the civil authorities until the latter have exhausted every means in their power to quell an insurrection. The county is responsible to the mill owners for the preservation of their property.

It is a very easy matter to talk about calling out the militia, but it is not so easy to call them in again. Witness the coke riots of last year when the militia was out for more than two months. The militia have a very salutary effect on turbulent strikers while they

Frick the Man

are present, but their withdrawal is exceedingly likely to cause a renewal of hostilities.

Mr. Samuel Gompers gravely doubted the Governor's right to call out the militia at all and politicians of both parties were disposed to complain for one reason or another, but the public generally coincided with the view expressed by the NEW YORK TIMES on July 11th to this effect:

> The calmness, prudence, and faithful effort to avoid resort to the military power of the State, if possible, that have characterized Gov. Pattison's conduct from the beginning give greater weight to the decision he now feels himself impelled to reach. And he has done well in that when he saw the time to act had come, he has resolved to use no half-way measures, but to employ all the force of the Commonwealth. There will be far less likelihood of resistance. There will be far greater certainty that resistance, if offered, will be overcome promptly and with the least possible injury to those who offer it.

Whatever doubts may have lingered in honest minds were, in any case, dispelled by the Governor himself when a few days later he appeared personally upon the scene and declared flatly that he would spend the entire six million dollars in the State treasury and mortgage the commonwealth itself "if necessary to maintain the National Guard here until law and order are restored." Incidentally he leased a house and announced his intention of remaining with the troops "until preservation of law shall be fully established and permanently guaranteed."

Thus was dissipated probably for all time any surmise that public authority could be defied successfully by a private organization, however strong in numbers or in wealth, within the boundaries of the United States.

The State Intervenes

The firmness of the Governor, emphasized by the resounding bugle notes and reverberations of sunset guns from historic Braddock Field, where eight thousand troops had pitched their tents, left no doubt of the elimination of rapine and murder as factors in the contest. Employers and employés now stood upon a level, obedient to the law, and all phases of contention were resolved to a single issue: Could the workmen compel the company to "recognize" and deal with the union?

Undismayed by their failure to force a second quick surrender by menace to life and property, the Amalgamated Association promptly expanded the field of controversy to comprise the entire force of men employed by the Carnegies by bringing the "sympathetic strike" into play. On the very day—July 13th—after the militia arrived, the union workers in three outside plants voted to break their agreement and strike unless Mr. Frick would confer with the union leaders of Homestead. Crisp and decisive came the laconic response: "Mr. Frick declines." Two thousand men promptly walked out of the Upper and Lower mills in Pittsburgh, and from Beaver Falls, thirty miles down the Ohio river, came the following telegram:

> We, the Amalgamated Association of Beaver Falls, the rod mill, wire mill, and nail mill, have come to the conclusion that we will refuse to work until such time as H. C. Frick, Chairman of Carnegie Steel Company, Limited, is willing to confer with the Amalgamated Association in order to settle the Homestead affair.
> ARTHUR THORNTON
> Chairman of Committee.

Frick the Man

Mr. Frick repeated this ultimatum to Superintendent Wrigley at Beaver Falls and added:

You will please say to Mr. Thornton, Chairman of the Committee, and ask him to so notify the men, that if they, composing the Amalgamated Association at Beaver Falls Mills, and who signed an agreement with us for one year, do not go to work on Monday (this was Friday) next, or when you are ready to start (the mills had been temporarily shut down for repairs) we shall consider their failure to do so as a cancellation of the agreement existing between us, and when these works do resume it will be as non-union, and former employés satisfactory to us who desire to work there will have to apply as individuals. You can say that under no circumstances will we confer with the men at Homestead as members of the Amalgamated Association.

The Carnegie Steel Company, Limited.
By H. C. FRICK, Chairman.

Simultaneously, with steam up in seven of the ten Homestead mills, Superintendent Potter addressed a personal note to each of the former employés inviting him to return to his old position on July 18th, and the following placard was posted conspicuously:

THE CARNEGIE STEEL COMPANY, LIMITED.

NOTICE—Individual applications for employment at the Homestead Steel Works will be received by the General Superintendent either in person or by letter until 6 p.m. Thursday, July 21, 1892. It is our desire to retain in our service all of our old employés whose past records are satisfactory and who did not take part in the attempts which have been made to interfere with our right to manage our business.

Such of our old employés as do not apply by the time above named will be considered as having no desire to re-enter our employment, and the positions which they held will be given to other men, and those first applying will have the choice of unfilled positions for which they are suitable.

The Carnegie Steel Company (Limited).
H. C. FRICK, Chairman.

The State Intervenes

On the 15th, 177 men had returned to work; on the 16th, 190; and on the 17th, 220; many applications from outsiders were under consideration; and, "on the whole," Mr. Frick wrote to President Morse of the Illinois Steel Company, "I am pretty well pleased with the situation"; adding, in response to another anxious inquiry, "You can rest assured that we propose to manage our own business as we think proper and right."

Referring to the innumerable rumors then rife, the correspondent of the NEW YORK TIMES said:

> There have been published numerous statements to the effect that Mr. Frick is constantly guarded by detectives. There is no sign of a guard in his office. He can be seen at his desk from the public hall of the building, and anybody can reach the hall by going up in the elevator.

Among Mr. Frick's many callers on the day when this report appeared was an alert, intelligent Russian who called himself Alexander Berkman and professed to represent a labor agency in New York. The interview lasted about half an hour and an appointment was made for further conversation, one week later, on Saturday, July 23rd, 1892,—the date of a memorable and tragic episode.

X

Attempted Assassination

ALEXANDER BERKMAN was a professed anarchist —"a violent and destructive opponent of all government"—and a disciple of the notorious Emma Goldman. He was born in the province of Vilna, Russia, in 1867, the son of a prosperous druggist, and while attending a college exploited views of such radical nature that he was expelled from the town by the authorities. He came to New York when nineteen years old and obtained a position on the FREIHEIT, an organ of discontent, but soon began to mouth doctrines so extreme that John Most and his associates, fearing that he might embroil them in penal offenses against the government, compelled him to resign.

After working for a short time as a compositor in New Haven, he obtained a place in the Singer sewing machine factory in Elizabeth, where he joined the Penkert nihilists who held that every individual was endowed with absolute right to do whatever he might please without regard to group opinion. Presently he drifted back to New York where he invented an "employment agency" under the name of Simon Bachman and it was in the guise of a representative of that imaginary concern that he sought an interview with Mr. Frick and obtained an appointment for Saturday, July 23rd. He was then

Attempted Assassination

twenty-five years old, of average height, slender, lithe, athletic, quick as a cat and sinewy as a leopard—a sanguinary fanatic, with all the cunning and daring of his breed, and yet a tyro.

His first call, made the week before to spy out the ground, had revealed Mr. Frick's custom of lunching more quickly and returning sooner than his office force. If Berkman had gone prepared on that occasion, when he arrived about half-past-one and found his quarry absolutely alone, unsuspecting and helpless in his desk-chair, he could have killed him with surety and ease. But inexperience, circumstances and nerves combined to defeat his purpose.

Too tense to bide his time, Berkman reached Pittsburgh on Thursday evening, and on Friday forenoon unable to restrain his impulses, he called twice at Mr. Frick's office on the second floor of the CHRONICLE-TELEGRAPH building but got only as far as the anteroom owing to the presence of other callers. At noon on Saturday he appeared a third time; but, when word came that Mr. Frick would be unable to see him for a few moments, he became so agitated that he left hurriedly and, apparently failing to calm his nerves sooner, did not return till nearly two o'clock, twenty minutes too late to find his victim alone. But this time he gave himself no opportunity to falter. Revolver in hand though still in his pocket, he brushed past the office boy, threw open the door and darted into the room drawing his weapon.

As it happened, Mr. Frick was not in his desk-chair but in another at the end of the long table conversing with Vice Chairman Leishman and, rising quickly, was

Frick the Man

turning to face the intruder when Berkman fired the first bullet, which pierced the lobe of his left ear, entered his neck near the base of his skull and passed down between his shoulders. Mr. Frick staggered and fell as Berkman quickly fired another bullet into the right side of his neck.

A third attempt to kill was frustrated by Mr. Leishman who leaped forward and struck up the weapon just as it exploded and then clinched with the assailant. While his partner was wrestling to get hold of the revolver Mr. Frick, dazed and bleeding profusely from his wounds, struggled to his feet and, seizing Berkman around the waist, brought all three to the floor with a crash; but, interlocked though he was, the fanatic wrenched his left hand loose and seizing from his pocket a dagger made from a file stabbed viciously at his weakening adversary, the first thrust piercing his hip, the second jabbing his right side and the third tearing open his left leg below the knee. By a supreme effort, however, Mr. Frick managed to pinion the man's arm and wrist to the floor and, throwing himself upon his body, held him fast till the clerks, aroused by the noise, rushed in and overpowered him.

But the nihilist had not yet reached the end of his resources. He was still struggling when a Deputy Sheriff, greatly excited, rushed into the room and was trying to get a clear shot at him without imperilling others when Mr. Frick, who had been leaning on his desk and watching keenly, made a gesture of dissuasion.

"Don't shoot," he ejaculated, "leave him to the law; but raise his head and let me see his face."

This demand having been complied with none too

Attempted Assassination

gently, the Sheriff, following the direction indicated by Mr. Frick's index finger, saw the culprit's jaw moving as if he were chewing something. Instantly his mouth was forced open and a capsule containing enough fulminite of mercury to blow all in the room to bits was extracted. This was too much for a carpenter who, having rushed in from his work hammer in hand, struck at, but missed, Berkman's head and was drawing back for another blow when again Mr. Frick interceded faintly:

"Don't kill him, I tell you; let the law take its course."

The effort of speaking, following loss of blood which was still streaming from his wounds, exhausted him and he would have fallen if those nearest had not sprung to his support and borne him to a couch in the adjoining room. By this time policemen had arrived and taken charge of Berkman, and surgeons and physicians were not far behind.

While the wounds inflicted by the nihilist's jagged dagger were being staunched Mr. Frick arranged for notification of his sick wife in such a way as to cause a minimum of anxiety and dictated the following telegram to his aged mother, who had been prostrated since the outbreak of violence:

Was shot twice but not dangerously.   H. C. FRICK.

A similar message was cabled to Mr. Carnegie with these words added:

There is no necessity for you to come home. I am still in shape to fight the battle out.

Meanwhile the physicians, preparatory to probing, were providing an anaesthetic, which Mr. Frick resolutely refused to have administered, saying that it was

Frick the Man

quite unnecessary and was inadvisable because he might help in locating the bullets. This surmise proved correct from the moment the surgeon inserted the instrument and pushed it forward gently and tentatively in pursuance of the patient's directions until in each of the two searches he heard "There, that feels like it, Doctor," and extracted both balls with unerring precision.

Mr. Frick, propped up in a chair at his desk after a brief rest, then proceeded to finish his day's work, specifying the final terms of an essential loan which he had been negotiating, signing several official documents and many letters which he had dictated in the forenoon and finally, just before submitting to be carried to an ambulance, he made the following statement to be given to the press:

> This incident will not change the attitude of the Carnegie Steel Company toward the Amalgamated Association. I do not think I shall die but whether I do or not the Company will pursue the same policy and it will win.

He did not reach home until nearly eight o'clock, then suffering intensely but able to sing out to Mrs. Frick, in response to a query from her, as he was being borne past her bedroom door on a stretcher:

"Don't worry, Ada, I'm all right; I may come in later to say good-night; how is the baby?"

Although not permitted to leave his bed that evening or for several days following, Mr. Frick summoned his secretary as soon as the doctors had left the next morning and dictated and signed this notice to the new employés, then numbering about five hundred:

Attempted Assassination

CARNEGIE STEEL COMPANY, (LIMITED):

NOTICE:—To all men who entered our employ after July 1st, 1892: In no case and under no circumstances will a single one of you be discharged to make room for another man. You will keep your respective positions so long as you attend to your duties. Positive orders to this effect have been given to the general superintendent.

By order of the board of managers,
The Carnegie Steel Company, (Limited)
H. C. FRICK, Chairman.

Homestead Steel Works, July 24th, 1892.

During the succeeding ten days, propped up in bed and swathed with bandages, with a telephone installed within reach and secretaries in constant attendance in defiance of the doctors' orders, ignoring pain and scoffing at the sweltering heat, Mr. Frick not only kept fully informed but personally dictated every move in the continuing contest and attended to all other details of the Company's business with customary thoroughness.

On Wednesday, August 3rd, he was summoned to behold the passing of the spirit of his little son and namesake, born less than four weeks previously, on the day of the battle at Homestead, and on Thursday afternoon his eyes rested upon the tiny coffin during a brief funeral service. The long evening, passed at the bedside of the stricken mother, finally wore away and he slept for a few hours.

Rising and breakfasting promptly on the following morning, thirteen days after he had been attacked, he walked alone across the lawn, stepped upon an open street-car, entered his office on the stroke of eight and rang for the morning's mail.

Frick the Man

"Those who hate him most," wrote the correspondent of the NEW YORK WORLD, his severest critic, "admire the nerve and stamina of this man of steel whom nothing seems to be able to move. He looked a little thinner and paler than before he was shot but the change was not so marked as had been expected. There is a mark on his left ear where a bullet passed through it and behind the ear is a hole stuffed with cotton in which the bullet buried itself. He was particularly interested in the hole in the ceiling made by the bullet when Mr. Leishman knocked up Berkman's arm and which, but for that act, would have ended his own career. But he was not worried when he was attacked nor while lying in his home during those terribly hot days when his recovery was anything but certain, and today, when he returned to work after thirteen days, he seemed just the same as ever. There was no bodyguard. Mr. Frick does not like bodyguards. When he saw the detective who had been watching the Company's offices ever since the shooting he frowned and the detective was sent downstairs, where he remained as long as the Chairman was in the building."

"If an honest American," he remarked to the TIMES reporter, "cannot live in his own home without being surrounded by a bodyguard, it is time to quit."

While he was in his office the WORLD correspondent asked how he was feeling.

"Very well, indeed, thank you," answered Mr. Frick. "I am nearly well, and in very good trim for work. I had too much to do to stay away from the office any longer and I am glad to get back again. I am going right along

Attempted Assassination

now attending to my affairs. Fortunately there is nothing behind, for during my absence the work has been done most satisfactorily by the officials and clerks. I could not ask any better management of this trouble than that of my assistants, and the results thus far are all that could be wished for. There have been many grave situations and complications and all of them have been successfully met. The outlook is most bright. I could not ask for anything better."

He lunched with the managers of the Company's various plants and left for home on a street-car unattended shortly after three o'clock. Half a dozen or more policemen were patrolling the block and at the gate he met Superintendent O'Mara and protested somewhat vehemently. The Chief replied that he had stationed his men upon his own notion that their presence would contribute to Mrs. Frick's peace of mind and possibly hasten her recovery.

"Very well," was the reply, "come in and we will find out."

While the Chief waited in the hall Mr. Frick went upstairs and returning in a few moments said to him:

"My wife asks me to thank you most kindly for your thoughtfulness but earnestly requests that you take the men away; she fears that their being here all the time might make the servants nervous."

The Chief laughed and complied, and thereafter Mr. Frick made his trips daily to and from his office alone on open street-cars at fixed hours without paying the slightest heed to the other passengers.

Frick the Man

Berkman meanwhile, having grievously injured the cause of the workmen whom, wholly without their consent or knowledge, he had meant to serve, remained in jail until the autumn when he was tried, convicted and sentenced to one year in the workhouse for carrying concealed weapons, and twenty-one years in the penitentiary for assault with intent to kill. At the expiration of twelve years, proposals to obtain commutation of his sentence were strongly urged and no less earnestly opposed by thousands of persons actuated by contrary motives, and both parties solicited Mr. Frick's support, which he declined to accord to either the one or the other upon the familiar ground based, so far as he was concerned, upon his own tenet to the effect that, once the law was invoked in any matter, no species of influence should be brought to bear upon the courts in their dispensation of justice.

The advocates of clemency finally won in 1905, and Berkman was released after thirteen years of imprisonment. Replying to a famous detective agency's proposition to furnish adequate safeguards against fateful possibilities, a secretary wrote:

New York City, April 14th, 1905.
Dear Sir:—
 Mr. Frick directs me to say, in reply to yours of the twelfth, that he is not at all interested in Berkman or in any of his class and has no fear whatever. All newspaper reports regarding arrangements made by him to keep track of Berkman, or anyone in connection with him, are unfounded.

Neither then nor thereafter did Mr. Frick take or permit anyone else to take the slightest precautions respecting his personal safety. When news of his death on

Attempted Assassination

December 2nd, 1919, reached the unrepentant anarchist, he remarked with brutal cynicism: "Well anyhow he left the country before I did."

At a later hour of the very same day, by an odd coincidence, Berkman, along with Emma Goldman, was deported by the United States Government.

XI
Politics

THAT politics should play a large part in the Homestead controversy was inevitable. The two leading candidates for President, Mr. Harrison, Republican, and Mr. Cleveland, Democrat, each standing for a second term, were unexceptionable and well matched in ability, character and experience. Of the two Mr. Cleveland possessed the stronger personal appeal but had won his election over Mr. Blaine in 1884 upon an issue of personal integrity by the narrowest conceivable margin, only to be beaten by Mr. Harrison in 1888 by a substantial majority.

As between the two organizations, the Republican party seemed to have demonstrated superior capacity to conduct a government successfully along constructive lines. The first Democratic administration since that which preceded the Civil War had proved unsatisfactory, lacking both definiteness of purpose and cohesion in action, "a thing of shreds and patches" ill fitted to establish and maintain prosperous conditions throughout the country. The party in national convention had disregarded its conservative candidate's wishes and had forced an issue, not between excessive and moderate tariff rates, but between Protection and the closest feasible approach to Free Trade as fundamental principles,—a far cry from the mere resent-

Politics

ment at the McKinley Bill which had overwhelmed the Republicans in the Congressional elections two years previously. Despite the apparent significance of that stinging rebuke in 1890, the country seemed likely to swing back to the Republican policy in 1892 unless some extraneous question should alienate a large block of normal partisans.

Upon the main issue Capital and Labor engaged in industrial pursuits were as one for mutual benefits derived from the protective system of which the great steel-manufacturing State of Pennsylvania was the citadel. But any change, however essential, fair and desirable, in the proportions of legalized gains shared by the beneficiaries in a time of marked prosperity could not fail to exasperate the class affected adversely. In the Homestead instance Labor seemed to be the sufferer, and workingmen throughout the country, disinclined to consider the merits of the case, were easily aroused to consciousness of injury, and large numbers of consumers, though still distrustful of Free Trade, began to question the soundness of Protection.

This gave rise to a situation most serviceable to the clever organizers, headed by Mr. Powderly, then engaged in an endeavor to create trades unions upon a vast scale, and they were quick to take advantage of it. Individually, probably a majority of the workingmen felt their natural affiliation to be with the Democratic "party of the masses," but the leaders preferred to deal with the Republican "party of privilege" as the more capable and better equipped for trading purposes.

One of the perplexing problems which confronted the Republican management at the outset had arisen from

Frick the Man

the strained relations existing between the NEW YORK TRIBUNE, the chief Republican organ, and the powerful Typographical Union No. 6. The TRIBUNE had been maintained as a non-union establishment for nearly fifteen years but in 1890 negotiations had been begun with a view to unionizing the office and were approaching a probable settlement when the Republican Convention nominated Mr. Whitelaw Reid for Vice-President. In point of fact an adjustment would already have been reached but for the circumstance that Mr. Reid was serving as Minister to France and unable to give the matter his personal attention.

Having returned from France, however, he was about to resume parleys when, quite unexpectedly and without expectation or desire on his own part, he was nominated as the Republican candidate in place of Vice-President Levi P. Morton. The conversations which had already begun between Mr. Reid and the officers of the Union were quietly continued without regard to his candidacy and a settlement satisfactory to both parties was reached without difficulty.

Mr. Reid's attitude, indeed, had been so friendly and considerate that, when Mr. Hugh O'Donnell, the head of the Amalgamated Association in Pittsburgh, realized that Mr. Frick was practically certain to win the contest, he appealed to Mr. Reid to intercede with Mr. Carnegie to propose a settlement upon his own terms, contingent only upon recognition of the Union.

Mr. Reid thereupon, after having communicated his purpose to Secretary of State Foster for the information

Politics

doubtless of President Harrison, addressed the following cypher communication, through Mr. John C. New, Consul-General in London, to Mr. Carnegie in Scotland:

Have received appeal from Hugh O'Donnell, for aid with you in reaching settlement Homestead difficulty. He says he does not ask in any political interest, or in that of organized Labor; but solely for the men, women and little children making up their distressed community; and he makes appeal to me because he thinks me, in consequence of our personal relations, in position to render efficient aid.

He believes you will be able to start your mills, but that the trouble will then have only begun. He thinks it to nobody's interest, either yours, theirs or the public's, that such a bitter warfare should be inaugurated and that you can well afford the only concession he asks.

He assures me that if your people will merely consent to reopen a conference with their representatives, thus recognizing their organization, they will waive every other thing in dispute, and submit to whatever you think it right to require, whether as to scale or wages or hours or anything else; and do all in their power to reestablish harmonious relations.

These assurances have been given to me in writing, over his signature, and have been repeated and emphasized in conversation, in presence of witnesses, during the two days' visit he has made to New York for this purpose.

I cannot rest under such an appeal, in a matter which has already cost many lives and threatens yet more bloodshed and misery, without transmitting his message direct to you; and without begging you to weigh it most carefully before deciding, for so small a reason as the objection to continued recognition of their organization, which you have heretofore recognized, to prolong this distressing and bloody strife which may spread so widely.

Mr. Reid received the following reply from Mr. New:

Proposition heartily approved here. Send copy of same to Frick and have Elkins and Wanamaker see him at once. Utmost importance.

Frick the Man

Simultaneously Mr. John E. Milholland, acting for Mr. Reid, by request of the Republican National Committee, arrived in Pittsburgh on July 30th and sought an interview with Mr. Frick at his house with a letter of introduction from Mr. Reid. Immediately following this conversation Mr. Milholland made the following report to Mr. Reid who forwarded it promptly to Mr. Harrison:

Mr. Frick was lying in bed when I called, his face and head swathed in bandages. He seemed, however, to be in a fairly vigorous condition and displayed considerable excitement when we opened the conversation. I had presented your letter of introduction, and he seemed to know all about my mission. I discovered later in the conversation that he had received some cablegrams from the other side informing him that somebody from you would call within a few days.

I briefly laid the correspondence in the case before him, that is to say, Mr. O'Donnell's letter, your despatch to Mr. Carnegie and Consul-General New's cablegram in reply saying that Mr. Carnegie approved the proposition and recommending that it be immediately laid before Mr. Frick.

I told Mr. Frick that Mr. Reid had cabled to Mr. Carnegie because he found it impossible to come in contact with him, Mr. Frick. He looked surprised and asked what I meant. I told him then of my visit to Mr. Schoonmaker, the New York representative of the firm. I told him that we had spent three days in endeavoring to get from Mr. Schoonmaker Mr. Carnegie's address or the use of the code. He told me that he had intended to transmit the message through Mr. Frick and also that our enquiries for Mr. Carnegie would have been the means of bringing us into relation with Mr. Frick. I further stated that finally Mr. Schoonmaker informed me after holding telephone communication with the Pittsburgh office, that is, with Mr. Frick, that they did not have Mr. Carnegie's address and they did not have the code there. There was of course but one interpretation to be placed upon such a reply, namely, that Mr. Frick did not care to meet Mr. Reid and

Politics

was evidently bent upon preventing any intercourse between him and Mr. Carnegie.

At this point, Mr. Frick declared emphatically that he would never consent to settle the difficulties if President Harrison himself should personally request him to do so. Notwithstanding the fact that he was a Republican and a warm friend and admirer of the President, the whole Cabinet, the whole leadership of the party might demand it but he would not yield. He was going to fight the strike out on the lines that he had laid down. I remarked, "If it takes all summer?" "Yes," he said, "if it takes all summer and all winter, and all next summer and all next winter. Yes, even my life itself. I will fight this thing to the bitter end. I will never recognize the Union, never, never!" He was considerably wrought up at this point, and noticing the despatch that I held in my hand, added "It makes no difference to me what Mr. Carnegie has said to General New or to anybody else. I won't settle this strike even if he should order me peremptorily to do so. If he interferes every manager that he has will resign and of course I will get out of the concern. But I do not think he will interfere."

Then he talked for some time on the favorable outlook for the situation from the Company's point of view. He believed that what he was doing was really in the true interests of the men themselves. The Amalgamated Association, he said, was one of the most tyrannous bodies on the face of the earth. He had put up with it as long as he could and proposed to stand it no longer.

Mr. Frick detailed some of his unpleasant experiences with the Association. I told him that I could fully appreciate the annoyance to which he had been subjected, as I knew something about trades-unions, but that it had not been the purpose of those who had interested themselves with a view to effecting a settlement to inquire into the merits of the case, or the right or wrong of it. A situation existed. It was of the most deplorable character. The practical question was, Could anything be done to bring about a settlement that would be satisfactory to both sides? It was simply with that end in view and only that end, that Mr. Reid had interested himself to the extent of transmitting O'Donnell's message to Mr. Carnegie. He had no sympathy with the lawlessness; he had no disposition to champion the cause of the strikers. His sole object was to bring about peace if it were possible to do so. His

Frick the Man

position in the matter, however, was so clearly defined in the telegram that it was unnecessary to dwell further upon it.

Mr. Frick, who by this time had seemed to take a less hostile view of the matter said that it was impossible to bring about peace by any way that involved a recognition of the Union. That could not be done, and there was no use discussing it. This position was unalterably fixed. He seemed to think that it was just as well to keep the matter of my visit a secret. I told him that I had no in tention of giving it publicity and while I could not speak for those whom I represented, yet I thought it would be perhaps best all round to say nothing of the matter at least for the present. Before leaving, however, I made it perfectly clear that I had not bound anyone to maintain secrecy.

I believe I have here stated the main points touched upon in the hour or three-quarters of an hour's conversation we had; there was some incidental conversation, but I do not think any important point touched upon has escaped me.'

The first intimation of what was going on had reached Mr. Frick in cablegrams from Mr. Carnegie dated July 28th and July 29th reading as follows:

Rannoch, July 28th, 1892.

We have telegram from Tribune Reid through high official London Amalgamated Association reference Homestead Steel Works. The proposition is worthy of consideration. Replied "nothing can be done. Send H. C. Frick document." You must decide without delay. Amalgamated Association evidently distressed.

Rannoch, July 29th, 1892.

After due consideration we have concluded Tribune too old. Probably the proposition is not worthy of consideration. Useful showing distress of Amalgamated Association. Use your own discretion about terms and starting. George Lauder, Henry Phipps, Jr., Andrew Carnegie solid. H. C. Frick forever!

The perplexing difference in Mr. Carnegie's attitude as revealed by his direct cablegram to Mr. Frick and as transmitted by Mr. New was not mentioned to Mr. Mil-

Politics

holland; nor was the incident recounted to Mr. Carnegie until August 23rd, when Mr. Frick confessed apologetically that in the stress of business he had neglected to write of it, and continued:

> I told Mr. Milholland that I did not think the matter had been placed before you correctly or you never would have entertained, certainly not heartily approved, any proposition to adjust matters with the Amalgamated Association, and that I was surprised that you had not availed yourself of the opportunity offered to tell Mr. Reid and Mr. O'Donnell emphatically that you did not propose then, nor at any time in the future, to urge your partners here to treat with law-breakers and assassins. I went over the situation very fully with him at the time, and am satisfied convinced him that it was most unreasonable for Mr. Reid to expect us to treat with the Amalgamated Association.
>
> He was very solicitous that the fact of his having called should be considered confidential. I assured him that the matter would go no further than my associates.
>
> From information received from time to time since then, I am inclined to the opinion that Reid has been keeping O'Donnell and his gang on the string, and leading them to believe he was still endeavoring to bring about a settlement through you. It is too late now, however, for you to say or do anything in the matter.
>
> As you know, I have always feared that the consolidation of our various companies would give us some trouble with labor where the Amalgamated Association was in charge, and I know that you could not have had any other idea but that sooner or later we would have to run non-union at all the works or union at all the works, and when the issue was once made, viewing it from any standpoint that you might, we could not afford to do otherwise than fight it through to the end, without regard to cost or time.

No more was heard of the matter until, while his account of the interview was on its way to Scotland, Mr. Frick received word that Secretary of War Elkins and Postmaster-General Wanamaker wished to make an ap-

Frick the Man

pointment for an interview with him upon a subject of great urgency. Whereupon he cabled Mr. Carnegie on August 26th:

> The fact that in your communication with New you advised "having either Wanamaker or Elkins see me" and the fact that they are both now wanting to see me leads to the conclusion that Whitelaw Reid is holding out to Laugh's (O'Donnell's) representative that some arrangement can yet be made. Would advise cabling Reid at once most emphatically to the contrary and that we will never consent to any compromise of any kind at Plunge (Homestead) and tell him to so notify Laugh's representative immediately as I know they think you will interfere sooner or later in their favor.

Mr. Carnegie replied promptly:

> Wired Reid as follows: Tell party no compromise possible. Over two thousand men working Homestead. Firm's honor pledged never to dismiss them. Every one of the twenty-three owners would sink works rather than dismiss one man. Party only bringing thousands to misery by allowing places taken by strangers after fight is lost.

"Frankly," wrote Mr. Frick with respect to this, "I do not think you sent the proper message to Reid. You should have said emphatically, in my opinion, that we did not propose hereafter, under any circumstances, to deal with the Amalgamated Association. Saying to him the number of men we had at work, and giving that as a reason really why we would make no compromise would, it seems to me, indicate that if we had not so many new men at work a compromise might be possible. Reid should have been given to understand that we not only would not compromise, but would never have any dealings with the Amalgamated Association. This is the way it strikes me."

Politics

Mr. Carnegie countered cleverly and good-naturedly on September 9th:

My dear Mr. Frick:

Yours received. I thought I had sent a rattling message to Reid, its form is yours and not mine. Your cable read: "Wire Reid we will never consent to any compromise of any kind,"—and these were the words I began with, and kept to it. To travel beyond them might not have suited your book.

You have no idea how much in the dark one is up here among the moors, twenty-three miles from a railway station, and a wrong word might easily be said, since I am so ignorant of conditions, and just what you wished to hit at the time and how to hit it.—Having wired your very words, I added the strongest proof why compromise was impossible, for to my mind, the firm's honor being pledged in that public notice renders any re-instatement of the Union simply impossible.

Had I known then that Mr. Reid had, or was going to change his office from a Non-union to a Union office, I could not have been so cruel as to put the matter in the way I did. It must have stung him hard. I ask for a clean dismissal on the count that the message to him was not what you "had a right to expect," being your own my boy.

Yours sincerely,
A. C.

No further appeals from the Republican leaders to "recognize the Union" were received by either of the partners. That nevertheless Mr. Frick had reason to anticipate further nagging was indicated in this lugubrious postcript to his letter to Mr. Carnegie:

At his request I am to meet Mr. Wanamaker on Monday night at Cresson. I don't know what about but surmise it may be on this business. If I find it is so, I shall promptly inform Reid that he must cease meddling in our affairs. He had no right to do so after my interview with his representative. I wrote to Mr. Elkins that I could not see him now.

Frick the Man

But Mr. Frick guessed wrong. As already noted, Mr. Reid had written the following letter to President Harrison on August 4th:

August 4th, 1892.

Private

Dear Mr. President;

As Mr. Milholland talked with you about the Homestead business, you ought to know the steps taken.

After fruitless efforts for a day or two, I at last found a method of sending the despatch which you saw, in cypher, through a commercial concern not likely to talk. General New transmitted it at once and on Friday last telegraphed me as follows:

> Proposition heartily approved here. Send copy of same to Frick and have Elkins and Wanamaker see him at once. Utmost importance.

It seemed to me unwise to involve the Administration in any way in this matter without first ascertaining the probable reception it would get; and in order to keep the matter for the time, within as few hands as possible, I sent the same messenger to Pittsburgh. You will find enclosed herewith his report of the conversation.

Seeing no opportunity for further useful action in the premises, I have not communicated with Messrs. Wanamaker and Elkins; but, if you should think otherwise, the matter is in your hands.

* * * * *

With high respect,
Always faithfully yours,
WHITELAW REID.

What Mr. Wanamaker really sought was a substantial contribution to the Republican Campaign fund—a proposition which Mr. Frick found, upon making inquiry, to be as distasteful to Mr. Carnegie as it was to himself.

That some contribution should be made was agreed and the amount was still under discussion by correspondence when Mr. Frick was called to New York on business, and meeting Secretary Elkins, settled the matter by hand-

Politics

ing him a check drawn to the order of Thomas Dolan, for $25,000, the sum he had suggested in lieu of $50,000 which Mr. Wanamaker had intimated had been promised by Mr. Carnegie, whose real view he found in a letter awaiting him upon his arrival home, to the effect that not more than $10,000 should be contributed.

"Mr. Elkins told me," wrote Mr. Frick on October 31st, "that Quay, Carter, Dolan and Clarkson felt very confident, to which I said I thought it a waste of money, but we wanted to do our duty and I hoped Mr. Harrison would be elected."

But Mr. Frick's wish was smothered by his expectation. Mr. Cleveland was elected and bore into power with himself Democratic majorities in both Houses of Congress. Letters dated November 9th crossed.

"I am very sorry for President Harrison," wrote Mr. Frick, "but I cannot see that our interests are going to be affected one way or the other by the change in administration."

"Cleveland! Landslide!" replied Mr. Carnegie. "Well we have nothing to fear and perhaps it is best. People will now think the Protected Manfrs. will be attended to and quit agitating. Cleveland is pretty good fellow. Off for Venice tomorrow."

"I fear," he wrote a week later from Venice, "that Homestead did much to elect Cleveland—very sorry—but no use getting scared."

On March 20th, 1893, following the inauguration of Mr. Cleveland, Mr. Carnegie addressed the following letter to Mr. Reid:

Frick the Man

Private

5 West Fifty-first Street
New York, March 20th, 1893.

My dear Mr. Reid:

I called upon you upon my return from Pittsburgh but found your house closed. Supposing you would soon return I waited, but learning from the woman at Mr. Mills' house (where I called to ask about you), that you might not be here until May I feel that it is too long to wait to express my sincere and heartfelt thanks for the noble effort you made to settle that deplorable Homestead blunder. I assure you my partners Messrs. Phipps & Lauder whom I had summoned to Scotland to confer with me, agree with me in feeling ourselves under a debt of gratitude to you. We supposed the matter would be promptly settled, as a consequence of your action.

I never suspected that the seven hundred men reported as at work were *new men*. I rested believing them to be our former employés. Between ourselves, no manufacturer is wise who attempts to employ new men. My partners thought the three thousand old men would keep their promise to work, and therefore opened the works *for them*. The guards were intended only to protect them. The workmen were terrorized and dare not appear. Here was the turning point. The works should then have been closed and the firm should have kept on negotiating, but never starting until matters were right.

For twenty-six years I ran all our various works and never had but one labor stoppage. I told the Committee they were right in saying "I would never fight but they had to learn one thing I could beat any Committee ever formed, *sitting down*, the works would start when they voted to ask me to start them." They voted soon enough—but I only started to express myself your debtor and to assure you that all three of the principal owners are very grateful to you.

This has been the hardest trial I ever had to endure (save when the hand of death has come)—I have been in misery since July, but am reconciled somewhat since I have visited Homestead and gone through all the works and shaken hands with the chief men.

No one knows the virtues, the noble traits of the true working man who has not lived with them as I have and there's one con-

Politics

solation in all my sorrow, Not one of them but said, Ah, Mr. Carnegie if you had only been here it never would have happened.

To add to my cup I know the mistake injured my friends, President Harrison and yourself, but I was powerless—after the riot and with Mr. Frick supposed to be dying no step could be taken that would not have complicated matters still more.

I was all ready to return by the first steamer, but as my appearance on the scene would have implied Mr. Frick's virtual deposition and he had begged me not to do this, I remained abroad. Excuse this long epistle. My kindest regards to Mrs. Reid and Mr. Mills and renewed thanks to you believe me always
Your friend
ANDREW CARNEGIE.

Mr. Frick said nothing. When the election was over he returned to business without apologizing to anybody for anything that he had done.

XII

"The Laird" and "The Man"

THE motives and the acts of both Mr. Carnegie and Mr. Frick were misunderstood or misrepresented from the beginning of the struggle at Homestead. One widespread impression respecting the conduct of the former was that he forsook the workmen whose friendship he had sedulously cultivated and "ran away to Scotland" in the nick of time to avoid facing the situation. This accusation, insofar at any rate as it bore upon the date of his leaving the country, had no foundation in fact. He sailed in April as usual, nearly three months before the expiration of the agreement, in pursuance of a routine which he had followed for years; and wisely, since postponement would have served only to evince apprehension which he did not feel, and to encourage the labor leaders in inciting disaffection among the men.

His withdrawal from directive responsibility, even from nominal membership of the Board, was attributable undoubtedly to his sincere desire to shift the entire executive and financial burden to the shoulders of THE MAN whom at last he believed he had found, and thus leave himself free to work at philosophy, experiment in philanthropy, indulge his fads and play betimes at publicity.

"The Laird" and "The Man"

The possibility of serious disturbance in one of many working organizations was incidental rather than unusual and in no sense a controlling influence over his activities.

In point of fact neither Mr. Carnegie nor Mr. Frick foresaw anything approaching in magnitude and consequences the terrific hurricane that was to follow; less than a month before the outbreak, they were planning a long conference in Scotland; but, as a practical matter, the two had agreed that whatever might arise in the form of strikes or lockouts, either at Homestead or elsewhere, could be handled most effectively by the Chairman alone, without interference by the chief or any other stockholder,—and so it was arranged to the satisfaction of both, the one assuming full responsibility and the other, content to aid by suggestion, pledging unqualified support of whatever decision might be reached by the management.

Although this understanding was observed faithfully, in most trying circumstances, throughout the entire contest, both were aware long before trouble began that their minds were not in accord with respect to either general policy, or specific methods. Mr. Frick stood for squarely upholding what he considered the absolute right of a corporation, no less than of an individual, to conduct its business as it might see fit. It might or might not deal with union officials as authorized representatives of masses of workmen, but it should not be compelled to do either through complicity or negligence on the part of the State, whose sole duty was to guarantee and to secure, by force if necessary, all "equal privileges" accorded by basic law to both Capital and Labor.

Frick the Man

Mr. Carnegie held contrary views acclaimed by some as "advanced" or "progressive" and condemned by others as "radical" or "socialistic." To Labor he was accustomed to accord rights that were "natural," equivalent to those depicted by Jefferson in the Declaration of Independence as "endowed by their Creator," thus clearly superseding rights of Capital derived from mere mundane authority. This doctrine appealed strongly, on humanitarian grounds, to those who perceived in its pronouncement by a leading employer evidence of great breadth and magnanimity, but it made slight impression upon dialectical minds for the simple reason that it applied solely to organized Labor in its unending struggle with Capital and barred from consideration the vastly greater number of individuals who were thus left out in the cold without recourse of any kind. But Mr. Carnegie, heedless of his own disregard not only of logic but of the very sympathy which he was striving to manifest for the toilers, did not hesitate to carry his theory to its irresistible conclusion with a dictum approximating an Eleventh Commandment to the effect that—

"Thou shalt not take thy neighbor's job."

Pronouncing this "the unwritten law of the best workmen," Mr. Carnegie bestowed upon it his benediction as being equally desirable from the standpoint of the best employers. To the logical mind of Mr. Frick it spelt conclusively nothing less than abdication by responsible managers of control of property from whose owners they had accepted virtual trusteeship. A sharper disagreement "in principle" could hardly be imagined.

"The Laird" and "The Man"

And yet the difference in application was even more vivid. Mr. Carnegie had already, in a letter to Mr. Frick, outlined the method which he reasoned would coincide with his theory, in these words:

> My idea of beating in a dispute with men is always to shut down and suffer; let them decide by vote when they desire to go to work —say kindly "All right, Gentlemen let's hear from you, no quarrel, not the least in the world, until a majority vote (secret ballot) to go to work—have a good time—when a majority vote to start, start it is." I am satisfied that the Employer or Firm who gets the reputation of adhering to that will never have a prolonged stoppage, or much ill feeling.
>
> A.C.

This was a private communication from controlling owner to responsible manager and, from its permanent abiding place in the office safe, could cause no embarrassment; but unfortunately the like could not be said of a sweeping generalization along the same line made public some time before.

"My idea," Mr. Carnegie then wrote, "is that the Company should be known as determined to let the men at any works stop work; that it will confer freely with them and wait patiently until they decide to return to work, never thinking of trying new men—never."

Later he added: "Workmen can always be relied upon to resent the employment of new men. *Who can blame them?*"

Taken in conjunction with "Thou shalt not seek thy neighbor's job," this naturally induced the labor leaders to believe that they might count upon the moral support and dominant influence of Mr. Carnegie in offsetting at least, and probably overwhelming, the stern deter-

Frick the Man

mination of the man whom they most feared as an enemy of labor organization.

This deduction was natural but erroneous. Mr. Frick felt that he had ample reason to distrust a union which, while holding that a company was bound by its contracts, had persistently repudiated its own agreements, but he was so eager to carry on peaceably the great undertakings which he had in mind that he not only welcomed but sought a continuance of the existing arrangement with the Amalgamated Association upon a wage scale which he and the labor leaders tacitly admitted to be fair and reasonable, even going so far as to offer at the last conference to split the immaterial difference of only two dollars per ton in the fixed minimum.

Nevertheless, in the face of this proposal, involving of course the "recognition" so ardently desired, the labor negotiators insisted that he was deliberately using a trifling disparity as a pretext for completely smashing the union, and a large portion of the popular Press denounced him bitterly upon this false assumption. The public misapprehension of Mr. Carnegie's purpose in going abroad was trivial by contrast with this misrepresentation of Mr. Frick's true attitude.

In point of fact, unrevealed for many years, it was not Mr. Frick but Mr. Carnegie who wanted to make open war on the union from the very beginning, and it was not Mr. Carnegie but Mr. Frick who vetoed the proposal.

Shortly before sailing in April, following several conferences in New York, Mr. Carnegie embodied his idea

"The Laird" and "The Man"

in a manifesto, or "ultimatum," as subsequently he described it, to be posted at a suitable moment, reading as follows:

NOTICE
TO EMPLOYEES AT HOMESTEAD WORKS.

These Works have been consolidated with the Edgar Thomson and Duquesne and other mills, there has been forced upon this Firm the question Whether its Works are to be run 'Union' or 'Non-Union.' As the vast majority of our employees are Non-Union, the Firm has decided that the minority must give place to the majority. These works therefore, will be necessarily Non-Union after the expiration of the present agreement.

This does not imply that the men will make lower wages. On the contrary, most of the men at Edgar Thomson and Duquesne Works, both Non-Union, have made and are making higher wages than those at Homestead, which has hitherto been Union.

* * * * *

This action is not taken in any spirit of hostility to labor organizations, but every man will see that the firm cannot run Union and Non-Union. It must be either one or the other.

Mr. Frick neither accepted nor rejected this plan; he simply pigeon-holed the document, and abided events, hoping that a sober second-thought would avert the necessity of engaging in altercation and possibly forcing an issue of control at a most inopportune moment. This policy quickly justified itself. Immediately upon his arrival at Coworth Park, Sunningdale, England, Mr. Carnegie was joined by two of his partners, Mr. Phipps and Mr. Lauder, his cousin, and on May 4th addressed to Mr. Frick a long communication which he labelled "a joint production," in the course of which he said:

You remember I gave you a type-written slip which I suggested you might have to use. It is probable that you will. But I hope you will make this change in it: I did not get it quite right,

Frick the Man

because I think it said that the firm had to make the decision of 'Union' or 'Non-Union.' This I am sure, is wrong. We need not meet that point, and we should not.

We simply say that consolidation having taken place, we must introduce the same system in our works; we do not care whether a man belongs to as many Unions or organizations as he chooses, but he must conform to the system in our other works.

* * * * *

One thing we are all sure of: No contest will be entered in that will fail. It will be harder this time at Homestead than it would have been last time when we had the matter in our own hands, as you have always felt. On the other hand, your reputation will shorten it, so that I really do not believe it will be much of a struggle. We all approve of anything you do, not stopping short of approval of a contest. We are with you to the end.

Mr. Frick accepted this assurance as approval of his determination as outlined in a letter dated April 21st, saying that if "a stubborn fight" should arise, it would be "fought to a finish without regard to cost or time." He made no reference to the proposed "ultimatum"; nor did Mr. Carnegie on May 23rd when he wrote, "No doubt you will get Homestead right as you can get anything right with your 'mild persistence.'"

On July 7th, the day following the pitched battle at Homestead, Mr. Carnegie cabled from Pitlochry:

Cable received. All anxiety gone since you stand firm. Never employ one these rioters. Let grass grow over works. Must not fail now. You will win easily next trial only stand firm law and order wish I could support you in any form.

Two days later a correspondent of the NEW YORK WORLD succeeded in tracing him to a secluded lodge in Perthshire and reported as follows:

Asked if he had anything to say concerning the troubles at his mills, Mr. Carnegie replied:

"The Laird" and "The Man"

"I have nothing whatever to say. I have given up all active control of the business and I do not care to interfere in any way with the present management's conduct of this affair."

"But do you not still exercise a supervision of the affairs of the company?"

"I have nothing whatever to say on that point, the business management is in the hands of those who are fully competent to deal with every question that may arise."

"Have you heard from Homestead since the riot occurred?"

"I have received several cables and among them several asking my interference with the parties in control."

"But you must have some opinion in the matter that you are willing to express."

"No, sir. I am not willing to express any opinion. The men have chosen their course and I am powerless to change it. The handling of the case on the part of the company has my full approval and sanction. Further than this I have no disposition to say anything."

Immediately following the arrival of the troops the union leaders sought to embarrass Mr. Carnegie and to effect a break between the two partners by cabling this message:

Kind master, tell us what you wish us to do and we shall do it for you.

"This," wrote Mr. Carnegie in his Autobiography, "was most touching but, alas, too late. The mischief was done, the works were in the hands of the Governor; it was too late."

Whether he meant to convey the impression that he might have intervened if the affecting appeal had reached him sooner, or simply availed himself of a plausible pretext to escape from a perplexing situation is perhaps a question since, in lieu of a direct answer, the following breath of apparent relief was flashed to Mr. Frick:

Governor's action settles matters all right now no compromise.

Frick the Man

"Much pleased with your cable, did not doubt your position," Mr. Frick promptly responded and amplified by letter in these words:

> Your cable of this morning was received, and I cabled a reply. Never had a doubt but that you would thoroughly approve of every action taken in this matter when you would once be made acquainted with all of the facts in the case, and have felt that you had sufficient confidence in the management here not to form an opinion unfavorable to it, even with the meagre information that you would receive or gather from newspaper dispatches.

Meanwhile, in the course of frequent reports, he was writing:

> We will lose no time in resuming operations at Homestead, but it shall be done with the greatest care, selecting the best men, and re-organizing the entire works, so that we shall not employ any more men than actually necessary.

Thus quite casually and without argument, Mr. Carnegie's favorite method of merely shutting down, waiting patiently for the men to return to work and "never thinking of trying new men—never," was ignored and no protest was forthcoming.

When Mr. Carnegie received news of the attempted assassination of Mr. Frick he cabled promptly:

> Too glad at your escape to think of anything. Never fear brave and dear friend my appearing upon scene as long as you are able to direct matters from house and unless partners call. We know too well what is due to you. Am subject your orders. Louise Stella myself all relieved by cables just received. Be careful of yourself is all we ask.

"I tremble yet to think of your escape, awful," he wrote but was reassured on August 5th by a cablegram

"The Laird" and "The Man"

reading, "At office feeling first-class, everything assuming good shape," and replied:

Hearty congratulations from all here, upon return to post of duty everything is right when you and Mrs. Frick are right every other consideration insignificant. You owe it to all your friends to be careful of yourself.

The first rift in the lute came on September 10th, when Mr. Frick wrote:

Had a cable yesterday evening from Mr. Lauder (Mr. Carnegie's cousin), who said he would be glad to come over if he could be of any use in any position whatever. Wired him not to come at present, and wrote him fully. There is a feeling yet that you will in some way interfere to settle this strike question, and Mr. Lauder's coming over now would only give them further hope. There is nothing personal in this matter, so far as I am concerned. I am, so far as I know, only doing what it seems to me to be for the interests of the owners of the property, and if we want to get the full benefit of all that we have gone through, there must be no deviation from the policy we have been pursuing all along. After it is all over, if it is thought somebody else can do bette , the position is open for him. I have never sought responsibility, nor to my knowledge have I ever shirked it.

The decisive note in this crisp utterance was unmistakable. There had been no interference in the past; there should be none in the present nor in the future; Mr. Lauder was recognized universally as Mr. Carnegie's personal representative; his appearance upon the scene, suggested undoubtedly by his Chief, would be hailed as a signal that the controlling owner was dissatisfied with the situation and was feeling his way toward taking a hand, as he had done on previous occasions; its immediate effect would be strengthening of the union and discouragement of the new men; the result might, and quite

Frick the Man

likely would, be defeat and disaster; Mr. Lauder ought not, and would not be permitted, to come.

When a precisely similar crisis arose during the coke strike Mr. Frick, refusing to carry out instructions which he considered ruinous, had conceded the right of majority stockholders to dictate a policy and had withdrawn from the management. His attitude had undergone no change. Owners held, and should be empowered to exercise, full control of their properties. Again he would retire voluntarily if his administration should prove unsatisfactory *"after it is all over,"*—a significant phrase which, stripping for an instant the velvet glove, revealed the hand of steel.

Whatever construction he may have put upon this plain intimation and whatever may have been his emotions, Mr. Carnegie, admittedly ill and obviously despondent, ignored it for the moment, but at the expiration of a week he wrote at great length, expressing his regret that Mr. Frick had misinterpreted "Mr. Lauder's volunteering to go to you," hoping that he had not alienated him by making "a curt reply," quoting Mr. Phipps as remarking that he was "too touchy" and arguing with great earnestness that "the more partners there are in the works the better" as showing that the firm was "a unit and bound to win."

Paying no attention to the general dissertation, Mr. Frick answered a specific question somewhat laconically in these words:

> It seems to me that you would enjoy a trip in Italy much more if you felt well satisfied with the way everything was running at

"The Laird" and "The Man"

home, and that you would be better satisfied with the situation here if you were to return in November, as you have counted on. You will find that things are not as bad in many respects as you imagine them to be. Curry and Leishman both think it would be better that you should postpone your return until next spring, and they have felt more strongly all the time than I have that it would be a mistake for either yourself, Mr. Phipps or Mr. Lauder to return until this matter is over. I merely say this to show that the decision reached in regard to Mr. Lauder was not made on my own responsibility, although I freely concur in it.

Meanwhile, having received Mr. Frick's response to Mr. Lauder, setting forth his reasons for declining the latter's proffer of aid, Mr. Carnegie wrote:

My dear Pard:

H. P. and I are delighted with *tone* of your reply to Lauder. Altho we don't agree with your decision—Lauder is a *partner*—big word, inside Homestead Works, and not a small word anywhere—His presence there could only tell strikers the firm was a unit—not a personal quarrel of any one member—If twenty of our young partners were inside Homestead encouraging new men so much the better.

This fight is too much against our *Chairman*—partakes of personal issue. It is very bad indeed for you—very and also bad for the interests of the firm.

There's another point which troubles me on your account—the danger that the public and hence all our men get the impression that it is *all Frick*—Your influence *for good* would be permanently impaired—You don't deserve a bad name, but then one is sometimes wrongfully got—Your partners should be as much identified with this struggle as you—think over this counsel. It is from a very wise man as you know and a true friend.   A.C.

Mr. Frick, on October 12th, summed up the situation in response to this peculiar epistle as follows:

I note the counsel you give, but I cannot see wherein I can profit by it, or what action could be taken by me that would change matters in respect to that which you mention.

Frick the Man

As you understand, the only objection to Mr. Lauder's returning now, or when he proposed it, was the fear that it might prolong the strike. For no other reason, I assure you.

So far as the strike is concerned, you will recollect, in your library, before you left for Europe, during my next to the last visit with you, when you gave me a memorandum expressing your views about the labor situation at Homestead, I told you then that I did not like to think of the labor situation at Homestead, etc., etc. If we had adopted the policy of sitting down and waiting, we would have still been sitting, waiting, and the fight would yet have to be made, and then we would have been accused of trying to starve our men into submission. This is the way I think.

Of course I may be wrong, and if we had eventually been compelled to make a deal with the Amalgamated Association just think what effect that would have had on Edgar Thomson and Duquesne, and when this victory is won it will not take very long to show our men at Homestead how much better it is to deal with us direct, and anything we do for them will not be credited to the Amalgamated Association, or any other Association, but to the one that we are most deeply interested in.

Mr. Carnegie, having decided to follow his inclination and seek diversion in Italy, proceeded by easy stages to Milan, Venice and Florence, where two cablegrams from Pittsburgh awaited his arrival:

Nov. 18.—Victory!—EARLY (H.C.F.).

Nov. 21.—Strike officially declared off yesterday. Our victory is now complete and most gratifying. Do not think we will ever have any serious labor trouble again, and should now soon have Homestead and all the works formerly managed by Carnegie, Phipps & Company, in as good shape as Edgar Thomson and Duquesne. Let the Amalgamated still exist and hold full sway at other people's mills. That is no concern of ours.

"Life worth living again!" Mr. Carnegie replied, and followed with:

Cables received—first happy morning since July—surprising how pretty Italia—congratulate all round—improve works—go ahead —clear track—tariff not in it—shake.

"The Laird" and "The Man"

"I am well," he wrote from Rome, "and able to take an interest in the wonders we see," and added:

> Shall see you all early after the New Year. Think I'm about ten years older than when with you last. Europe has rung with Homestead, Homestead, until we are all sick of the name, but it is all over now—So once again Happy New Year to all. I wish someone would write me about your good self. I cannot believe you can be well.
>
> Ever your Pard, A.C.

Mr. Carnegie returned home in January deeply distressed by consciousness of the contemptuous attitude of the public toward him for what was regarded mistakenly as the craven part which he had played. But he did not flinch. Proceeding straightway to the battle-ground, he published a carefully prepared statement with "I did not come to Pittsburgh to rake up but to bury the past, of which I knew nothing," reiterating his numerous assertions that he had "retired from active business" for all time four years previously and closing with this striking tribute to his partner:

> And now one word about Mr. Frick. I am not mistaken in the man, as the future will show. Of his ability, fairness and pluck no one has now the slightest question. His four years' management stamps him as one of the foremost managers of the world—I would not exchange him for any manager I know.
>
> People generally are still to learn of those virtues which his partners and friends know so well. If his health be spared I predict that no man who ever lived in Pittsburgh and managed business here will be better liked or more admired by his employees than my friend and partner Henry Clay Frick, nor do I believe any man will be more valuable for the city. His are the qualities that wear; he never disappoints; what he promises he more than fulfils.
>
> I hope after this statement that the public will understand that the officials of the Carnegie Steel Company, Limited, with Mr. Frick at their head, are not dependent upon me, or upon any one

Frick the Man

in any way for their positions, and that I have neither power nor disposition to interfere with them in the management of the business. And further, that I have the most implicit faith in them.

Many years later, it is true, Mr. Carnegie, actuated by motives not then existent, said and did many things difficult to reconcile with this unqualified encomium, but the fact remains that he did play the game to the finish and emerged from the "most terrible experience" of his life unscathed save in popular repute.

The relations of THE LAIRD and THE MAN, having thus miraculously survived the ordeal, remained unimpaired.

XIII

Victory's Cost and Gain

CONDITIONS at Homestead and elsewhere in the district improved steadily, from the company's standpoint, during the summer months. The sympathetic strikes, inaugurated with great reluctance by union men at the Upper and Lower mills in Pittsburgh and by non-union men at Fort Duquesne lasted only a few weeks and work was resumed by the men individually all along the line on a non-union basis. Nearly two thousand new men half filled the Homestead mills in August without serious menace from the former employés.

But one dastardly performance marked this period under the direction of Master Workman Hugh Dempsey of District Assembly No. 3 of the Knights of Labor. An unaccountable epidemic broke out among the workmen who obtained their meals inside the mills and completely mystified the physicians, until, after several deaths had taken place, suspicions of poisoning were confirmed by helpers who confessed that they had been paid by Dempsey and an associate to put certain yellow powders into the soup and coffee supplied to the men. Analysis showed that these powders contained croton oil and arsenic varied with powders of antimony.

Dempsey was arrested, indicted, convicted in due time

Frick the Man

and sentenced, with others, to seven years in the penitentiary. At the expiration of three years, besought as in the case of Berkman, by both advocates and opponents of clemency to intercede, Mr. Frick addressed the following communication to the Board of Pardons:

> I have been requested to write you upon the subject of the application of Hugh Dempsey for pardon. If the application is put upon the ground of clemency, it would not seem proper to protest. There is no desire to interfere, and indeed it would be improper to attempt to interfere with the exercise by the Board of Pardons of its power so long as its exercise is invoked in the name of mercy, but the claim of innocence and unfair trial heretofore made is so manifestly untrue as to call for a protest from every well-informed and law-abiding citizen.
>
> Very Respectfully yours,
> H. C. FRICK.

The cynical effrontery of the Knights of Labor in upholding Dempsey and keeping his name on their rolls after he had been sentenced to the penitentiary contributed materially to the breakdown of the organization under Mr. Powderly and its supersession by the American Federation of Labor which was guided wisely and successfully for more than forty years by Mr. Samuel Gompers.

The troops were withdrawn gradually until October 13th, when the last instalment departed, and immediately assaults upon the non-union employés were renewed vigorously though only in a few individual instances effectually.

"The firmness with which these strikers hold on," Mr. Frick wrote to Mr. Carnegie on October 31st, "is surprising to every one, but I think after the election we will see a decided change. There is not much that I can

Victory's Cost and Gain

say about Homestead except that we are gradually improving. This strike, of course, will cost us a large sum of money but we will get it all back in the next two or three years, and, as you know, Homestead has never been well managed; always something going wrong, and a large amount of money has been wasted by poor management. The mills have never been able to turn out the product they should, owing to being held back by the Amalgamated men, but this is a chestnut, etc."

This diagnosis proved to be correct. The political culmination pulled the last prop from under the Amalgamated Association and dissipated the faint lingering hopes of the former employés, two hundred of whom broke away on November 17th and were followed by large groups of different classes on the following day, all of whom were cordially greeted personally and few turned back by Mr. Charles M. Schwab, who had been brought by Mr. Frick from the Edgar Thomson works to become Manager of the mills. Three days later the local lodges of the Amalgamated Association formally abandoned the contest and released their members.

The struggle had continued five months less one week, and had cost the company in necessary expenditures and loss of profits $2,000,000, the workmen in loss of wages $1,200,000 and the State for militia service $1,600,000,—a grand total of approximately five millions of dollars.

After notifying Mr. Carnegie that all expenses had been charged up, "so that we swallowed the dose as we went along," Mr. Frick summed up tersely:

Frick the Man

We could never have profited much by any of our competitors making and winning the fight we have made. We had to teach our employés a lesson, and we have taught them one that they will never forget, but we will talk this all over when we meet. It is hard to estimate what blessings will flow from our recent complete victory, both to the owners and the employés of the Carnegie Steel Co. Ltd., I am sure that I never want to go through another such fight.

Thereafter the company dealt with all their workmen as individuals to mutual benefit and satisfaction and never had a strike or a lock-out to mar their harmonious relationship, with the result that in 1900, the last year of its separate existence, its net profits amounted to $40,000,000, thus fully verifying the prediction of Mr. Frick contained in a letter to Mr. Carnegie dated September 8th, 1892, and reading as follows:

I do not agree with you, as stated in your cable, that we are going to suffer for years at Homestead, as we surely would have suffered if the struggle had not taken place.

Notwithstanding the heavy loss entailed by the shutdown at Homestead, the net profits of the Carnegie Steel Company for 1892 fell off only $300,000 from the gains of 1891—from $4,300,000 to $4,000,000—and still showed 16% upon the entire expanded capital of $25,000,000.

The reinstatement of the Democratic party in full power on March 4th, 1893, was preceded by symptoms of much uncertainty respecting continuance of prosperous conditions. Business began to slacken early in the year and misgivings became so strong when President Cleveland insisted in his inaugural message that solemn pledges of substantial tariff reductions must be kept that manufacturers, caught between enhanced timidity of capital and

Victory's Cost and Gain

unusual caution of consumers, were thrown back upon their own resources for money with which to fabricate products which they could not sell. The consequence was not actually the "panic" that it was termed but rather a universal and irresistible business depression which settled like a pall over the entire country. Many industrial establishments "closed for repairs" and all "slowed down" to curtail production until the storm should blow over.

The Chairman of the Carnegie Steel Company found himself in a most trying position. His aims were threefold: (1) To guide the Company through the critical period with a minimum of loss or sacrifice: (2) To demonstrate that workingmen fare better in co-operation with their own employers than under direction of labor unions and (3) To meet the financial requirements of the Company without calling upon the controlling owner for assistance.

The experience was less exciting than that of quelling a terrific outbreak in the previous year but the task was hardly less difficult. All thought of expansion or advancement fell inevitably before the absolute necessities of working capital and most rigid economy to provide living wages. Day by day and hour by hour throughout the blazing summer time Mr. Frick patiently and, so far as anyone perceived, happily paced the treadmill. Oddly the most revealing glimpses of that dreary period appear in cheery comments from Mr. Carnegie, with whom he was still in full accord, written in England and Scotland, and ending with the following:

Frick the Man

I know you have been having a hard time, but, under the circumstances, the tenor of your letters and also your cables has been reassuring. It did me great good to get the words that, "all things considered, we are getting along comfortably." You took in the situation promptly, I must say, upon your arrival, and have added even to your unsurpassed reputation as a financier.

The Chairman, meanwhile, evinced no desire for the controlling owner's return and brought into play the ingenuity developed years before in hiring money. He not only stood ready whenever requested to endorse personally any note offered for sale but also did not hesitate to pledge the backing of his friends.

"I took considerable liberty," he wrote appealing to Mr. John Walker on August 10th, "in promising Mr. Arbuckle your individual guarantee, but I really do not think I could have secured the money without it, and I trust you will have no hesitancy in doing this for us. As you know every dollar I have or any of us have would always be used to protect you against loss of any kind, and while things are bad I am sure we can get through this with unimpaired credit."

Although Mr. Andrew W. Mellon was so fully occupied in protecting their mutual interests in outside undertakings, he could always be relied upon to fill temporary gaps; but Mr. Frick's most noteworthy *coup*, when the firm's credit was finally exhausted, consisted of pledging in lots of varying amounts the entire resources of the H. C. Frick Coke Company and realizing no less than six million dollars for the "accommodation" of the Carnegie concern. This happy stroke, achieved hardly less upon his own high financial rating than upon the record of

Victory's Cost and Gain

the company of his own creation, really tided over the financial crisis and won the confidence of the full force employed while neighboring mills were shutting down.

But Homestead continued to be a thorn in his flesh. Young Mr. Schwab's zeal, charm and vivid personality had proved of inestimable value in restoring good feeling between the various groups so recently incensed at one another but, from the company's standpoint, his methods did not satisfy the pressing need of rigid economy in operation at such a time and the Chairman felt constrained to institute many reforms while the Manager was in Scotland visiting Mr. Carnegie. Happily Mr. Schwab proved wholly tractable upon his return and, by promptly renewing his full support, Mr. Frick achieved his immediate purpose without impairing the full usefulness of the "great ability" which he ungrudgingly accorded his youthful coadjutor.

The salutary effect throughout the entire organization of this evidence of unflinching determination to carry out the company's policy could hardly be overestimated. A substantial reduction in salaries was decreed and accepted by all affected without a whimper. Mr. Frick had already forwarded an outline of the percentage basis which he had adopted when he received Mr. Carnegie's suggestion that reductions should apply to all salaries beginning with the Chairman's; so that, in making acknowledgment, he merely remarked somewhat drily that "No sensible person would expect anything else than that a reduction when made should include everybody,"—an observation which drew no response.

Frick the Man

Mr. Carnegie returned to New York early in September and went immediately to the White Mountains in search of relief from a slight indisposition and a few weeks later proceeded as far west as Chicago, whence he returned to New York by way of Pittsburgh, to facilitate consultation with Mr. Frick. But there was no imminent or important question to discuss. The condition of the Company, compared with that of the country, was satisfactory and, contrasted with other steel concerns, as a consequence of shrewd financiering and enforced economies, was absolutely pre-eminent. There was no pressing need for money, no sign of labor disturbances and nothing, in fact, to do but to hold fast and mark time in hopeful anticipation of the general recovery in business which was bound soon to come.

After all, as Mr. Carnegie had predicted, the bark of the Wilson tariff had proved worse than its bite and toward the end of December the Chairman was able to report to the controlling owner that, despite all drawbacks, the dreary year would show a net profit for the Carnegie Steel Company (Limited) of not less than $3,000,000, a decrease of only one million dollars from 1892.

Whereupon Mr. Carnegie promptly decided to go to Europe for the winter and on the eve of sailing wrote to Mr. Frick:

> Good-bye—If I had been as well two weeks ago as I am now I should not have thought of deserting you for several months, but I am subject to cable, recall or conference and I have faith in your judgment which keeps me easy. Yours ever, A.C.

Victory's Cost and Gain

The year 1894 opened more auspiciously for business and manufacturing than had been anticipated. Results for January clearly evidenced the upward trend and so delighted Mr. Carnegie that he wrote immediately from Luxor insisting that the Frick family visit Scotland in the summer.

Differences of opinion among coke operators as to the method of meeting a labor crisis prevented the Chairman from leaving in early summer but, finally yielding to Mr. Carnegie's persistent importunities, he sailed late in July and proceeded directly to Cluny Castle for a few days' visit, which ended with mutual consciousness that perhaps never before had the two viewed all problems and policies so nearly eye to eye.

A return visit to Pittsburgh in November seemed to tighten even more closely the bonds of understanding and friendship.

Mr. Carnegie looked back upon it "with rare pleasure," —indeed, "we never enjoyed ourselves so much."

During the latter part of 1894, a difference in opinion respecting methods of dealing with competing coke operators so nearly caused a break between the two partners that each offered to sell his interest to the other, but a satisfactory adjustment of all points in dispute was finally effected at an unrecorded personal interview. Undoubtedly, when this meeting took place, sober second thoughts had implanted the conviction in both minds that each needed the other and that full separation would involve enormous mutual sacrifices. Assuredly Mr. Carnegie could not have failed to contrast the $4,000,000 net

Frick the Man

profit of his company in the previous year with nearly $1,000,000 actual loss incurred by its chief competitor, the Illinois Steel Company, as a direct consequence of Mr. Frick's surpassing management, and had written frankly:

"Last year was really fine under the circumstances. This year may not be better but a year comes after when I think double."

Mr. Frick, too, for his part, at forty-six, in full maturity of his powers and broadened by experience, could not have failed to recognize the wider opportunity afforded himself as the head of the commanding combination.

So one may readily surmise that the atmosphere of the conference—wherever held and by whomsoever initiated—was from the beginning far less antagonistic than it was assuasive. Despite the unacceptable offer of each to sell out to the other, there was no disagreement in principle; the difference which had so nearly caused a complete severance of relations was found, after all, to have been one of degree only. Mr. Carnegie had been even more insistent than Mr. Frick himself that the time for a respite for the working partner had come as a matter of both personal right and corporate policy, and it is altogether probable that, at the peace meeting, he evinced willingness to accept any solution that would ensure continuance of the single-headed management.

In any case, Mr. Frick proposed the creation of a new post, to be filled by an official designated as President, who should superintend operation without interference but under the supervision and general direction of the

Victory's Cost and Gain

Chairman of the Board. Mr. Carnegie approved unhesitatingly and the arrangement, since adopted by nearly all great corporations, was initiated and Mr. Leishman was appointed President.

While relinquishing his purpose to dispose of his entire interest in the Carnegie Company, Mr. Frick nevertheless felt constrained to rid himself of all financial obligations. From the day when he borrowed two thousand dollars from his sister to begin business with he had never been out of debt and now, after a full quarter century, seemed an opportune time to free his mind of consciousness of a fact which, though not important in itself, ought no longer to exist. The thought was not new. As long before as 1892 he had offered to sell to Mr. Carnegie at a low price a sufficient amount of his most cherished possession, stock in the H. C. Frick Coke Company, to take up the notes he had given in payment for his interest in the steel company, writing somewhat plaintively in the midst of the Homestead warfare:

"I should like to feel that I was out of debt for once, and that is what moves me to make this proposition to you."

But Mr. Carnegie declined, saying:

"Remember you are not really *in debt*—the collateral given up frees you or your estate—I don't think you should lessen your interest in Frick Company—It is *You*, and the only trouble about it is its not being a Limited, so all dead wood can be lopped off."

—and Mr. Frick responded with full candor that on the whole he was "not at all disappointed."

Frick the Man

But the wish had persisted and Mr. Carnegie reluctantly accepted a fresh proposal to purchase 5 per cent of the 8 per cent interest in the Carnegie Steel Company which he held as collateral security for Mr. Frick's obligations to himself, at 1.344 on the $1,250,000 involved, and to cancel the notes.

This transaction reduced Mr. Frick's total interest in the steel company from 11 per cent to 6 per cent, but left the remainder along with his large holdings in the coke company and in many other concerns conjointly with Mr. Mellon, free from incumbrance of any kind.

So the controlling owner and the controlling director continued their business relationship upon the new and even basis of neither feeling under the slightest legal or moral obligation to the other.

XIV

Oliver and Frick

THE ensuing five years—1896-1900—comprised a period of successful expansion of the Carnegie Steel Company unsurpassed in the history of industrial development,—net earnings increasing eightfold, from $5,000,000 to $40,000,000 a year, and actual values of properties owned in yet greater proportion, without the addition of a dollar of cash capital.

Chief among the contributions to this amazing result, meeting at lowest costs enormous demands for steel products, was the acquisition of mines capable of yielding huge quantities of Bessemer ore. Very early in his management Mr. Frick had realized that control of sources of supply of raw material was essential to full independence of the manufacturing unit into which he was welding the segregated and competing plants. Its own coke, the company had; its own ore, it must have. The Tyrone region of Pennsylvania had promised well prior to the Chairman's advent but in practice its product had proved deficient in both quantity and quality, and prospecting had approached a standstill when a gleam of light appeared in the northwest.

Iron ore had been discovered in the Lake Superior region as early as 1860, but it lay in ranges so distant that min-

Frick the Man

ing was impracticable except in so small a way, with primitive tools transported through a hundred miles of forest from Duluth, that the first railroad to the nearest Vermilion range was not built until 1884. Although production was restricted to this section and development lagged for years, the extraordinary purity of the mineral did not escape notice, and only a rumor to the effect that Mr. John D. Rockefeller was making large investments in the region was needed to attract widespread attention.

Among the most alert and energetic of investigators was Mr. Henry W. Oliver, of the big Pittsburgh firm of plow and shovel manufacturers, who lost no time in forming the Oliver Iron Mining Company to operate the first mine opened up on the famous Mesabi range, which soon became and continues to be the most fruitful in the world.

This was in 1892, the year of the Homestead trouble, but Mr. Frick was not so busy as to neglect an opportunity whose coming he had been awaiting for years and, immediately upon his return to his office partially recovered from the effects of Berkman's murderous assault, he opened negotiations with Mr. Oliver for participation in his mining enterprise. His approach was cordially welcomed. The primary purposes of their two companies were identical. Both desired above all else to be assured adequate supplies of high-grade Bessemer ores for their blast furnaces; each, moreover, would gain through a combination providing a market for the entire product of the mine and the lowest transportation rates for guaranteed tonnage; and the new company itself would be susceptible of unlimited expansion through unequalled

Oliver and Frick

advantages in the purchase of products of other mines upon a royalty basis. True, the Carnegie Company would profit more largely, in proportion to its greater consumption; but this could be offset by provision of money needed for development purposes.

Quick trading between friends who held each other in highest esteem proved feasible, and Mr. Oliver agreed to give the Carnegie Company one-half of the mining company's capital stock in return for a mortgage loan of $500,000 to the latter for development purposes.

Fully convinced that this combination was the most advantageous that ever had been, or probably ever could be made, for the Carnegie Company, Mr. Frick hastened to notify the controlling owner of his accomplishment, in confident expectancy of winning his enthusiastic approbation. But Mr. Carnegie, despondent over the prolongation of the shutdown at Homestead and possibly chilled by the failure of his own costly experiments in the Tyrone region, had reached the conclusion that "pioneering don't pay."

"Oliver's ore bargain," he responded from Rannock Lodge, "is just like him—nothing in it. If there is any department of business which offers no inducement, it is ore. It never has been very profitable, and the Mesabi is not the last great deposit that Lake Superior is to reveal."

Although the Chairman had made the bargain with full authority and insisted upon strict adherence to its terms, Mr. Carnegie strove persistently to prevent compliance by the company and, in the face of his opposition, development of the property was seriously retarded

Frick the Man

through 1893 into 1894, when the activities of the Rockefeller managers produced a disturbing effect upon his mind.

"Oliver," he wrote from Sorrento on March 16th, 1894, "hasn't much of a bargain in his Mesabi, as I see it, but in view of threatened combination it is good policy to take the half as independent of its intrinsic value; it gives us a wedge that can be driven in somewhere to our advantage in the general winding up. In less strong hands, the Oliver would be squeezed. Remember Reckafellows & Porter will own the R. R. and that's like owning the pipe lines—*Producers* will not have much of a show. We are big enough, however, to take care of ourselves and if *forced* could make another outlet somehow.

"Taking half with Oliver means we have all the risk, must furnish all the capital—not a small amount, etc., etc.; besides, Oliver isn't a good manager and mining needs just that thing. It's a pity we have to go in at all, still I cannot but recognize we are right in flanking the combination as far as possible—There are no doubt others in Oliver's position who will offer to do as he has, with us. I don't think Standard people will succeed in making ore a monopoly like oil, they have failed in every new venture and Rockefeller's reputation now is one of the poorest investors in the world. His railroads are almost worthless. Note Troy, Cotton Seed, etc., etc. Still I favor *taking* the Oliver half gratis."

This obviously reluctant assent was qualified within a fortnight when he wrote that he should "not be sorry if you miss one-half of Oliver mines," was "not greatly

Oliver and Frick

scared about Rockefellow," did "not want any business managed by Harry (Oliver), good fellow though he is" and that "really" in any case Mr. Carnegie himself "should stand for controlling interest." The hint thus conveyed evoking no response from the Chairman, on April 18th, 1894, he addressed a formal communication to the Board of Managers to this effect:

> You will find that this ore venture, like all other ventures in ore, will result in much trouble and less profit than almost any branch of our business. If any of our brilliant and talented young partners have more time, or attention, than is required for their present duties, they will find sources of much greater profit right at home. I hope you will make a note of this prophecy.

Simultaneously, as revealed by Mr. J. Frederick Byers in an address delivered on February 26th, 1927, thirty-three years later, he was advising his friend, Mr. A. M. Byers, "against investment in association with Messrs. Oliver and Kimberly because of the hazards of the undertaking." So, despite the astounding fact that, through the introduction of huge Oliver steam shovels, the output of the Mesabi range was increased from 29,245 tons in 1892 to 1,913,234 tons in 1894, the mining company continued to languish from inadequate capital for another two years.

But in 1896, Messrs. Oliver and Frick, still persisting in the face of constant discouragement, effected an arrangement with Mr. Rockefeller's managers to lease his properties upon a royalty basis of 25 cents a ton, as against 65 cents a ton then universally paid, in consideration of a guaranteed output of 600,000 tons a year and a like amount from the Oliver mines, to be shipped over the

Frick the Man

Rockefeller railroad and steamship lines to Lake Erie ports at a total rate of $1.45 a ton. The contract, running for a period of fifty years and indicating a visible saving to the Carnegie-Oliver interests of $500,000 a year, a total of twenty-five millions, was made subject to approval by the Boards of the two companies and required the consent of Mr. Carnegie as controlling owner of the steel company.

Mr. Oliver waited upon him in New York shortly after his return from Europe and submitted the agreement with a strong recommendation of acceptance from Mr. Frick, to whom Mr. Carnegie wrote immediately upon the conclusion of the interview:

> Oliver called today. He has got matter really in good shape—so HE SAYS. Hope he will have final papers to submit when you come. He may be too sanguine about closing on basis reported.

Apparently all misgivings in Mr. Carnegie's mind as to the advisability of engaging in mining operations were dissipated by the obvious merits of the proposition. But then arose another question, for which probably Mr. Oliver was prepared, in the light of the hint conveyed two years previously that he was "really" entitled to a controlling interest, without which he was never content for long to continue association with any corporation. Mr. Oliver acquiesced. And then the trading began, with the astute Scotchman in his element. The two interests, he thought, ought to be revised to correspond to the percentages of consumption. That seemed undeniable. In any event, Mr. Oliver was in no position to dispute it.

On the other hand, of course, Mr. Oliver should be

Oliver and Frick

reimbursed to the extent of the actual cash he had paid in. The trading continued, as related by Mr. Carnegie:

> Oliver Mining Company made, say, $400,000.
> Now he says his ½— $200,000
> Now he got half his cost
> $120,000   60,000
> He wants his $260,000   2, 3, 4, 5,
> years with interest—for this he sells us $\frac{2}{6}$th making us $\frac{5}{6}$ths.

He asked $120,000 but when I showed him he had given us $60,000 ½ and that this was "gone"—He agreed. He wanted 1 2 3 4 5 years. I said we could not pay anything shorter than 2 years. No doubt the interest sold will net this before it is due.

> $\frac{2}{6}$th of $400,000 is $133,333
> to begin with—then we
> have only to pay   133,333

One year like last would pay it entire.

The next year did, in fact, "pay it entire" and much more; with the net result that the Carnegie Steel Company acquired five-sixths and, of course, full control of the Oliver Mining Company, after it had proved highly successful, for literally nothing.

"Pretty good, I think," Mr. Carnegie complacently remarked.

But better yet was to ensue immediately. The reduction of royalties paid on the Rockefeller output from 65 cents to 25 cents a ton, resulting in a corresponding lowering of selling prices at the Lake Erie docks, greatly alarmed the stockholders of other mining companies who, foreseeing only disaster, began to throw their shares upon the market, only to discover that purchasers could not be found. A rare opportunity thus presented itself and early in the summer of 1897, when the demoralization

Frick the Man

was at its worst, Messrs. Oliver and Frick concluded that the time was ripe to gather options upon the shares of the three most important companies.

It was a difficult task, owing to the wide distribution of the stock throughout the country, but Mr. Oliver undertook it with characteristic energy and succeeded so well from the beginning that, warned by previous experience, Mr. Frick went to Scotland laden with facts and figures calculated to avert conceivable opposition from the controlling owner. But Mr. Carnegie continued to balk at "pioneering" and, even after having studied the final report showing the acquisition by Mr. Oliver of more than four hundred options at astoundingly low prices, he vetoed the proposition with a jocular quip at the enthusiasm of his partners.

Mr. Oliver was in despair. The options were about to expire and he was only too well aware that extensions could not be obtained. Although knowing that nothing effective could be added by way of argument to the Chairman's strong presentation of the case, he also realized that the time had passed when Mr. Frick would plead with Mr. Carnegie for consideration of any kind. Having no such compunctions himself, he hung his last hope upon the slender thread of personal entreaty and, on September 25th, 1897, sent the following telegram:

To CARNEGIE   LAGGAN

I am distressed at indications here that Norrie options expiring on Monday, are to be refused. It would be a terrible mistake. The good times make it that I could not possibly secure these options again at fifty per cent., advance. The Norrie mine controls the whole situation. They have sold over one million tons this year.

Oliver and Frick

With the additional property we will get from the fee owners, we secure fifteen to twenty million tons of the ore that the Carnegie Company are purchasing this year five hundred and fifty thousand tons. I will guarantee, counting the surplus they have in their treasury, to return in profits every dollar we invest in two years. Do not allow my hard summer's work to go for naught.

HENRY W. OLIVER

This beseeching message added the requisite touch to Mr. Frick's impressive reasoning; Mr. Carnegie replied promptly agreeing to abide by the decision of the Chairman and the Board of Managers and, in the nick of time, Mr. Oliver was authorized by unanimous vote to declare the options. By so small a margin, the Carnegie-Oliver interests gained a position which enabled them to acquire within two years sufficient additional lands to give them exclusive ownership of two-thirds of the greatest high-grade Bessemer ore deposit in the world.

Once the deal was made, Mr. Carnegie quickly awoke to realization of the wisdom of overriding his own whim against "pioneering."

"I am happy," he wrote frankly to Mr. Frick as early as October 9th, "that we are now secure in our ore supply; it was the only element needed to give us an impregnable position."

Rejoicing in the Carnegie and the Oliver offices naturally was boundless but even there none, from the farseeing Frick and the indomitable Oliver to the sanguine young partners headed by the buoyant Schwab and the canny Morrison, comprehended fully the vastness of the potentialities of the commonplace transaction.

A very few figures suffice to indicate the concrete re-

Frick the Man

sults. From less than 30,000 tons of ore in 1892, the output of the Mesabi range increased to 9,303,541 tons in 1901 and reached 40,396,711 tons in 1918; the known supply turned over to the United States Steel Corporation by the Carnegie Company in 1901 was valued by Mr. Schwab at $333,000,000; and the total known reserve of the Mesabi region in 1920 was reported by the Institute of Mining and Metallurgical Engineers to be 1,400,000,000 tons.

After noting in his book, "The Story of Steel," published in 1926, the recent increase in national wealth from 220 billions of dollars to 350 billions, Mr. J. Bernard Walter, Editor Emeritus of the SCIENTIFIC AMERICAN said:

> If the writer were asked to name the principal agent in the enormous growth in wealth of this country during the past two decades, he would unhesitatingly name the vast iron deposits of the Lake Superior region and the consequent phenomenal growth of our steel industry.

To this extent at any rate the dictum of Mr. Walker seems to be justified by two warrantable deductions, regardless of the relative economic merits of competition and combination, to wit:

(1) But for the acquirement of the Mesabi mines obtained for the Carnegie Company by Messrs. Oliver and Frick, with the assent of Mr. Carnegie, in the manner noted, the colossal United States Steel Corporation, with its later huge net earnings of $200,000,000 a year, could not have been organized; and

(2) Without the subsequent intervention of Mr. Frick alone, as presently we shall show, in the expert opinion of Mr. John D. Rockefeller, the Corporation could hardly

Oliver and Frick

have survived the first crisis of its infancy. The Carnegie Company was now assured an abundant supply of iron ore and cheap transportation from its mines to Lake Erie ports, but one essential connecting link was yet to be provided. That was conveyance by rail for two hundred miles from lakes to furnaces. The Pennsylvania railroad was the natural medium but its virtual monopoly had emboldened its management to exact excessive rates for inadequate service while dealing separately with the various Pittsburgh manufacturers. Both Mr. Carnegie, originally, and Mr. Frick, subsequently, had chafed under this domination for years in vain. Impervious alike to the repeated threats of the former to arouse public opinion in behalf of justice to the city and of the latter to project a competing line, the powerful corporation had calmly assumed itself to be so strongly intrenched politically that there was no cause for apprehension.

The acquirement of the Oliver Mining Company and the making of the Rockefeller alliance effected a complete change in this situation overnight and Mr. Frick lost no time in pointing out that the Carnegie Company was now in a position to finance a new railroad by agreeing to furnish ample shipments and, if necessary, by guaranteeing construction bonds, without itself contributing a dollar in cash. He no longer pleaded, he flatly demanded, the privilege of operating over Pennsylvania tracks the Carnegie Company's trains of ore, with its own locomotives and crews, on its own schedules.

This was reprisal for past injuries with a touch of vengeance, but it seems to have been justified and the

Frick the Man

discomfited Pennsylvania management was hesitating when word came from Mr. Carnegie to the effect that he had quietly acquired control of the rusty rails called Pittsburgh, Shenango and Lake Erie railroad through arrangements with Mr. Samuel B. Dick, its President, and Mr. Frederick H. Prince, the Boston capitalist, who had saved the company from actual bankruptcy by paying its coupons.

Although naturally peeved at secret intervention which might have put him in an equivocal position, Mr. Frick perceived two reasons for rejoicing,—first, that fortunately he had made no commitment and, secondly, because no conceivable project could have served better his purpose to attain complete independence for the Carnegie Company. So it came to pass that, in less than fifteen months, the old road was reorganized, rechristened the Pittsburgh, Bessemer and Lake Erie, rebuilt throughout, extended forty-two miles to join the Company's Union railway, and trains of thirty-five steel cars were running from the Company's docks at Conneaut over its new steel bridge, two-thirds of a mile long, across the Allegheny, and delivering 175,000 tons of ore to the big blast furnaces at Braddock, Duquesne and Pittsburgh.

Thus was completed the thousand-mile chain, stretching from the bowels of the earth north of Lake Superior to the salesrooms south of Lake Erie, which established the invulnerable preeminence of the Carnegie Steel Company; and every link was unassailable save one. While the contract with Mr. Rockefeller's steamship company affording conveyance of 1,200,000 tons of ore per annum for fifty years met immediate requirements fairly well, it

Oliver and Frick

neither provided for the needs of probable expansion nor ensured the perpetuity of ownership, and incidentally still left the company even then partially dependent upon the service of unsubstantial shipping concerns.

To safeguard the situation fully, Mr. Frick enlisted the services of Mr. Oliver and, at the end of fifteen months, that patient and skilful negotiator had purchased for the Oliver Mining Company a fleet of six vessels, along with the ore mines on the Marquette range owned by the Lake Superior Iron Company, and had formulated a plan for financing the undertaking through the issuance of bonds by a new subsidiary Pittsburgh Steamship Company.

The securities found a ready market and the transaction was completed so expeditiously and admirably that Mr. Carnegie, then abroad, so far from interposing objections, as in the previous instance already noted, promptly ratified the arrangement and, frankly reversing his opinion of the desirability of Mr. Oliver as a partner, offered him a valuable interest in the Carnegie Steel Company.

Ten years of arduous labor, attended by many vicissitudes, had been required to fulfil Mr. Frick's ambitious project of unification and expansion, but the great constructive effort, fortified by amazingly efficient executive capacity, now began to find its reward in an increase in tons of steel ingots produced from 332,111 in 1889 to 2,663,412 in 1899 and in net profits from $1,900,000 to $21,000,000, of which, incidentally, $1,253,853 was earned on the company's 30 per cent interest in the H. C. Frick Coke Company and no less than $1,067,000 on its five-sixths interest in the Oliver Mining Company.

XV

Negotiations

THE year 1899 was the most eventful in the history of the Carnegie Steel Company, not only revealing clearly for the first time its enormous earning capacity of more than 80 per cent upon its inflated capital, equal to 400 per cent upon its original paid-up shares, but also marking a complete severance of the personal and partnership relations of its two creative and guiding spirits.

The three years following the reconcilement of Mr. Carnegie and Mr. Frick were not marred by serious altercations. Correspondence was renewed promptly and frequently educed differences of opinion respecting both policies and men, but contrary views were advanced tentatively, and expressed courteously, though plainly and frankly, with obvious design to avoid offensiveness.

Early in 1896 a rift seemed imminent in consequence of Mr. Carnegie's recurrence to negotiating with outsiders upon a basis differing from that adopted by the firm, without consulting or even notifying his partners. It was his yielding to this inclination that had just caused the rupture which came so near being complete and Mr. Frick felt that he could not tacitly assent to continuance of the practice by permitting the episode to pass unnoticed. But his remonstrance was mild indeed as compared

Negotiations

with the caustic protest that would surely have been forthcoming before the two had pledged the mutual confidence essential to better understanding.

"True," he wrote, "we did shake hands but there is a difference in the way of stating things: don't you think so? On Sunday morning you had reached a different conclusion, and were so set in your idea that you would not even discuss the matter, and this is certainly not what that open book above your mantelpiece says. I never told you what you say about the Bessemer Coke rate nor could anybody else have done so and told you the truth, as I said to you recently when you referred to the matter."

And, looking to the future, he added:

> Suppose you deal frankly with me. Don't put words in my mouth that I never uttered.
>
> You do not find me putting you in a compromising position when we get into discussion with outside people. I have stood by you in this matter just as loyally as you could wish and my suggestions as to appointments, etc., have not weakened your position. I may view the whole matter differently from you, but there is no reason why we should quarrel about it. What we are both after is the ultimate best interest of the Companies in which we are interested. We should not allow feeling to enter into such matters, as you have often said. You may not care for the dollars but your partners do.
>
> In all my dealings want of frankness with you on all subjects has not been a failing. It might from some points of view be considered a fault.

What, if any, response was evoked by this temperate avowal is not of record; quite likely none other than of a jocose and conciliatory nature; in any case, the pleasing change in tone proved effective, and Mr. Carnegie gave no further cause for complaint. Almost immediately,

Frick the Man

moreover, his most businesslike letters, though bearing no longer the familiar superscription "My dear Pard," began to reflect the temperamental buoyancy, good fellowship and friendliness of former scribbled communications, after this fashion:

Suppose you put your "gigantic intellect" on this and write me freely.

Don't let us fail now and you can buy $60,000 more pictures per year and remember me in your prayers.

Douched, massaged—fine! "No family should be without it."

Paid my bill at Aix out of capital, sorry you couldn't arrange dead-head!

We are all hoping for a visit from the Fricks this season at Skibo. I have my eye on adjoining estate, castle and all—tell Helen about this—I am anxious for her to come to MY side.

How goes the struggle for European trip? I can give you plenty of fishing in salt or fresh water. P.S. Can you not get more land adjoining Illinois Steel?

And so forth, by frequent reiteration, through the year 1898.

The advent of the year 1899 synchronized with a crisis in the entire steel industry. Competing companies suddenly awoke to realization of the fact that they had been so skilfully outgeneralled by the Carnegie management that the very existence of several, if not all, was imperilled. The menace was widespread, involving, in hardly less degree than the shareholders of the various corporations, the bankers who had floated their securities. Not only were hundreds of millions of dollars and the priceless prestige of scores of investment brokers at stake but all stock values might be seriously affected by a general crash in steel shares.

The pre-eminence of the Carnegie Company in resources,

Negotiations

plants and organization, fortified by ownership of all agencies contributing to manufacture and by absolute financial independence, was undeniable, and a vastly greater earning power than had yet been revealed was shrewdly suspected. Only the few men in full control could compute the potentialities of the young industrial giant. But those few had access to accurate foreknowledge in the estimates of their Chairman which had never failed of realization.

Mr. Carnegie called them together at his house in New York on the evening of January 5th to consider the situation. Messrs. Carnegie, Frick, Phipps, Lauder, Schwab, Lovejoy and Peacock reported present and, by request of the controlling owner, the Chairman announced his judgment that the net profits of the coming year would reach $20,000,000 and might be expected to double that sum in 1900. In the event of these anticipations being verified by results—as subsequently they were—the company would inaugurate the coming century with an earning capacity of 160 per cent upon its outstanding stock, the equivalent of 800 per cent upon its entire cash-paid capital.

Two questions, said Mr. Carnegie, confronted the partners present, representing practically all of the shareholders:

(1) Should a price be fixed upon the entire property, including 30 per cent of the stock of the H. C. Frick Coke Company, for submission to a syndicate of New York and Chicago capitalists who had made overtures for its purchase? and

Frick the Man

(2) In the event of a sale upon that basis failing of consummation, should steps be taken to consolidate the Steel Company and the Coke Company on terms to be agreed upon?

Both proposals were unanimously decided in the affirmative, and the price was fixed at $250,000,000, payable one-half in cash and one-half in fifty-year, five-percent gold bonds.

This offer was declined by the Syndicate which, it was reported, had hoped to make partial payment in the stock of a new company.

Two plans were then drawn for the consolidation of the Steel and Coke Companies,—one by Mr. Frick providing for the purchase of both properties by a new company with $60,000,000 capital and $100,000,000 bonds and another by Mr. Carnegie increasing the proposed capitalization to $150,000,000 of preferred and common stock and the bond issue to $150,000,000. These and other proposals were under consideration when a fresh proffer was made by a syndicate headed by Former Judge W. H. Moore, looking to the purchase of Mr. Carnegie's majority holdings in both companies for $157,950,000, payable in $100,000,000 first mortgage bonds and $57,950,000 in cash.

This sum was pronounced satisfactory by Mr. Carnegie, but as a consideration for an option he required a cash deposit of $1,170,000 to be paid to himself if the Syndicate should fail to consummate the transaction within ninety days. The amount thus fixed he reckoned as his percentage of a total option price of $2,000,000. Mr.

Negotiations

Moore offered to put up $1,000,000, the Carnegie partners waived payments for their percentages in the total option price, Messrs. Frick and Phipps contributed the additional $170,000 required by Mr. Carnegie, and all parties to the agreement signed the papers on April 24th.

Mr. Carnegie, having publicly proclaimed his intention to sell out to his partners when he should retire from business, preferred not to deal with outside parties personally and gave his power of attorney to Messrs. Frick and Phipps, his senior partners, to execute the agreement and to complete the entire transaction on his behalf. He then sailed for England after having arranged with Mr. Frick to keep him fully informed, regarding the progress of the Syndicate's endeavors.

There then seemed to be a perfect understanding between Mr. Carnegie and his designated agents but later developments indicated much confusion in the former's mind from the beginning. On May 4th, the following cablegram was sent from New York:

Carnegie, Langham Hotel, London.

Option money deposited today. We furnish one hundred and seventy thousand. Except Lauder, your partners underwrite largely and look to you for kind aid.

PHIPPS.   FRICK.

Testifying before the Congressional Investigating Committee in January, 1912, however, when asked by Chairman Stanley if he "did not know at any time" that his partners "had any interest in that option," Mr. Carnegie replied, "No sir, I did not suspect it," and the colloquy continued:

Frick the Man

THE CHAIRMAN. Was not the amount put to your credit, when the option was not carried through, $1,180,000?

MR. CARNEGIE. When I returned from Europe I found that they had deposited the amount due me, which I got.

THE CHAIRMAN. Which was $1,180,000 was it not?

MR. CARNEGIE. I think so. About that.

THE CHAIRMAN. Did you not know at that time that a part of that money was contributed by your partners? Were you not told that at that time?

MR. CARNEGIE. Part of what money?

THE CHAIRMAN. A part of the $1,180,000 that was put up for that option.

MR. CARNEGIE. I was in Europe, and I did not hear anything. I sailed before the option money was deposited.

THE CHAIRMAN. Were you not told in Europe that your partners had put up a part of that money?

MR. CARNEGIE. When the option was not executed, I lost all interest in it, and things that came to me bearing upon it I never read.

THE CHAIRMAN. Did you not stipulate at the time, or promise at the time, or make a statement at the time, or send a letter from Europe at the time, stating that if your partners had put up any of this money they would be refunded their portion of the money?

MR. CARNEGIE. I do not remember that at all.

THE CHAIRMAN. I will hand you a letter here, and ask you if this is not your handwriting, containing a statement with reference to this option, that you will demand this money and that—

"Of course any part paid by my partners
I shall refund."

I will ask if that is in your handwriting. That is a photographic copy of the letter (handing paper to Mr. Carnegie). The main part of it is written by an amanuensis, but the line across the middle is what I refer to. I will ask you if that is not in your handwriting?

MR. CARNEGIE. Yes; of course. I have never seen this since I wrote it. I wrote this. I shall have to study it a moment. I never knew of the deposit of my money until I came back, and no partner ever asked me for any money that I can think of.

Later he declared his willingness "to refund to all of them today, but if Mr. Frick and Mr. Phipps entered

Negotiations

into a contract with the Moore Brothers by which they assumed to make $5,000,000 apiece, and never told me about it, why, I do not think I am obligated to pay them anything now."

Mr. GARDNER. Do you mean half a million dollars or $5,000,000? You said $5,000,000 the other day, I think.

Mr. CARNEGIE. Now, it may be half a million or it may be $5,000,000. I think I said five millions, did I not? If I were asked what I thought, I should say it was half a million each. I can only state what I heard about this.

Mr. GARDNER. I think you said day before yesterday five millions. Am I right, Mr. Reed?

Mr. REED (Mr. Carnegie's attorney). Five millions of the stock of the new company was to go to them, he said.

Mr. GARDNER. Was it $5,000,000 each or $5,000,000 in all?

Mr. REED. I do not know.

Mr. CARNEGIE. Well, that is the best of my recollection.

* * * * *

Mr. GARDNER. The testimony was, as I remember it, that the option ran in the name of Judge Moore for your share in the company.

Mr. CARNEGIE. I never knew Judge Moore was a party to it. If I had known it, I would not have given them an option upon any account.

The records, nevertheless, show that on May 10th, 1899, Messrs. Frick and Phipps cabled an outline of the Syndicate's plan of reorganization and clearly identified it ten days later in a second cablegram reading as follows:

New York, May 20th, 1899.

CARNEGIE   CLASHMORE   SCOTLAND.

Moore's plan cabled was not made public but requiring our aid consented to Pennsylvania charter. Present plan capital Two hundred and fifty millions of one kind of stock to be sold at par subject to bonds. Proceeds of fifteen millions stock go into treasury and fifteen millions to bear expenses. One-third of the balance to Moore, one-third to us and one-third to be held for deserving young men,

Frick the Man

thus carrying out your long cherished idea. Expect to offer public soon. After allowing fair premium on bonds you will see we are offering the stock at less than paid you. Bonds are a serious objection, perhaps fatal. The sum needed is immense, hence uncertainty.

FRICK.   PHIPPS.

This cablegram was amplified three days later in a letter from Mr. Frick to Mr. Carnegie at Skibo Castle reading in essential part as follows:

May 23rd, 1899.

I beg to enclose a copy of the agreement reached last Friday, after a hard struggle, and after an offer to Mr. Moore to return his money, which he refused to accept.

We endeavored to limit Moore's share of the profits in promotion to one-fifth of the amount left of $15,000,000, but finally compromised on one-third.

This agreement puts the matter in control of Mr. Phipps and myself, and is on a very conservative basis, in view of what has been agreed to pay you, and on a basis where our employés and friends can safely invest. It is astonishing the demand there is from that source.

I propose having all of our partners who take stock in the new Company join in an agreement not to sell any of their stock for two years, unless otherwise mutually agreed.

These communications certainly seem to show that, if Mr. Carnegie was kept in ignorance (1) of Mr. Moore's connection with the enterprise, (2) of the participation of Messrs. Frick and Phipps in both the general undertaking and the promotion profits and (3) of the expectation that the junior partners would partake of the underwriting, the fact could hardly be attributed to any attempt at concealment on the part of Messrs. Frick and Phipps.

These strange misapprehensions on the part of Mr. Carnegie, however, being unsuspected by anyone else,

Negotiations

had no effect upon the negotiations and all signs pointed to success of the undertaking when suddenly there fell a bolt from the blue in the complete demoralization of the money market caused by the unexpected death of Former Governor Roswell P. Flower, then head of the most active and most seriously extended brokerage firm in Wall Street. All values shrank so sharply overnight that the great number of banks and bankers involved, already overloaded with underwritings, were in no position to make further commitments.

While the partial panic thus created was not expected to be of long duration, it was a virtual certainty that the Moore Syndicate would be unable, even with the powerful aid of Mr. George F. Baker, to raise the many millions required to take up the Carnegie option within the time allotted. A reasonable extension, such as was being generally allowed in like enterprises, Judge Moore had reason to believe, would suffice to meet the temporary crisis, and in the circumstances he did not doubt that it would be granted. Mr. Frick and Mr. Phipps were far less confident and promptly cabled to Mr. Carnegie proposing a conference at Edinburgh. On May 29th Mr. Frick wrote to Mr. Moore in Chicago:

> On Saturday we received a cable from Mr. Carnegie, in reply to the one which you saw sent him on Friday. He said he would be delighted to see us, not, however, at Edinboro: we would have to go to Skibo, as he was doing strictly an office business. As you are of opinion that October would be the most propitious time for renewing our efforts to put this matter through, and as our option expires about August 4th, it seems to me that your interest, being so large, should induce you to go abroad and join Mr. Phipps and myself in the interview with Mr. Carnegie regarding an extension

Frick the Man

of the same, and a modification of some of its terms. I personally should feel much better if you would join us at Mr. Carnegie's castle on the 21st of June. If you should decide to go, it would be well to keep it entirely quiet, and not let the newspapers know that you are going abroad to see him. I have grave fears that Mr. Carnegie will decline to extend the option. He will regard it as a cold business transaction, so that the result, as far as you are concerned, would be to lose the money you have paid, and I have serious doubts about Mr. Carnegie's willingness ever to return it. Please think this over and let me hear from you.

Mr. Moore replied that the necessity of attending to other matters at home would prevent him from going. Even though circumstances were otherwise, moreover, he should doubt the advisability of making the trip.

"Of course," he said with shrewd insight, "I do not care to lose the money and Mr. Carnegie would undoubtedly believe that the long distance travelled was for the sole purpose of saving it. If you and Mr. Phipps cannot convince him that he will be a loser if he does not take advantage of this opportunity, I feel certain that he cannot be convinced."

Reluctantly but frankly concurring with this judgment, Mr. Frick and Mr. Phipps sailed and put forth their best endeavors, with the disappointing result that, at the end of a month, Mr. Frick cabled to Mr. Moore:

Carnegie refuses to extend or modify option. Impossible.

So the deal fell through and, on the day following the expiration of the option, the forfeited $1,170,000 was credited to Mr. Carnegie's personal account on the books of the Carnegie Steel Company.

The breakdown of negotiations with the Moore Syndicate, marking failure of the third attempt to enable

Negotiations

Mr. Carnegie to withdraw from active business, was most disappointing naturally to his partners who, under the final arrangement skilfully effected by Mr. Frick, would have gained control of the great property which jointly they had built up. Obviously, however, there was nothing to do but to take up anew the various plans which had been suggested for consolidation of the Steel and Coke Companies. Having reached this conclusion, and divining further that parley with the controlling owner at that stage would prove surely futile and possibly acrimonious, the two chief senior members of the firm separated, Mr. Phipps returning to his place in Scotland and Mr. Frick to Aix les Bains for rest and meditation, with the understanding that the latter should return to America for consultation with the junior partners and the formulation of a fresh proposal.

It was a disheartening renewal of what seemed to have become, for no apparent reason, a hopeless undertaking. The real motive of Mr. Carnegie was wholly conjectural. Was he, like his partners, disconcerted by the collapse of the latest trading which would have brought to him a fortune greater probably than any other in the world and given to him the freedom which he craved? If so, why had he refused to grant the brief extension of the option which everybody believed would produce that result? Or did he consider $1,170,000 in the hand worth $157,950,000 in the bush? One per cent upon so huge a sum realized surely could not be reckoned as excessive even though it should be sacrificed; it could not, moreover, be lost in case of a second forfeiture of the

Frick the Man

option, whose price was already in hand and would remain there under the identical terms of the original agreement.

Had Mr. Carnegie's attitude changed since he sold the privilege of purchase to persons then unknown but subsequently revealed to him, though not that he could recall, as chiefly his own associates? Had he really wished to pass control of the entire property to his partners, with Henry Clay Frick at their head?

This was the question that puzzled the two senior members because it bore directly upon the problem of consolidation. It is hardly conceivable that either of them had forgotten that the first words of Mr. Carnegie's prospectus which accompanied the plan submitted by him were these:

> In pursuance of a decision of long standing, the four principal owners of the Carnegie Steel Company, Limited, and the H. C. Frick Coke Company (Messrs. Carnegie, Phipps, Frick and Lauder) now retire from active business.

—a statement true as to Mr. Phipps but a complete surprise to Mr. Frick and then quite contrary to his desire.

And yet, somewhat contradictory of this "decision of long standing," as Mr. Frick must have recalled, Mr. Carnegie had simultaneously pencilled on the back of a memorandum sent to Mr. Lauder and the junior partners the following personal note:

> H. C. F.—Have written Lauder as desired. Let them decide whether to include our Frick Coal Company stock or not. I don't care. It's good enough to hold as long as I can have you as my pard looking after it. I'm not going to force it on my partners.

Negotiations

And there the matter had been left. What was the portent of it all? Did Mr. Carnegie really favor the consolidation for which he, in common with his associates, had voted? Or was it his underlying purpose to segregate the two companies and, by relegating the Chairman of both to coke production, to eliminate him from steel manufacture? Or did he truly care as little, one way or the other, as he had seemed to mind smashing the trade with the Moore Syndicate? Or what?

Bewildered by the strange workings of a mind which he was never able fully to comprehend, Mr. Frick sailed for home on August 30th to evolve a reorganization through anticipated "consolidation," harassed, dubious and mistrustful, with only the consciousness of the establishment of a closer personal relationship with Mr. Phipps which might, as in fact it did, prove to be of inestimable value.

Henry Phipps, Jr. was not merely the second largest owner of the Carnegie Company; as the only surviving partner of the brothers Kloman whose one little engine and single trip-hammer constituted the basis of the great plant, he was its oldest member, preceding Mr. Carnegie by four years,—from 1861 to 1865, when the Union Iron Mills Company was organized with a capital of $500,000 to take over the firm's property and the Cyclops mill, in which Mr. Carnegie had acquired an interest.

The partnership of the two young men—Mr. Phipps was then twenty-six and Mr. Carnegie thirty—continued through many vicissitudes for thirty-six years, at the end of which they sold their holdings to the United States

Frick the Man

Steel Corporation for colossal sums. During this long period, until toward the very last, they were to each other "Andrew" and "Harry," and no serious disturbance of their amicable relations had arisen when the transaction with the Moore Syndicate fell through.

Nevertheless, although from the beginning subordinate to Mr. Carnegie as controlling owner, Mr. Phipps scrupulously maintained his full independence in thought and action. His undeviating course, indeed, could not be better depicted than by himself, in a letter addressed to "My Dear Andrew" in 1890 protesting against what he considered the unfairness of a virtual edict of the controlling owner, to this effect:

> With regard to the sale of undivided stock, if it were in my possession, I would do pretty much as you would wish, as it always gives me pleasure to concur with you—when I can properly do so. A right decision in this matter is less important to me in its effects upon my pocket than its influence upon my mind. To feel that I have been rightly treated is a greater pleasure to me than any probable or possible gain in money; That is subordinate, the first is everything; and next to it is the feeling that the business in which my heart has ever been, has been dealt with on timehonored, safe and just business principles.

"You have not forgotten," he interjected, careful to voice his own appreciation of his partner's consideration, "the time I had to get Frick in, but on my arguments and strong urging you consented, with the proviso that I should represent his stock. Your overcoming your powerful convictions so long held was very clever and I ever held it as a notable instance of your reasonableness."

It was frank recognition of his own responsibility undoubtedly that impelled Mr. Phipps to uphold Mr. Frick

Negotiations

in the trying early days of his management but it is no less certain that, once the new executive had won his spurs, his every act was judged upon its merits; that was Mr. Phipps's conception of perfect fairness to both shareholders and management. In point of fact, the two men apparently never disagreed upon any point of policy or method but, owing to Mr. Phipps's prolonged absences, they were not brought into close personal contact until Mr. Carnegie deputed them to act for himself, as well as for the Company, in the negotiations with Mr. Moore. The outcome of the ensuing difficulties on all sides was an arousal of mutual respect and faith which led them to see eye to eye from that time forward.

It may be well believed, therefore, that Mr. Frick welcomed the wise counsel of his sympathetic associate contained in the following letter which awaited his perusal on the steamer:

Beaufort Castle, August 26th, 1899.

Dear Mr. Frick:

Though I gave my views strongly and fully to my three senior associates, yet I consider it a duty to put them in a more enduring form.

The price at which it is proposed that we take over the properties of the firm is far too high; unless it is intended to make a quick sale and get out of business, which appears to be the intention of mainly one member. You suggested $250,000,000, and I think you spoke wisely. Perhaps it will be necessary to give more, but we should not pay the $320,000,000. We cannot defend the transaction to the community now, nor in later years to ourselves.

My aim is to make the securities good enough to keep. Our friend only wants to make them good enough to give away.

The senior says we can prick the bubble of trusts. Where is there one that is burdened with fixed interest charges exceeding $8,000,000. Time taken now to negotiate will bring better results than perhaps years of earnings.

Frick the Man

We should want the basis on which we start, one to inspire confidence instead of derision.

As Mr. C., in many letters and conversations, has stated his desire to benefit the firm, when, if not now, is he to do it? Good times like the present, make bad times; a law sure as the swing of the pendulum. We have experience to know these elementary truths. Have we the sense to put them into practice?

If a fair value was agreed upon, probably we would be willing to give the retiring partner all bonds; otherwise, I think I will take my share, and advise my friends to do likewise.

I reserve the same right that any of the other partners possess as to a final decision.

The quiet and time for reflection on the voyage, gives you a good chance to think carefully over the foregoing. Upon you will rest the great responsibility, which, in respect to the value of the property, few men in the world have ever had to meet. Reputation and profit alike require that you should pause before you take this serious step.

Yours very truly
HENRY PHIPPS.

Enheartened by this assurance of firm support by the most powerful partner other than the controlling owner, without regard to the latter's wishes, of a prudent and conservative programme such as had always appealed to his own judgment, Mr. Frick, while on the ocean, made a rough draft of a plan upon the lines suggested by Mr. Phipps, whipped it into shape immediately upon arrival, obtained the written approval of all the junior partners within reach, comprising Messrs. Schwab, L. C. Phipps, Clemson, Gayley, Singer, Peacock, Curry, Morrison and Lovejoy, and one week after landing cabled to Mr. Phipps:

Unanimous favoring reorganization two hundred fifty millions without bonds but will write fully after further meeting next week.— H.C.F.

Negotiations

On September 28th he wrote to Mr. Phipps:

The enclosed plan is the outcome of many conferences and much consideration on the part of all. From what I know of your views, I am inclined to think you will not approve of some features of it on first reading. However, I should like you to give it serious consideration, and on your return home, before you take the matter up, you will give me an opportunity of talking it over with you. Even if you should not sail, as your last letter to me would indicate, before the middle of November, we would have ample time to talk it over before it need be taken up with the Senior, or others.

P.S.—Mr. Lovejoy is mailing Mr. Carnegie a copy of the enclosed, signed by all today.

"We would not favor any plan that would contemplate bonding the property," were the final words of the proposed agreement signed by the junior partners.

That settled it. Mr. Carnegie rejected the plan instantly. He wanted bonds.

XVI

Mr. Frick Receives His Resignation

MR. CARNEGIE returned to New York in October and shortly after his arrival attended a meeting of the Board of Managers in Pittsburgh. He was in high spirits and never more jovial. If he detected a certain tenseness in the atmosphere, the fact was not apparent. He fairly radiated goodfellowship, sweetness of spirit, appreciativeness of his associates and kindliness for all men.

The meeting itself was harmonious throughout, only one subject out of routine being considered. Mr. Frick announced that he had recently acquired, partly in exchange for other real estate that he had owned for years, certain lands above Peter's Creek which he contemplated putting on the market.

Before doing so, however, in view of Mr. Schwab's opinion that the Company would need the property before long, he felt that he should offer the privilege of purchase to the Board. Personally he doubted that the Company could utilize it advantageously for many years and the only reason for acquiring it would be to prevent construction of a large competitive plant or to hold in reserve to meet possible contingencies. Mr. Lawrence Phipps, the Manager most familiar with real estate, had valued it at $4000 an acre, which probably could be

Mr. Frick Receives His Resignation

obtained, but the price to the Company would be $3500.

The Board, with Mr. Carnegie's sanction, voted unanimously to buy the land. Subsequently, however, Mr. Frick felt constrained to impose an unacceptable condition upon the transaction and presently sold the property to outsiders for $500,000 more than he would have obtained from the Company.

The condition referred to consisted of a peremptory demand for nothing less than an apology from Mr. Carnegie.

Following the highly agreeable meeting of the Board, Mr. Carnegie chatted gaily with individual members, made a few desultory remarks privately to Mr. Frick concerning a new plan for consolidation, in the course of which he casually submitted a mystifying proposal to exchange for the latter's coke stock an additional interest in the Steel Company, "dollar for dollar," and conversed at length with Mr. John Walker, former manager of Carnegie, Phipps & Co., and still a large holder of Frick Company stock. No sooner had he reached his home in New York than the purport of his various observations, divulged to Mr. Frick, caused deep resentment. Chief among the aspersions reported was an alleged insinuation that the Chairman had wrongfully exacted from the Company an undue profit on the sale of his land to the Board of Managers.

Nothing imaginable could have offended Mr. Frick more deeply and, having decided to retaliate by making his refutation of what he considered a personal insult a matter of record, he addressed a formal communication to the Board reading in part as follows:

Frick the Man

Mr. Carnegie also stated, I am told, while here, that he had purchased that land from me above Peter's Creek; that he had agreed to pay market price, although he had his doubts as to whether I had any right, while Chairman of the Board of Managers of the Carnegie Steel Company, to make such a purchase. He knows how I became interested in that land, because I told him so in your presence, the other day. Why was he not manly enough to say to my face what he had said behind my back? He knew he had no right to say what he did. Now, before the Steel Company becomes the owner of that land, he must apologize for that statement.

Harmony is so essential for the success of any organization that I have stood a great many insults from Mr. Carnegie in the past, but I will submit to no further insults in the future.

There are many other matters I might refer to, but I have no desire to quarrel with him, or to raise trouble in the organization, but, in justice to myself, I could not at this time, say less than I have.

A copy of the statement was sent to Mr. Carnegie and was followed by a notice that, at its next meeting, the Board had approved the minute. As soon as he received this information, Mr. Carnegie entrained for Pittsburgh on December 3rd, called for an immediate meeting of the Board, which Mr. Frick refrained from attending, and demanded that the Managers sign a paper requesting the Chairman to resign, saying that he should not use it unless it became necessary to do so.

Armed with this document, he then waited upon Mr. Frick and reminded him of his repeated assertions that he had no desire to retain for a moment an executive position, contrary to the wishes of a shareholding majority. What more he may have had in mind to say can only be surmised, as Mr. Frick brought the interview to an abrupt conclusion by a nod of acquiescence and, on

Mr. Frick Receives His Resignation

the next day, the following entry was made in the minute book of the Company:

At a meeting of the Board of Managers of The Carnegie Steel Company, Limited, held at the General Offices of the Association, Carnegie Building, Pittsburgh, Pa., at 12:30 p.m., Tuesday, December 5, 1899, there were present MM. Schwab (president), Peacock, Phipps, Morrison, Clemson, Gayley and Lovejoy (secretary); and MM. Carnegie, Henry Phipps, George Lauder and W. H. Singer.

The following communication was read:

December 5th, 1899.

Gentlemen:

I beg to present my resignation as a member of your Board.

Yours very truly,

H. C. FRICK.

To the Board of Managers,
The Carnegie Steel Co., Ltd.,
Pittsburgh, Pa.

On motion, (MM. Clemson and Peacock), the resignation was accepted, with the sincere thanks of the Board of Managers, both as such and as representing the Shareholders; for efficient, zealous and faithful service as a member of this Board from January 14, 1889, to the present day; The vote being unanimous, and all present concurring.

So ended peaceably an arduous service of ten years and eleven months, but not the struggle of two determined men. Mr. Carnegie's war proved to be one of extermination and Mr. Frick had not yet begun to fight.

Of vastly greater importance than a mere question of propriety involved in a minor real estate transaction was the "coke difference" mentioned in Mr. Carnegie's letter to Mr. Frick. The price which the Carnegie Company should pay the Frick Company for coke had been a bone of contention for ten years, the former as by far the largest purchaser quite properly demanding a preferen-

Frick the Man

tial rate and the latter insisting with equal justness that the charge should not be so low as to warrant criticism by its minority shareholders.

Each year the officers of the respective companies had experienced increasing difficulty in satisfying all concerned and, early in December, 1898, Mr. Carnegie and Mr. Frick personally took the matter in hand with a view to effecting a permanent arrangement. Each naturally favored the company which bore his name, but the question quickly simmered down to $1.50 per ton asked by Mr. Frick as against $1.20 offered by Mr. Carnegie and a compromise at $1.35 per ton for a period of five years, beginning on January 1st, 1899, was agreed upon.

Pending formal action by the two Boards of Managers, Mr. Carnegie gave notice through Messrs. Lauder and Schwab that a clause must be inserted in the contract providing that if at any time the market price should fall below $1.35 per ton, the charge to the Carnegie Company should be reduced accordingly. Mr. Frick promptly rejoined through the same intermediaries that the understanding did not comprise any such arrangement and he could not recommend the execution of a contract on that basis. Nevertheless he stood ready to make any reasonable concession to effect a settlement. Perhaps it would be well to let the matter rest until Mr. Carnegie should make his promised visit to Pittsburgh when another effort might be made to reach a definite agreement.

But Mr. Carnegie did not go to Pittsburgh and, when Mr. Frick raised the question in New York on the eve of his sailing, he refrained from discussing it, and Mr. Frick

Mr. Frick Receives His Resignation

pressed its consideration no further, chiefly no doubt because the Moore option was then uppermost in the minds of both.

Meanwhile, quite paradoxically, the Coke Company was selling large quantities of fuel to the Steel Company at one price and the Steel Company was buying the same product from the Coke Company at another. That is to say, the seller was charging the market rate, less about 20 per cent preferential, as usual, and the purchaser was accepting at $1.35 per ton, under a contract which Mr. Carnegie declared he had made with Mr. Frick. The difference in favor of the steel company was exceeding $600,000 for the year 1899 and seemed likely to amount to millions annually for years to come.

Such was the confused and dangerous condition of affairs when the Chairman returned from Europe following the Moore Syndicate fiasco and called a meeting of the Board of Directors of the Coke Company for October 25th to make official record of the company's position. President Lynch submitted the following:

RESOLVED, That the president be authorized and instructed to notify the Carnegie Steel Company, Limited, that the existence of any contract is denied and that no claim to settle in accordance with the terms of the alleged contract for past, present and future deliveries of coke to the said Carnegie Steel Company, Limited, will be recognized or entertained by this Company.

Messrs. Frick and Lauder, Mr. Carnegie's representative, refrained from voting because of their partnership in the steel company and the resolution was adopted by the votes of Messrs. Walker, Lynch and Bosworth, whose interests were in the coke company exclusively.

Frick the Man

This action afforded Mr. Frick an opportunity to incorporate in his "Minute" filed with the steel company, following Mr. Carnegie's conversations in Pittsburgh, the following:

> I learn that Mr. Carnegie, while here, stated that I showed cowardice in not bringing up question of price of coke as between Steel and Coke Companies. It was not my business to bring that question up. He is in possession of the Minutes of the Board of Directors of the Frick Coke Company, giving their views of the attempt, on his part, to force them to take practically cost for their coke.
>
> It is the business of the Presidents of the two Companies to make contracts of all kinds. Mr. Carnegie has no authority to make a contract that would bind this Company. Neither have I any authority to make any contract that would bind the Frick Coke Company, and, at any rate, why should he, whose interest is larger in Steel than it is in Coke, insist on fixing the price which the Steel Company should pay for their coke?
>
> The Frick Coke Company has always been used as a convenience. The records will show that its credit has always been largely used for the Steel Company, and is to-day, to the extent of at least $6,000,000. The value of our coke properties, for over a year, has been, at every opportunity, depreciated by Mr. Carnegie and Mr. Lauder, and I submit that it is not unreasonable that I have considerable feeling on this subject.
>
> He also threatened, I am told, while here, that, if a low price did not prevail, or something was not done, he would buy twenty thousand acres of Washington Run coal and build coke ovens. That is to say, he threatened, if the minority stockholders would not give their share of the coke to the Steel Company at about cost, he would attempt to ruin them.

While Mr. Carnegie's real attitude in those days was more frequently conjectural than assured, there seems to be no doubt that the quick change in his state of feeling toward Mr. Frick was caused by this indignant "Minute." With respect, for example, to the very dispute out of

Mr. Frick Receives His Resignation

which the final rupture grew, we find him writing, just before the displeasing paper was filed, with all his former sprightly and ingratiating pungency:

There's one question I wish you would fix up—coke prices. With market price 1.50 and idle ovens I think 1.35 is the fair price to C.S.Co. Now you said 1.35 was right. Surely you and Lauder and Lawrence can figure this out. The best plan is to get a fixed price for all time and relieve the friction which has arisen.

Do get at this and fix it and always remember that none of your partners can or will regard you as only the representative of a seller company to them, they will not argue or object freely but they *think* all the same. None of them want to stir up things with F. & Co.—very foolish when its only business with nothing personal in it. Isn't it? Yet so it is.

Do get at a permanent arrangement and greatly oblige. You want to make your pard a Christmas gift anyhow. I'll not look for a $40,000 thing. Give me a settlement permanent on coke and I'll bless you.

A.C.

We never had friction before—it annoys me more than dollars—even than Phillippines.

And then, a few days later, in reply apparently to a letter from Mr. Frick, not in evidence, noting an unsettled misunderstanding of precise terms:

H.C.F., Esq.

Excuse me, I have no time to waste upon the Prest. of the F.C. Co. who begins saying he didn't know the bargain—that's all I read—Its gone to waste basket. It is all settled anyhow. Schwab writes me they are all willing to pay 1.35 permanently. I think its high. It is your own terms and ends it.

My friend, you are so touchy upon F.C.Co. (fortunately the only point) you are, and we all have our "crazy bones"—you know where Roslander, thanks to you for him, gets his finger sometimes and oh it hurts, doesn't it? But now all's over and you have a mighty good bargain and a big profit. I had no part fixing price.

Frick the Man

It's all the same to me provided there is no more dissatisfaction. I believe all back things are also settled—so now all's well.
A.C.

This is all the Christmas gift I ask.

But all was not over and nothing was well. The immovable object had not yet felt the impact of an irresistible force.

XVII

The Final Dramatic Break

MR. HENRY CLAY FRICK, Chairman of the H. C. Frick Coke Company and former Chairman of the Carnegie Steel Company, Limited, was seated at the desk in his private office in the Carnegie building at midday on January 8th, 1900. He had finished dictating answers to various business communications and, having lighted a fresh cigar, was reading leisurely a personal letter from his friend, Mr. A. R. Whitney, who was then sojourning in Colorado Springs. Raising his eyes upon hearing the door open and close, he beheld without appearance of emotion the familiar figure of Mr. Andrew Carnegie poised at the entrance. Half rising, he stood in an attitude of expectancy while the unheralded visitor, with a cheery "Good morning, Mr. Frick," stepped jauntily forward and, in response to a grave bow, placed himself gingerly upon the edge of a chair obviously assigned to callers. Having simultaneously resumed his own seat, Mr. Frick, without speaking, looked at him inquiringly.

Mr. Carnegie readily announced his mission. He had dropped in to see if they could not reach a definite and final settlement of the coke dispute between their two companies. Personally, as he had said over and over again, he could perceive no reason why a satisfactory contract

Frick the Man

should not be executed at once. The price had been agreed upon and he stood ready to close the matter and be done with it.

"If you had stood by our arrangement originally," quietly remarked Mr. Frick, "it would have been closed long ago."

Well, in the opinion of Mr. Carnegie, expressed with a hint of impatience, there was no use in going over all that. Let bygones be bygones! The present situation was the one to be considered. He had thought the matter out. In fact, he had decided upon a plan. $1.35 was mutually satisfactory. Very well, let it stand for two years. At the end of that time both parties would know whether they wanted to go on or to make other arrangements. Each could do what he liked.

The Steel Company must have coke of course. Everybody knew that. And it must take no chances. It must provide for all contingencies. But two years would afford ample time to acquire fifteen or twenty thousand acres of coal lands to be mined if necessary. That would be only prudent. The Coke Company too could make any provision for the future it saw fit. So the arrangement would be perfectly fair all around.

"Is that the contract you propose to have made?" asked Mr. Frick.

"It is perfectly fair; what do you say?"

"But if I object, it is your intention to put it through anyway?"

"That plan or something similar will undoubtedly be adopted. You may as well make up your mind to that."

The Final Dramatic Break

"Mr. Carnegie, would you like to sell your interest in the Coke Company at a price to be fixed by competent and disinterested business men? If so, I will buy it."

"I will have nothing to do with outsiders."

"Will you buy my interest in the Steel Company at a price to be fixed in the same way? If so, you can have it."

"Nothing to do with outsiders. Never have had. If the company wants to take over your interest, the way is provided and you have signed for it."

"At the sum appearing on the books, you mean, without regard to its actual value?"

"As provided by the contract."

"And if I do not accept your proposed agreement between the two companies, or whatever else you may suggest, you intend to take over my interest in the way you have indicated?"

"It's not my business; it's the company's."

"And the company will try to do it?"

"Why not? The company has the right."

"And you will advise the company to exercise its power?"

"Your interest will surely be taken over by the company; you can depend on that."

The colloquy had been carried on thus far,— by Mr. Frick in notably distinct but even tones, by Mr. Carnegie toward the end impatiently. There was nothing more to be said by way of explanation. The case was closed, the verdict rendered. Mr. Frick looked long and intently into Mr. Carnegie's defiant eyes while, one cannot doubt,

Frick the Man

the steel was creeping slowly into his own. Then, speaking still evenly but with steadily rising inflection, "his anger," writes Mr. Bridge in his History of the Carnegie Steel Company, "burst out into flame," and his pent-up indignation was finding full vent when Mr. Carnegie, who had been edging toward the door, suddenly hastened his steps and dashed into the hall, closely followed by Mr. Frick.

During the ensuing nineteen years, from 1900 to 1919, when both passed away, the elder in August and the younger in December, neither Mr. Carnegie nor Mr. Frick spoke to the other.

Mr. Frick returned to his desk, looked at his watch, reverted to his custom of clearing his desk before luncheon, rang for his secretary and dictated a reply to Mr. Whitney, whose letter he had been reading when interrupted, in the course of which he said incidentally:

> Everything here moving along very pleasantly. All concerns are making money and the outlook is quite bright for the coming year along all lines. I hope that this will find your daughter much improved.

Five minutes later Mr. Carnegie, appearing distressed, entered the Board room of the Carnegie Company and directed his associates awaiting him to proceed with the work in hand.

On his way back to his office from luncheon at the club, Mr. Frick dropped in on his old friend and associate Mr. John Walker.

"John," he remarked meditatively, "I lost my temper this morning."

The Final Dramatic Break

"Oh, well," smilingly observed Mr. Walker, "I knew you had one."

"For the first time in years."

"Washington lost his once, you know. Carnegie, I suppose. Proceed."

Whereupon Mr. Frick depicted the episode in detail and quietly awaited comment.

"All right!" ejaculated Mr. Walker. "That will clear the air. We shall soon be out in the open now. It is high time."

They had not long to wait. The month intervening between December 5th, when Mr. Carnegie obtained Mr. Frick's resignation, and January 8th, when he reappeared in Pittsburgh, had been one of ominous silence on the part of the controlling owner and of anxious waiting by his partners. Only Mr. Carnegie himself could tell where the next blow would fall or what its nature might be, and he confided in none of his associates barring possibly his cousin, Mr. Lauder, his oldest comrade, Mr. Phipps, and his most valued manager, Mr. Schwab, having already revealed their lack of sympathy with his programme by pleading with him to refrain from taking the first step.

On Sunday, December 3rd, with the acquiescence of Mr. Phipps, the following communication from Mr. Schwab was delivered to Mr. Frick:

My dear Mr. Frick:

I write you confidentially. I just returned from New York this morning. Mr. Carnegie is en route to Pittsburgh today—and will be at the offices in the morning. Nothing could be done with him looking towards a reconciliation. He seems most determined. I

Frick the Man

did my best. So did Mr. Phipps. I feel certain he will give positive instructions to the Board and Stockholders as to his wishes in this matter. I have gone into the matter carefully and am advised by disinterested and good authority that, by reason of his interest, he can regulate this matter to suit himself—with much trouble no doubt, but he can ultimately do so.

I believe all the Junior members of the board and all the Junior Partners will do as he directs. Any concerted action would be ultimately useless and result in their down-fall. Am satisfied that no action on my part would have any effect in the end. We must declare ourselves. Under these circumstances there is nothing left for us to do than to obey, although the situation the Board is thus placed in is most embarrassing.

Mr. Carnegie will no doubt see you in the morning and I appeal to you to sacrifice considerable if necessary to avert this crisis. I could say much on this subject but you understand and it is unnecessary. Personally my position is most embarrassing as you well know. My long association with you and your kindly and generous treatment of me makes it very hard to act as I shall be obliged to do. But I cannot possibly see any good to you or any one else by doing otherwise. It would probably ruin me and not help you. Of this as above stated I am well advised by one most friendly to you. I beg of you for myself and for all the Junior Partners, to avoid putting me in this awkward position, if possible and consistent.

I write you this instead of telling you because I cannot under the circumstances well discuss this subject with you at this time, and I wanted you to know before tomorrow. Please consider confidential for the present, and believe me

As Ever
C. M. S.

This was a fair warning which was heeded by Mr. Frick, partly no doubt in consideration of the perplexities of others, to the extent at least of acceding to Mr. Carnegie's demand for his resignation without protest or argument. But the indirect effect upon Mr. Carnegie himself was to strengthen his confidence that he could safely ignore his junior partners, whom he had terror-

The Final Dramatic Break

ized, his senior partners, whom he mistakenly thought he had cowed and, last but far from least, the Company's distinguished counsel, Knox and Reed, who refused to appear in any legal proceedings against Mr. Frick.

Calling other lawyers into service, he perfected his plans during that holiday month and, when he reappeared before the Board, he felt fully equipped to meet any contingency. Clearly, to his mind, his recent experience left no alternative to proceeding to the extreme limit of possibilities, namely, to eject Mr. Frick from partnership and forcibly seize his interest at virtually whatever price he himself might see fit to pay.

All this Mr. Carnegie seems to have believed he could do legally under the terms of various agreements and he proceeded forthwith to execute his purpose.

At the annual meeting of the stockholders of the H. C. Frick Coke Company, on the following day, the number of directors was increased from five to seven; Messrs. Frick, Lynch and Lauder were re-elected, Messrs. Walker and Bosworth were dropped and Messrs. Gayley, Moreland, Clemson and Morrison, to whose names qualifying shares had been transferred by the Steel Company, were chosen; giving the Carnegie interests control by a majority of three. Mr. Lynch was continued as President and the office of Chairman, previously held by Mr. Frick, was abolished by unanimous consent.

The only significance of this action, barring of course the change in control, lay in the dropping of Mr. John Walker, who was not only the largest stockholder having no interest in the Steel Company but was guardian of

Frick the Man

Andrew Carnegie Wilson, a minor who had inherited his share of Mr. Carnegie's deceased partner, whose widow and daughter he also represented. In view of these circumstances and of the common knowledge that Mr. Carnegie and Mr. Walker had been on friendly terms for years, the exclusion of the latter from the Board caused surprise.

Presently, however, the fact transpired that, in the course of the recent interview between the two, Mr. Walker had rejected Mr. Carnegie's proposal that he exchange his coke stock for an interest in the steel firm and a position on the Board, feeling that such an act would constitute a betrayal of Mr. Frick, who alone had tried to protect the minority stockholders. Subsequently, moreover, when assured that Mr. Carnegie would guarantee full recompense in some form for any loss to his personal interests if he would withdraw his opposition to the coke contract which he had voted to repudiate, he had spurned the suggestion with words that virtually enforced his deposition by Mr. Carnegie and added another doughty foe to the latter's swelling galaxy of adversaries.

Immediately following its organization on the same day, the new Board voted—five to two—to rescind the resolution of October 25th denying the existence of a contract to deliver coke to the Carnegie Steel Company at $1.35 per ton, and, two weeks later, on January 24th, adopted the following resolution, over the protests of Mr. Frick and President Lynch:

> Whereas this Company acting by H. C. Frick, then chairman of the Board of Directors in December, 1898, entered into an agree-

The Final Dramatic Break

ment with the Carnegie Steel Co. (Ltd.), whereby this Company agreed to sell and Steel Company agreed to purchase all the coke required for the furnaces of said Steel Company for the period of five years, beginning January 1, 1899, at the price of $1.35 per ton of 2,000 pounds delivered f.o.b. cars at oven, payable on or before the 20th day of each month for the preceding month's shipment, and pursuant to said agreement the shipment of coke began January 1, 1899; and

Whereas said agreement, though acted upon by the parties, was never formally set forth in writing.

Resolved, That the said agreement be, and the same is hereby, ratified and confirmed as fully and completely as if the same had been originally entered into under authority of a resolution of this Board, and the officers of this Company are hereby authorized and directed to reduce said agreement to writing, and to execute and deliver the same in the name and on the behalf of this Company, taking effect as of January 1, 1899.

A proposed contract with the Carnegie Steel Company, embodying the terms recited and already executed by President Schwab was then submitted and President Lynch, by direction of the Board, executed it under protest.

It is interesting, at this point, to note that if Mr. Carnegie had not insisted originally that his understanding with Mr. Frick comprehended the inclusion of a clause giving the steel company the advantage of a lower price if such should appear "at the market,"—a provision which he now abandoned—the contract would have been executed at the time for a period of five years, and the Coke Company would then have been forfeiting to the Steel Company the difference between $1.35 and the market price of $3.50 per ton, or $2.15 on 2,500,000 tons, no less than $5,375,000 a year.

Frick the Man

Truly, a costly inadvertence, which deprived Mr. Carnegie of an enormous advantage and enabled Mr. John Walker to bring a promising injunction suit,—which, however, need not be considered since, for reasons presently to be disclosed, it never came to trial.

XVIII

Mr. Frick Wins His Fight

Having been thus quietly ousted from the Chairmanship of both companies, Mr. Frick no longer had a voice in the management of either. To make the severance complete, however, it was incumbent upon Mr. Carnegie to acquire his 23 per cent of stock in the Coke Company and his one-sixth interest in the steel firm.

There seemed to be no insuperable obstacle in the way. Mr. Frick was as eager to sell as Mr. Carnegie was willing to buy. His holdings in the two concerns constituted the bulk, although not the sum total, of his fortune, which he naturally desired to keep within his own control for investment in enterprises, the management of which he would share. There was no question of his full ownership of his coke stock for which he stood ready to accept any price fixed by disinterested persons as its fair value.

His title to his interest in the Steel Company, also fully paid for, was equally clear but the holding itself, Mr. Carnegie maintained, was subject to recapture by the Company for the sum at which it was carried on the books at the time. The difference between this price and the actual value, as appraised by disinterested persons, which Mr. Frick offered to accept, was very large. The "book

Frick the Man

value" of his one-sixth interest, as determined by Mr. Carnegie, was "approximately $4,900,000"; his own estimate of its real value was "upwards of $15,000,000"; two years later, following transformation through the new Carnegie Company, it was exchanged for securities of the United States Steel Corporation having a market value at the time of not less than $25,000,000.

Although nobody foresaw this quick quintupling, all realized that the amount of money involved in the controversy could not be less than six millions of dollars and might easily prove to be twice that sum.

While the representatives of the Steel Company were assuming control of the Coke Company and ratifying as a valid contract the tentative verbal arrangement made by Messrs. Carnegie and Frick thirteen months previously, Mr. Carnegie was personally directing the recapture by his Board of Managers of Mr. Frick's interest in the steel partnership.

The procedure was based upon the following clause in an "Iron-clad Agreement" signed by Mr. Frick and other members of the firm under date of July 1st, 1892:

> This agreement, Made this first day of July, A.D., 1892, and on certain dates thereafter, as shown, between The Carnegie Steel Company, Limited, party of the first part, and each one of the members of that Association who has hereunto affixed his name, party of the second part, witnesseth:
>
> (I) That the party of the second part, for and in consideration of the execution and delivery of this agreement by each of the other active members of said Association, The Carnegie Steel Company, Limited, and in consideration of the sum of One Dollar in hand paid by the party of the first part, the receipt whereof, by the signing hereof, is hereby acknowledged, as well as for other good

Mr. Frick Wins His Fight

and valuable considerations, to him moving, does hereby covenant, promise and agree to and with the party of the first part, that he, the party of the second part, at any time hereafter when three-fourths in number of the persons holding interests in said first party, and three-fourths in value of said interests, shall request him, the said party of the second part, to do so, will sell, assign and transfer to said first party, or to such person or persons as it shall designate, all of his, the said party of the second part, interest in the Limited partnership of The Carnegie Steel Company, Limited. The interest shall be assigned freed from all liens and encumbrances or contracts of any kind, and this transfer shall at once terminate all the interest of said party of the second part in and in connection with the said The Carnegie Steel Company, Limited.

(II) The request of the requisite number of members and value of interests shall be evidenced by a writing signed by them or their proper agents or Attorneys in Fact; and a copy thereof shall be either served upon the party whose interest it is proposed to buy, or mailed to him at his post office address; at least five (5) days before the day fixed in said request to make said transfer and assignment.

(III) The party of the first part covenants and agrees that it will pay unto the party so selling and assigning, the value of the interest assigned, as it shall appear to be on the books of said The Carnegie Steel Company, Limited, on the first day of the month following said assignment.

Said payment shall be in manner as follows:

If the interest assigned shall exceed four (4) per centum, but shall not exceed twenty (20) per centum of the Capital Stock at par, then the same shall be paid for as follows: One-fourth cash within six months after the date of the assignment, and the balance in five equal annual payments from the date of the assignment, to be evidenced by the notes of said party.

(IV) This agreement, and the option the party of the second part hereby gives to the party of the first part, is hereby declared to be irrevocable, and that it may be carried out in good faith, and notwithstanding any effort on the part of the party of the second part to evade it, the party of the second part does hereby appoint the person, who, at the time he is called upon to act, is Chairman of the party of the first part, the Attorney in Fact for said party of the second part, for him and in his name, place and stead to assign and transfer the said interest in said The Carnegie Steel Company, Limited, whenever under this agreement it would be the duty of said party of the second part to do so.

Application of this method of recapture would have resulted in payments by the company to Mr. Frick as follows: On or before September 1st, 1900, $1,225,000; On March 1st, 1901, 1902, 1903, 1904 and 1905, each, an instalment of $735,000; total, $4,900,000, a sum practically certain to be exceeded materially by the profits accruing during that period to the credit of the one-sixth share, which consequently would have paid for itself, with a net gain to Mr. Carnegie, as the holder of a majority interest, of many millions.

In point of fact, the net earnings upon Mr. Frick's one-sixth interest, in that very year of 1900 alone, surpassed the "book value" of $4,900,000 by $1,766,666.

Technically, however, though hardly perhaps in fairness, this extraordinary circumstance had no bearing upon the question at issue. Either the company had or had not a legal right to appropriate the share upon the terms specified in the option quoted, when three Iron-clad Agreements, each differing from the others, were really involved. Of these the first was between Carnegie Brothers & Co., a constituent concern, since liquidated, and its partners, executed on September 1st, 1887; the second was between its successor, the Carnegie Steel Company, Limited, and some of its partners, dated July 1st, 1892, and signed by Mr. Frick and others but never executed by several, including Messrs. Carnegie, Phipps

Mr. Frick Wins His Fight

and Lauder; and the third was of the same parties, dated September 1st, 1897, but executed by Mr. Carnegie alone.

To recapture Mr. Frick's interest at "book value" and obtain legal title, it was considered necessary preliminarily (1) To abrogate the resolution of 1897; (2) To revive the original agreement of Carnegie Brothers & Co., of 1887, bearing the signatures of all the partners, thus establishing mutuality of benefit and obligation; (3) To validate the agreement of 1892, signed in part only, in order to obtain Mr. Frick's signature and (4) To obtain additional signatures to this agreement in order to provide the "three-fourths in number" as well as the "three-fourths in value" required to take over the interest desired.

Resolutions designed to accomplish these purposes were produced by Mr. Carnegie immediately following the conclusion of his spirited interview with Mr. Frick on January 8th, and were promptly adopted by the Board of Managers. The resolution of 1897 was rescinded, the original agreement of 1887 was recognized simply as "appearing in the Minutes" of an unidentified company, the agreement of 1892 was referred to for the first time as "Supplemental" instead of the entirely new partnership compact which previously it had been considered to be, and the secretary was instructed to obtain all signatures not yet attached to the document.

All of these except Mr. Henry Phipps's and Mr. A. R. Whitney's having been secured readily, Mr. Carnegie, either thinking that the task would be distasteful to Secretary Lovejoy, who was not in sympathy with the movement, or surmising that President Schwab would

Frick the Man

speak more influentially as his personal representative, deputed the latter to obtain the three-fourths required for the formal demand and, on January 15th, the following notice was served on Mr. Frick:

> Under the provisions of a certain Agreement between The Carnegie Steel Company, Limited, and the partners composing it, known as and generally referred to as the "Iron Clad" Agreement, we, the undersigned, being three-fourths in number of the persons holding interests in said Association, and three-fourths in value of said interests, do now hereby request Henry C. Frick to sell, assign and transfer to The Carnegie Steel Company, Limited, all of his interest in the capital of The Carnegie Steel Company, Limited, said transfer to be made as at the close of Business January 31, 1900, and to be paid for as provided in said Agreement.

Messrs. Phipps and Frick, having already protested separately at the action of the Board on January 8th, joined in notifying the company that the "fair and true value" of its properties was not shown on its books, expressing their belief that it exceeded "considerably" $250,000,000 and declaring their willingness to accept the appraisal of three disinterested men as "final and conclusive." Receipt of these communications was not acknowledged, and on February 1st, the following letter was delivered by hand:

Mr. H. C. Frick,
        Building.
Dear Sir:
    I beg to advise you that pursuant to the terms of the so called "Iron-clad Agreement" and at the request of the Board of Managers, I have to-day acting as your Attorney in Fact executed and delivered to The Carnegie Steel Company, Limited, a transfer of your interest in the capital of said Company.
                                      Yours truly,
                                      C. M. Schwab.

Mr. Frick Wins His Fight

The stage was now set for trial of the most famous lawsuit ever brought in Pennsylvania. There had been a sharp competition for the services of John G. Johnson, Esq., the foremost lawyer of the country, as senior counsel, but Mr. Frick's retainer was the first to arrive. The great man's distinguished associates were Esquires D. T. Watson and Willis F. McCook. Mr. Carnegie's solicitors were Esquires George Tucker Bispham, Richard C. Dale, Clarence Burleigh and the firm of Dalzell, Scott & Gordon.

Mr. Frick's Bill of Complaint in his Equity Suit against the Steel Company and its shareholders and the joint and several answer of the defendants headed by Mr. Carnegie were filed with the Court of Common Pleas of Allegheny County promptly upon the opening of the Spring term early in March. Eleven years later, in his testimony before a Congressional Committee, Judge Reed of Knox & Reed, the company's attorneys who had refused to represent their most affluent client in any legal proceedings against Mr. Frick, set forth tersely the main point at issue.

"The fundamental question in the case," he informed the committee, "was whether Mr. Frick could be put out at all under the agreement. The next question was, how much was his interest worth? The attorneys who drew this answer—I had nothing to do with it—drew it with the main object in view, namely, to show that Mr. Frick, as one of a committee, had fixed his own valuation and was committed to it. How they found that I do not know. I hate to say it, but they stated rather carelessly that it was a full and accurate value of the assets when

Frick the Man

they should have said that it was a full and accurate account of the method adopted by the parties."

"Do you understand it, Judge?" asked Congressman Gardner.

"Sometimes I think I do and sometimes that I do not. I do not know what they did with the profits except that I think they depreciated things to about the extent of the profits and never allowed their book values to rise at all."

"Let me tell you, gentlemen," interjected Mr. Carnegie with rare insouciance, "since you have mentioned the name of Mr. Frick, that the quarrel was not between us. I never had a quarrel with Mr. Frick in my life. It was with the partners he quarreled. I tried to go in and settle it."

Asked how he personally accounted for the assertion in his sworn Answer to the Bill that the "book value" of the entire assets of the company was "full, fair and accurate," Mr. Carnegie replied:

MR. CARNEGIE. As to the value of our property, No. Everything I have said here shows you that the property did not go into that account at all.

MR. BEAL. Then this statement in this answer, as you understand it now, is not a correct statement?

MR. CARNEGIE. It is misleading.

MR. BEAL. It is a misleading statement?

MR. CARNEGIE. Surely.

MR. BEAL. Can you not go further than that and say that it is an incorrect statement?

MR. CARNEGIE. Yes; certainly it is an incorrect statement. Have you any doubt about it yourself? (Laughter).

MR. BEAL. Not at all.

Mr. Frick Wins His Fight

The Chairman. It is sworn to.
Mr. Carnegie. Yes.
The Chairman. By you?
Mr. Carnegie. Yes. My partners sent this on as an answer prepared by our lawyers. I no doubt glanced over it and signed it, but I did not read it all.

There was no casualness in the preparation of the brief for the plaintiff. Mr. Frick gave his undivided attention to the matter, not only gathering the data required down to the minutest detail but sifting and analyzing it with the p instaking thoroughness of a trained mind; inviting and even suggesting innumerable questions for himself to answer; proposing lines of bold attack supported by facts and arguments; and generally laying a broad foundation for comprehensive presentation of a case punctuated and enlivened by severe and caustic phrasing of his own devising.

The purely legal aspects of the controversy hardly call for consideration in view of their failure to attain judicial determination, but if Mr. Carnegie had thought to intimidate Mr. Frick into full submission, in line with the tender of his resignation without a protest, his hope was rudely dispelled by this defiant and scornful attitude, and his feelings were deeply hurt.

"Frick has filed an abusive Bill against me," he confided to Mr. Elbert H. Gary on a railway train, "and here is the reply which I want you to read."

"I did so at once," Judge Gary told his own biographer, "and found that Mr. Carnegie had excoriated Mr. Frick in violent language. I advised him not to file that reply; it was too abusive. Mr. Carnegie was plainly disappointed,

Frick the Man

for he believed he had done a fine thing, but he agreed to show the paper to his counsel, and it was never filed in that form."

Simultaneously with the filing of Mr. Carnegie's Answer in Part I of the Court of Common Pleas appeared the Bill of Complaint in the coke suit of his lifelong friend and associate, the redoubtable Mr. John Walker, in Part II. Compared with the scathing terms of this grim indictment, Mr. Frick's denunciation was less personal and almost indulgent. Contemptuously depicting the added directors as mere tools of their master, designated and qualified by him to act in his interest, in "utter and fraudulent disregard" of the rights of the minority stockholders, Mr. Walker pinned the entire responsibility upon Mr. Carnegie personally for "the execution of their evil design to cheat and defraud, not honestly or in good faith for the Coke Company but dishonestly and in bad faith for the benefit of said Carnegie," thereby becoming "guilty not only of constructive but also of actual fraud."

Since it was obviously "vain and useless" to look to such "representatives of the Steel Company and Carnegie for any redress for the aforesaid wrongs and grievances," Mr. Walker, on his own behalf and as guardian of Andrew Carnegie Wilson, was driven to pray the Honorable Judges for equitable relief.

While these blunt accusations from such a source made highly unpleasant reading, particularly when spread over the first pages of the newspapers, yet another defection, although relatively unimportant, bore perhaps even

Mr. Frick Wins His Fight

greater significance to Mr. Carnegie's mind. All but two of the junior or "debtor" partners accepted Mr. Schwab's judgment that Mr. Carnegie could, and "would probably," ruin them if they should disobey his orders, and bowed submissively, but of these two one was Mr. F. T. F. Lovejoy, Secretary of the company, who was more familiar with the intricacies of the various Iron-clad Agreements than anybody else and had served as special counsellor to the controlling owner in constructing and interpreting them.

While acting under instructions to make a thorough investigation of the proposed Agreement of 1897 with a view to perfecting it in every detail, he was informed by the company's attorneys that, to make it legally binding beyond question, it would be necessary to give to each shareholder the privilege of taking up his interest for cash and to secure the signature of every partner without exception in order to establish full mutuality of the pledge to surrender an interest upon demand. The latter requirement was supposed to have been met in the original Agreement of 1887, but inquiry developed the fact that the name of Mr. Vandevort was not appended. Mr. Frick promptly apprized Mr. Carnegie, who was then in Scotland, of this fatal defect.

"The fact is," he wrote on June 10th, 1898, "that the present Iron-clad Agreement (that of 1892, unsigned by Mr. Phipps and dependent for validity upon assumed continuance of the Agreement of 1887) is not binding on anybody and never has been; while we have purchased interests of deceased partners under it, if objection had been raised by their estates, it could not have been enforced."

But time was pressing, owing to the imminence of a conference at Skibo Castle designed to win Mr. Phipps's assent to the new Agreement, and Mr. Lovejoy had drawn a paper, for the debtor partners to sign, fully covering the point, and a copy was enclosed "for your consideration and FOR MR. PHIPPS'S CONSIDERATION."

No cablegram being received in response, however, no further step was taken and Mr. Frick sailed, as planned to find awaiting him at Liverpool the following communication:

SKIBO CASTLE, DORNOCH, N.B.
27th June, 1898.

My dear Mr. Frick,

Just occurs to me perhaps much better not to talk over new Ironclad Agreement until Squire (Mr. Phipps) comes here with you.

I do not agree that the present one is not binding,—better avoid that point.

The Squire and Mr. Curry expect to come up here with you. We are looking forward with the greatest pleasure to the arrival of you all.

Hastily yours
ANDREW CARNEGIE.

H. C. Frick, Esq.,
White Star S.S. "Germanic,"
Liverpool.

The intimation was plain that Mr. Phipps was to be kept in ignorance of Mr. Lovejoy's discovery that he was not, as he had been led to believe, bound by his signature to the 1887 Agreement,—at least until he could be induced to accept the new one which superseded it. But the precaution was to no purpose. Mr. Phipps could not be persuaded to sign.

Although Mr. Lovejoy, in common with the other junior partners, invited the loss of fortune foreseen by

Mr. Frick Wins His Fight

Mr. Schwab if he should disobey Mr. Carnegie's orders, he could not conscientiously join with his fellow managers in an effort to enforce an agreement which the distinguished counsel of the company had pronounced invalid, calling for the resignation of Mr. Frick and providing for recapture of his interest "for a consideration virtually nominal." Consequently he resigned as Manager and Secretary and filed a separate Bill setting forth that the agreement was "null and void," that "even if it were in full force and effect, no cause existed for the plaintiff's expulsion" and that, in any event, "justice and equity required that he should not be compelled to accept such payment as the purchasers themselves might fix."

However grieved he may have been by this singular action on the part of a junior partner whose fortune, he considered, was attributable to his own generosity, Mr. Carnegie not only betrayed no resentment but was so deeply impressed by Mr. Lovejoy's legal opinion, based upon the defect in the original agreement discovered and reported nearly two years previously, that, having commissioned an associate to make, on his own account, tentative advances looking to a settlement, he advertised indifference by going to Florida.

In vain. Mr. Frick continued imperturbable, Mr. Walker implacable, Mr. Lovejoy undisturbed, Messrs. Knox & Reed courteously aloof and the renowned Esquire Johnson smilingly unapproachable. Mr. Carnegie returned.

It was an anomalous situation. The Carnegie Steel Company was piling up profits at an undreamed-of rate but its prestige was diminishing, its superb organization

Frick the Man

was quaking, its rivals were chortling, bankers were beginning to look askance, customers were showing signs of dismay, and rumors were rife of prospective disclosures compelling governmental rending of the very foundations of its industrial supremacy. Clearly, all concerned, from the most affluent shareholder to the humblest yet highly prosperous wage-earner, had everything to lose and nothing to gain from protraction of the bitter struggle between its masterful guiding spirits. Again with the full acquiescence of Mr. Frick, and undismayed by his recent failure, Mr. Phipps intervened.

Nobody living was so well fitted for the role of peacemaker as he; none other could have appealed so effectively to the sentimental side of Mr. Carnegie's better nature; none could meet him on the same level; the two had toiled shoulder to shoulder as partners for nearly forty years and had shared a prosperity far surpassing any registered in the dreams of either; each admired and respected the other; between them was no jealousy; their friendship had never been seriously shaken; they were growing old.

There was a touch of pathos in the meeting. They were still "Harry" and "Andrew" to each other, but for how long? Appearances had been safeguarded scrupulously. Mr. Carnegie had shown, perhaps had felt, no resentment at what he must have considered a personal defection and Mr. Phipps had confined the protest which he felt bound to make to the smallest formal compass. The public detected no more than a difference in judgment; their associates, with minds possessed by self interest,

Mr. Frick Wins His Fight

prudently perceived nothing. But the two concerned knew that at last a rift was opening which must be closed quickly or it would widen beyond possibility of repair. The one must have been as surely conscious as the other was clearly aware of the entrance into their relationship of the fatal element of mistrust.

Mr. Phipps was not accustomed to champion the causes of others in public; privately, with Mr. Schwab, he had urged upon Mr. Carnegie the unwisdom of deposing Mr. Frick as Manager, but he seems to have raised no objection when he heard the controlling owner direct his Board to demand the Chairman's resignation; that was not his affair. Nor was Mr. Frick's suit at law; he had not sought an interview to discuss the merits of that; his grievance was his own, as he had indicated plainly to Mr. Frick himself, and it was based, not upon legal rights, but upon personal honor, mutual friendship and identical interests.

He had signed the original Iron-clad Agreement of 1887 most reluctantly and only upon the definite understanding that it "should apply only to debtor partners or employés" and under no circumstances to those classified as "Senior Partners" who had bought and paid for their shares.

"Of course," he added in a memorandum filed with Mr. Frick on January 17th, 1900, when the latter was threatened with ejectment and partial confiscation of his interest, "much was left to the honor of the Managers, in whom it was not unreasonable for me to impose implicit confidence, and I am confident that the agreement would never have been made an engine of oppression and robbery."

A second time, in 1892, "when the consolidation papers were agreed to by Mr. Carnegie and me at his place near Windsor, England," he received personal reassurance to the same effect with respect to "the intent of the paper of 1887."

Still further confirmation of Mr. Carnegie's commitment to this view was afforded by both word and deed of Mr. Carnegie himself in 1897, when he began a letter designed to allay Mr. Phipps's apprehensions respecting the proposed new Agreement with these words:

Sept. 29th, 1897.
My Dear Pard:
   Surely you are a little "off."
   I know of no reason why the Iron-clad is not pleasing to you.
   Did you not suggest that the power to expel should not apply to such as own their interests, and hasn't your wish been granted?

Mr. Phipps discovered upon examining the revised document that his desire to have the restriction to debtor partners clearly specified instead of being left indefinitely a matter of honor between partners had, indeed, been heeded, the "party of the second part" being explicitly designated as an "active member of the Association whenever, and at any time he shall be indebted in any sum to The Carnegie Steel Company, Limited, or to any member thereof for the purchase of Capital in said Association," thus relieving all actual owners from any commitment whatever.

This clause Mr. Phipps found wholly satisfactory and most comforting. His refusal to sign the last Agreement

Mr. Frick Wins His Fight

of 1897, executed by the company and by Mr. Carnegie alone of all the partners, and rescinded by the latter's direction on the memorable 8th of January, was based upon other grounds.

"I replied," Mr. Phipps continued in his Memorandum to Mr. Frick, "that there were clauses in the agreement that were unjust, and he replied 'Harry, I am ill, and am going abroad, and fix it to your satisfaction'—On such a promise, so clear and explicit, I would have done anything for my friend, and especially in his condition."

"I am very sorry to say," he concluded mournfully, "that since then he has shown no willingness to correct the agreement as promised."

Mr. Phipps carried out the plan of the interview precisely as agreed upon by Mr. Frick and himself. He scrupulously refrained from uttering a word that might give cause for offense but he spoke with a frankness equivalent to his friendliness. For himself, he had burned his bridges; there had been nothing else to do in justice to himself and his family; if one owner's interest could be seized by the company at fictitious book value, another's could be; continued possession of his own would be a matter, not of right, but of favor. Personal altercations between partners he viewed only with deep regret; he had never engaged in one; he never should; but it was only fair to say that Mr. Frick and himself had confided fully in each other from necessity in mutual defense.

He frankly accepted the responsibility for suggesting that Mr. Frick search the records of the settlement with Superintendent Abbott and Mr. Frick had done so and

Frick the Man

had found in a letter addressed to him in Mr. Carnegie's own handwriting these words:

Mr. Abbott came from Washington to see me as his friend.
He thought that if he retired his half was worth far more than the books and I could not say otherwise.
I said of course it was worth 20% more than the books and if he decided to retire and sell, I should see he got that for it.

And he got it and, by seeing that he did, Mr. Carnegie had upheld the very principle for which Mr. Frick and he were contending. Mr. Carnegie had forgotten all about this act of generosity, no doubt, as he had forgotten many other kindnesses of like nature, but there stood the admission. It might or might not have legal effect; but, to his mind, it surely did have moral force which no honorable man could, and he did not believe Mr. Carnegie would, ignore.

While plainly surprised at this bit of information, Mr. Carnegie welcomed the opportunity to respond to his lifelong associate's freshening of their friendship and his reiteration of faith in himself.

"Make your own plan, Harry," he finally said, "I only want what is fair."

So the interview ended to mutual satisfaction and Mr. Phipps immediately reported to Mr. Frick, whose sole comment was:

"It is useless now to talk about anybody buying or selling. The fair thing to do is to make the consolidation of the two companies upon the terms agreed to by everybody a year ago before the Moore offer was received. That will solve the whole problem justly and honestly. I am willing."

Mr. Frick Wins His Fight

At a meeting quickly arranged to take place at Mr. Carnegie's house in New York, on the evening of March 17th, attended by Mr. Carnegie, Mr. Phipps, Mr. Schwab and Mr. Lovejoy, representing Mr. Frick, Mr. Phipps submitted the latter's suggestion and it was favorably received. Three days later it was adopted by all parties in interest at a larger gathering in Atlantic City which became famous and, on March 21st, the following communication was delivered by hand:

THE CARNEGIE STEEL COMPANY, LIMITED.
PITTSBURGH, PA.

Mr. H. C. Frick,   March 21st, 1900.
Pittsburgh, Pa.
Dear Sir:

Referring to the tentative Agreement made at Atlantic City, March 19th and 20th, 1900, by Messrs. Carnegie, Phipps (Henry), Schwab, Phipps (L.C.), Lovejoy, Morrison, Clemson, Gayley and Moreland, covering a plan for the consolidation of the Carnegie Steel and Frick Coke interests recommended by all the signers:—

To prevent any misunderstanding as to the terms of said tentative Agreement as to one particular, on which you advise me that you do not consider the language sufficiently explicit: I would say that it is the understanding of all the persons making said Agreement that the transfer of six per cent. of the Capital of The Carnegie Steel Company, Limited, made by me (as Attorney in Fact under the "Iron-clad Agreement") out of your Capital Account, February 1st, 1900, shall be cancelled to the end that you shall be entitled to and shall receive your full share (6%) of the Dividend declared by The Carnegie Steel Company, Limited, to adjust the relative Book-Values of the Stocks of The Carnegie Steel Company, Limited, and of the H. C. Frick Coke Company and its subsidiary Companies, as provided in said Agreement, and of any and all other Dividends, if any, declared by The Carnegie Steel Company, Limited, between January 31st, 1900 and the date upon which the consolidation is consummated and the balance of surplus turned over to the new Companies.

You shall receive out of this merger the same moneys, bonds, stocks and other properties as if no attempt had been made to transfer such interest.

We hope to be able to complete said merger in all respects by May 1st, 1900, and we now agree to do so by June 1st, 1900, at furthest.

This to be without prejudice in case the Agreement referred to be not approved by all concerned.
Yours truly
C. M. SCHWAB.
President

The settlement was heralded, by unanimous assent, for courtesy's sake as a "compromise"; it was really a complete surrender by Mr. Carnegie and an unqualified triumph for Mr. Frick, who received from the new company precisely $15,000,000 for the interest whose value he had estimated at "upwards" of that sum, and who celebrated the event by sending a single telegram to his friend, Mr. Whitney, reading:

Settlement made. I get what is due me. All well.

I, of course, have not met this man Carnegie and never expect nor want to. It is not my intention to be officially connected with the reorganized concern.

In point of fact, by arrangement, neither Mr. Carnegie nor Mr. Frick was included in the directorate, but the former assumed full control from Scotland and the latter kept a sharp eye on operations in Pittsburgh. The month of March, 1900, the last of separate operation, showed net profits: of the Carnegie Steel Company, $4,394,588.48; of the Frick Coke Company, $666,142.41; a total of more than $5,000,000,—at the rate of $60,000,000 per year.

"Pretty satisfactory figures, are they not?" wrote Mr. Frick to Mr. Mellon in London.

But he chafed at signs of what he considered loose and wasteful management and late in August, on the day when

Mr. Frick Wins His Fight

President Schwab left the great concern headless to sail for Skibo, he sent the following cablegram,—the last message ever sent by him to his former partner:

CARNEGIE, *Clashmore.*

You being in control, stockholders and public look to you to see that the great Carnegie Company is managed successfully and honestly. Five year contracts for coal fifty per cent above the lowest price paid, and six per cent above prices now currently paid by smaller concern. Ruinous. Scrap unloaded on you at fancy prices, while others were selling, now being sacrificed abroad. Look into these and other matters yourself. Do not let them hide things from you. You cannot trust many by whom you are surrounded to give you facts. You need commercial rather than professional ability to cope with concerns managed by brainy and honest men trained to the business. You are being outgeneralled all along the line, and your management of the Company has already become the subject of jest.

FRICK.

Simultaneously he wrote a long letter to Mr. Phipps, then in England, specifying many instances of losses aggregating millions per year incurred unnecessarily and calling him sharply to task, as a director, for inattentiveness to his obligations.

Meanwhile the consolidation of the two companies had been effected under the name of The Carnegie Company and $160,000,000 bonds and $160,000,000 of stock had been issued proportionately to the original owners, resulting in the delivery to the three chief shareholders of the following securities:

	STOCK	BONDS
Andrew Carnegie	$86,382,000	$88,147,000
Henry Phipps	17,227,000	17,577,000
Henry C. Frick	15,484,000	15,800,000

the remainder going to sixty junior partners and heirs of deceased members of the firm.

XIX

The United States Steel Corporation

THE Carnegie Company died a yearling. It began operations on April 1st, 1900, and passed out of existence on March 31st, 1901. The time had then come for Mr. Carnegie to realize his cherished ambition to retire by forcing a sale of his property upon his rivals, and he proceeded with unexampled skill and audacity to accomplish his purpose. A way had been opened through the enormous successes of the steel and coke concerns which enabled the new consolidated company to earn interest upon a thousand millions of dollars, which it might either pay in full or use in part to crush its competitors. In any case, whatever disposition might be made of profits, the credit of the Company was limitless and its power as resistless as its position was impregnable.

That its policy was to be one of expansion along new lines was clearly indicated by the announcement, early in the summer, of immediate construction of a $12,000,000 tube plant upon land already purchased at Conneaut on Lake Erie. This was a dagger thrust at the very heart of corporate finance. What was about to happen to the National Tube Company, just formed and floated by no less a firm than J. P. Morgan & Co.? Mr. Carnegie made light of the undertaking.

The United States Steel Corporation

"The policy of the Carnegie Company," he declared, "is to coöperate in every way with its fellow manufacturers in the industrial world, and not to push itself into any new field save in self-defence. We did not leave the National Tube Company. They left us, which they had a perfect right to do, of course. Now we are ready to shake hands and coöperate with them in the most friendly spirit. We are better for them than a dozen small concerns, conducted in a small jealous way. We believe there is room enough for the two concerns," etc.

But the misgivings of the security holders, instead of being dispelled by this naïve declaration, were greatly enhanced when it transpired that Mr. Schwab had brought back from Skibo a message to his partners from the controlling owner containing these significant phrases:

> If I were czar (of the Carnegie Company), I would make no dividends upon common stock, save all surplus, and spend it for a hoop and cotton-tie mill, for wire and nail mills, for tube mills, for lines of boats upon the Lakes for our *manufactured* articles, and to bring back scrap, etc. . . . Put your trust in the policy of attending to your own business in your own way and running your mills full, regardless of prices, and very little trust in the efficacy of artificial arrangements with your competitors, which have the serious result of strengthening them if they strengthen you. Such is my advice.

This clearly presaged aggressive and ruinous competition, not merely for the National Tube Company, but for eight other near-Trust metal concerns, which had been organized during the previous few years and financed in Wall Street through the sale of more than five hundred millions of stock,—all over-capitalized and all vulnerable.

Frick the Man

"It is all Carnegie bluff," sneered brokers who still had stock for sale.

But responsible bankers, directors and managers were less confident. True, bluffing had constituted a large part in the canny Scotsman's shrewd trading with the new corporations but that was no secret; he had admitted the fact with a frankness which they had found most disconcerting.

"Inform these people," he had openly instructed his managers, "that we do not propose to be injured; on the contrary, we expect to reap great gains from it; that we will observe an 'armed neutrality' as long as it is made to our interest to do so, but that we require this arrangement—then specify what is advantageous for us, very advantageous, more advantageous than existed before the combination, and we will get it. If they decline to give us what we want, then there must be no bluff. We must accept the situation and prove that if it is fight they want, here we are 'always ready'. Here is a historic situation for the Managers to study—Richelieu's advice: 'First, all means to conciliate; failing that, all means to crush'."

This relentless policy he was now in a position to adopt with every prospect of success, and his pronunciamento indicated only too distinctly that he meant to enforce it promptly and rigorously. It was the stern reality of the actual situation, in vastly greater measure than either the eager pleading of Judge Gary recounted by his biographer or the eloquent portrayal of possibilities by Mr. Schwab at a celebrated dinner party, that finally

The United States Steel Corporation

impelled Mr. Morgan to essay the greatest undertaking of his career. Obviously the only solution of the problem lay in amalgamation of the segregated Trusts upon a larger scale than had ever been dreamed of, and Mr. Carnegie held the key to success or failure in his whiphand.

Mr. Schwab, who had reported that Mr. Carnegie would sell, was commissioned to obtain his price, and quickly returned with a pencilled memorandum embodying his terms. Characteristically, Mr. Morgan accepted the figures as final and, taking the option sum as a basis, himself fixed arbitrarily the amount, chiefly in securities, to be allotted each of the desired constituent companies. His liberal proposals were accepted promptly by the frightened owners and plans for the United States Steel Corporation were actually published when a singular and possibly vital omission was noted with deep concern. To "round out" the enterprise, the Rockefeller ore properties must be acquired and included.

There then took place an extraordinary episode shedding interesting sidelights upon various personalities.

"Morgan growled" that they "had all they could attend to," records Judge Gary's biographer, but the Judge persisted and, continues the biographer:

"How are we going to get them?" Mr. Morgan asked.
"You are to talk to Mr. Rockefeller."
"I would not think of it."
"Why?"
"I don't like him."
"Mr. Morgan," said the Judge, "when a business proposition of so great importance to the Steel Corporation is involved, would you let a personal prejudice interfere with its success?"
"I don't know," he replied.

Frick the Man

The next morning, however, he came in excitedly, throwing up his arms in exultation and shouting to Judge Gary, "I have done it."

"Done what?"

"I have seen Rockefeller."

"How did he treat you?"

"All right."

"Did you get the ore lands?"

"No. I just told him that we ought to have them, and asked him if he would not make a proposition. How much do you think we ought to pay?"

"I am not prepared to say. It would take me a week to figure out what I would consider a reasonable price."

"Well, tell me offhand what you think we ought to pay."

The Judge worked for half an hour, and finally announced, "there's an *outside* figure—so many millions."

Mr. Morgan made no response and there the matter rested for several days. Mr. Rockefeller, having originally declined a request from Mr. Morgan for an interview at his office upon the ground that he never went downtown, replied to a second suggestion that he would be happy to see Mr. Morgan at his residence at the latter's convenience, with the understanding that only strictly personal matters were to be considered, as he supposed the fact was generally known that he had retired from business.

Notwithstanding this restriction, Mr. Morgan called and, having briefly depicted the situation, told Mr. Rockefeller, precisely as he had recited to Judge Gary, that the new Steel Corporation ought to have his iron ores. Mr. Rockefeller expressed regret that Mr. Morgan had put himself to unnecessary trouble, owing doubtless to a misunderstanding of his previous message, and sug-

The United States Steel Corporation

gested that he talk with his son, who had charge of such matters and would undoubtedly be pleased to wait upon him.

Having obtained Judge Gary's judgment of a suitable price, Mr. Morgan invited Mr. John D., junior, to call, and at the appointed hour, the young man—he was then only twenty-seven—appeared for his first interview with the lion of Wall Street. The two sat down.

"I understand," said Mr. Morgan brusquely, "that your father wants to sell his Minnesota ore properties and has authorized you to act for him. How much do you want for them?"

Young Mr. Rockefeller rose from his chair and, with an evenness of tone suggestive of his father's, replied:

"It is true that I am authorized to speak for my father in such matters, Mr. Morgan, but I have no information to the effect that he wishes to dispose of his ore properties: in point of fact, I am confident that he has no such desire."

"And what did Mr. Morgan say?" quietly asked Mr. Rockefeller when his son repeated his remarks.

"Mr. Morgan said nothing; he sat quite silent."

"And what did you do?"

"I picked up my hat and, bowing as courteously as I know how, I said 'If that is all, Mr. Morgan, I bid you good afternoon,' and walked out. Did I do right, sir?"

Mr. Rockefeller meditated for an instant and replied thoughtfully:

"Whether what you said was right or wise, I would not venture to judge; time alone can answer that ques-

Frick the Man

tion; but I may say to you, my son, that if I had been in your place, I should have done precisely what you did."

Negotiations were at a standstill. Obviously no approach could be expected from Mr. Rockefeller and Mr. Morgan could not reopen the subject without sacrifice of dignity. But Wall Street was agog with excitement, subscriptions to the syndicate underwriting were being held up and publication of the completed plan was in the printer's hands awaiting inclusion of the essential ore properties. The whole project was endangered and time was pressing. Mr. Morgan sent for Mr. Frick and putting the situation before him, asked what, if anything, could he suggest?

Mr. Frick said he would think the matter over and went home. His acquaintance with Mr. Rockefeller was slight. Years before he had been introduced to him by Mr. Carnegie in words of fulsome praise and had received hearty congratulations upon the "intelligence, courage and firmness" which he had displayed in the Homestead controversy. The two had met once or twice more recently but their conversation had been only casual and the best assurance that Mr. Frick could feel was that Mr. Rockefeller regarded him favorably as one who had rendered signal service to all corporate interests, and that their relations were friendly.

Proud and sensitive himself, he disliked to invite a rebuff, but he had voluntarily proffered his services to Mr. Morgan if in any way they could be utilized to advantage and, after due consideration, without consulting anybody or even notifying Mr. Morgan, he decided to take the

The United States Steel Corporation

initiative and, through a trustworthy intermediary, he sought an interview with Mr. Rockefeller which should be regarded as wholly private and confidential.

The response was prompt and cordial. Mr. Rockefeller would be happy to see him respecting any matter of mutual interest and suggested that he come quietly to Pocantico Hills the following morning. Accordingly, shortly before 10 o'clock, Mr. Frick, leaving his carriage to wait on the main street, walked up the driveway to Mr. Rockefeller's residence and, just within the entrance, found Mr. Rockefeller himself strolling thoughtfully through his spacious grounds. Mr. Frick joined him in his walk and, briefly apologizing for what he feared might prove to be an intrusion, set forth the purpose of his mission. Mr. Rockefeller listened attentively to a concise, accurate and straightforward statement, such as had first won the approbation of Judge Mellon years before, and then said:

"Mr. Frick, I naturally suspected what you had in mind. My understanding of the situation coincides in all respects with yours. As my son told Mr. Morgan, I am not anxious to sell my ore properties, but, as you surmise, I never wish to stand in the way of a worthy enterprise. I do frankly object, however, to a prospective purchaser arbitrarily fixing an 'outside figure' and I cannot deal on such a basis. That seems too much like an ultimatum. Now I want to ask you a question. Nobody is more familiar with those properties than you are. Do you or do you not agree with me that the price these gentlemen propose to pay is less by several millions than their true value?"

Frick the Man

Mr. Frick replied that unquestionably, if payment was to be made chiefly in securities of the new company, and taking into consideration the allotments made for other properties, the sum suggested was far too small.

"I thought that would be your answer," said Mr. Rockefeller. "Now, Mr. Frick, I will tell you what I will do. I want only a just and fair price. You know what that is, certainly better than those gentlemen do, and quite likely than I do. I know your judgment is good and I believe you to be a square man. I am willing, Mr. Frick, to put my interests in these properties in your hands."

Amazed at this proposal, Mr. Frick, while expressing full appreciation of the compliment, hesitated to assume the responsibility.

"You need not hesitate, Mr. Frick," calmly remarked Mr. Rockefeller. "My confidence is implicit. You will receive no complaint from me. Now you will wish to be on your way. I thank you for coming to see me."

The two men shook hands and parted. The outcome of their conversation is recorded by Judge Gary's biographer in these words:

"To my surprise," Judge Gary says in telling the story, "Mr. Frick brought in a figure from Mr. Rockefeller a few days later—$5,000,000 more than my outside figure. 'That is a prohibitive proposition' I said.

" 'Judge Gary,' exclaimed Mr. Morgan, 'in a business proposition as great as this would you let a matter of $5,000,000 stand in the way of success?'

" 'But I told you, Mr. Morgan, that mine was the outside.'

" 'Well, put it this way: would you let these properties go?'

" 'No.'

The United States Steel Corporation

" 'Well, write out an acceptance.' "

And so it happened that when on April 2 another circular came out, addressed to the stockholders, the Lake Superior Consolidated Ore Mines were included in the amalgamation.

Years afterwards Mr. Rockefeller, recalling the incident, said "The price seemed wholly fair at that time and was entirely satisfactory to me. It was not long either before the purchasers themselves realized that it was really very low."

"I doubt, as I recall the circumstances," he added reminiscently, "if anybody but Mr. Frick could have effected the transaction."

"And if it had not been effected?" he was asked.

"Then, in my opinion," he replied slowly, "the United States Steel Corporation could not have survived the stress of its formative period."

In view of the tremendous enhancement of the new company's prestige through the subsequent inclusion, arranged by Mr. Frick, of both Mr. Rockefeller and his son, in its first directorate, this deduction seems more nearly certain than probable. In any case, Mr. Frick, greatly to his credit, permitted no mention of the part he had played in achieving the reconcilement and, as late as 1903, with his consent and approval, the historian Bridge summed up the great accomplishment from the standpoint of the Carnegie shareholders with this undivided encomium:

> It was the most masterly piece of diplomacy in the history of American industry, and formed a fitting climax to Andrew Carnegie's romantic business career.

Frick the Man

Mr. Frick received in exchange for his interest in the Carnegie Company these securities in the United States Steel Corporation, to wit:

Bonds	$15,800,000
Preferred stock (7%)	23,767,940
Common stock	21,832,440

representing substantially the net combined recompense for his services to the H. C. Frick Coke Company for thirty-one years and to the Carnegie Steel Company for twelve years.

He was elected a member of the first Board of Directors of the United States Steel Corporation as a matter of course.

And so it came about that, barely sixteen months after he had been ousted, by Mr. Carnegie's orders, from the management of the two great companies which he had done so much to build, Henry Clay Frick was brought back, through Mr. Carnegie's retirement, into a position soon to become hardly less potent in the controlling Committee of both, and retained it to his dying day.

XX
A Capitalist

WITH completion of the processes which transformed his ownership in the steel and coke companies into bonds and shares of the great Corporation, the career of Mr. Frick as an executive ended and he emerged, at the age of fifty-two, a capitalist of the first rank whose interests were no longer confined to a manufacturing town but now lay in the financial center of the country. He never forsook and frequently occupied his handsome residence in Pittsburgh but in 1905 he leased for the family an additional residence in New York City and two years later took possession of the magnificent country estate which he had acquired at Pride's Crossing, Massachusetts.

Their first house in New York, at No. 640 Fifth Avenue, was admirably located and most comfortable, but it did not quite fill Mr. Frick's fixed requirement of "always the best." He had known for years precisely what he wanted. Away back in 1880, while Mr. Mellon and himself were waiting to embark on their first trip to Europe, they took a drive up Fifth Avenue. Pausing in front of the cathedral, Mr. Frick directed his friend's attention to the new brownstone Vanderbilt houses across the street.

Frick the Man

"I suppose," he remarked meditatively, "those are really the best residences in the city."

"I think they are so considered," rejoined Mr. Mellon.

"I wonder how much the upkeep of the one on that corner would be."

Mr. Mellon ventured no estimate.

"Say three hundred thousand dollars a year? I should think that would cover it."

"It might."

"That would be 6 per cent on five millions or 5 per cent on six, say a thousand dollars a day; that is all I shall ever want," Mr. Frick remarked, and they walked along.

So, as a matter of course, twenty odd years later, Mr. Frick rented the residence of Mr. George W. Vanderbilt and the family occupied it until 1914, when they moved into the palace which he had built at a cost of $5,400,000 on the site of the Lenox library to serve primarily as a residence and ultimately as an art gallery for the public.

Meanwhile he entered upon his new vocation. Weary of the exactions of desk work after thirty years of close application, he took no office but shared that of his friend Mr. Schoonmaker until 1914, when he provided a small study for his personal use in his new residence, while retaining his rooms in the Frick Building, Pittsburgh, for transaction of business. His waking hours quickly and automatically resolved into three approximately equal parts: (1) Investments, (2) Art, (3) Recreation,— and they continued to be allotted in about those proportions during the ensuing years.

A Capitalist

The first problem which demanded prompt attention was financial. Nine-tenths of Mr. Frick's entire fortune, estimated at $50,000,000, was held in United States Steel securities and the stock exchange prices justified the valuation when Mr. Morgan, by a stroke of genius, had carried the Corporation successfully through its first crisis by personally settling the strike which was called coincidentally with its launching. The Syndicate still controlled the market, under the adroit manipulation of Mr. James R. Keene, and the prospect at the beginning of 1902 appeared auspicious.

But Mr. Frick was unquiet. He not only had too many of his eggs in one basket, but he appreciated the danger of the company's heavy over-capitalization and was still most distrustful of the management of which he had complained to Mr. Carnegie the year before. As he was not a member of the Syndicate and was a director only in name, having declined to participate in the management even to the extent of attending meetings of the Board, he was under no commitment with respect to the disposition of his shares. He had no wish to sell but careful study from his expert knowledge of results and methods of operation convinced him that declines in earnings were inevitable, and he began to liquidate his holdings.

The accuracy of his judgment was quickly confirmed by the gyrations of the stock market, to wit:

	1902 High	1902 Low	1903 High	1903 Low	1904 High	1904 Low
U.S. Steel, Preferred	$97\frac{3}{4}$	79	$89\frac{3}{4}$	$50\frac{1}{4}$	$95\frac{5}{8}$	$51\frac{1}{4}$
U.S. Steel, Common	$46\frac{3}{4}$	$29\frac{3}{4}$	$39\frac{7}{8}$	10	$33\frac{5}{8}$	$8\frac{3}{4}$

Frick the Man

Mr. Frick sold slowly and circumspectly on temporary rebounds, but the time came when he had disposed of his entire block of 218,324 shares of common stock and all but 10,000 of his original 237,679 shares of preferred.

The bottom was reached in January, 1904, when the common struck 8¾ and the preferred shivered around 50.

It was indeed a desperate situation. Business was bad. Dividends, which had been paid regularly at the rates of 7 per cent on the preferred stock and 2 per cent on the common were not being earned. Twenty-one thousand employés had been discharged and the average wage of the 147,000 remaining had been reduced from $716 to $677. Thousands of these had bought from the company at 82½ preferred stock which was now quoted at 50. The "profit-sharing" plan seemed to have resolved into a "loss-sharing" plan devised by Wall Street promoters to unload their worthless shares upon their own workingmen, who might lose every dollar of their hard-earned savings. Rumors were rife of a receivership and foreclosure, confirming Mr. Carnegie's reported expectation that the entire property would fall to him as owner of the bonds by default. A semi-panic was already hatching on the stock exchange.

Only a Morgan could hope to stem the tide and weather the storm. Again the great banker called upon Mr. Frick for advice and assistance.

The meeting took place on Mr. Morgan's yacht the CORSAIR. After having depicted the true situation with the lucidity of which he was a master, Mr. Frick recommended: (1) Stoppage of dividends on the common stock,

A Capitalist

(2) Reduction of dividends on the preferred, and (3) Complete reorganization of the operating force. Mr. Morgan had just rejected Judge Gary's fervent plea to pass dividends on the common stock but, upon Mr. Frick's presentation of the case, he would now assent. Mr. Schwab having resigned, he would approve a thorough reorganization if Mr. Frick would contribute his energy and experience to make it effective.

To this Mr. Frick could not consent. Mr. Mellon and himself had been driven by a disagreement with Mr. Carnegie into expansion of a small wire enterprise to steel manufacture on a large scale as the Union Steel Company, which had not been included in the big combination. With Mr. Mellon's consent he had lent the use of his name as a director to the Corporation, but he could not properly participate actively in the management of a competing concern. To Mr. Morgan, however, this did not appear as an insurmountable obstacle.

"For the purpose of inducing Mr. Frick to become active in the Steel Corporation," said Mr. George F. Redmond in his *Financial Weekly*, "Mr. Morgan purchased the Union Steel Works" at a price which, Mr. Mellon declared, "yielded a fair profit to all concerned."

There remained only the question of continuing dividends upon the preferred stock. Mr. Redmond continued:

> Mr. Frick pleaded earnestly and Mr. Morgan listened intently. Finally, rising from the breakfast table and going on deck with Mr. Frick, he said to him, with tears in his eyes, that if the dividends were not paid on the preferred stock, he could not face going down town on the following day. Mr. Frick was deeply touched.

Frick the Man

He then realized how keenly Mr. Morgan felt upon the subject and assured him that not another word should be said. At once he threw himself energetically into the task of aiding in steering the great organization through its trouble.

The other directors were enheartened by Mr. Frick's action; internal dissensions ceased; certain influential directors, who had induced Mr. George F. Baker unwillingly to convey to Mr. Morgan a proposal that Judge Gary be deposed, accepted his refusal to acquiesce, without resentment; all joined in firm determination to avert further disaster.

Good fortune attended earnest endeavors. Business began to pick up, the working shareholders accepted the passing of the common dividend as evidence that their interests were being safeguarded, and all other preferred stockholders naturally took heart.

Inevitably the market responded slowly but steadily. Before the close of 1906, when dividends were resumed, the preferred stock had climbed from $50\frac{1}{4}$ to $113\frac{1}{2}$ and the common from $8\frac{3}{4}$ to $50\frac{1}{4}$. The crisis had been met successfully and incidentally, at the end of the three-year period of resuscitation, Mr. Frick, now assured good management and convinced of sound conditions, according to Mr. Albert W. Atwood, the financial expert, "was down on the books of the company as the owner of 100,000 shares of preferred and 50,000 shares of common stock," the amounts which he had quietly acquired as suitable for permanent investment.

During the anxious period which immediately followed public announcement of his resumption of activity in

A Capitalist

steel manufacture, Mr. Frick was deluged with letters of inquiry from anxious investors, all of which he answered with painstaking care, with a view to spreading warranted reassurance without conveying undue encouragement. His first replies were somewhat perfunctory, of the "wait and see" order, but toward the end of 1904 he became more explicit.

"I know you are wrong," he wrote in December to Mr. E. T. Earl of Los Angeles, "in suspecting that Mr. Morgan has in any way intentionally deceived investors. Of course some things were done that should not have been done, but it is a great property and I think it is now well managed."

Striving to inculcate caution, he wrote anonymously to Mr. Charles W. Barron of the Boston *News Bureau*:

November 7th, 1904.
Dear Sir:

Are you sure of your position on the Steels?

Does the Corporation have any cash surplus applicable to dividends?

Is not their surplus invested in improvements made on their properties, and which from time to time should be charged against earnings, especially so in view of the high capitalization of the Company?

Can you not ascertain for a regular

READER

But he did not withhold words of encouragement from his co-laborers.

"I very much regret," he telegraphed to the new President, Mr. W. E. Corey, "my inability to be present at the dinner to the Presidents of the constituent

Frick the Man

Companies this evening. I congratulate them, one and all, upon their efficiency during this trying year, the splendid condition of their organizations and the present bright outlook."

Those were busy years, leaving little time for discriminative purchase of paintings or for recreation, although neither of those pursuits was wholly neglected. Many millions of dollars derived from sale of his steel securities were awaiting judicious investment and his concentrative policy forbade haphazard purchases of dissimilar properties. He must place his money where he could watch and guide it without encroaching too heavily upon his time. Inquiry and reflection finally evolved a programme.

"Railroads," he concluded, "are the Rembrandts of investment."

And railways began and continued through life to constitute his chief financial interest, to the virtual exclusion of all other considerations. But first he acquainted himself with all of the intricacies of values, present and prospective, of natural growth and forced development, of increase, decrease and distribution of earnings, of transportation and rate-making with which as a large shipper he was already familiar, of judicious extravagance as compared with false economies, of financing through issuance of shares or bonds, of general conditions which presaged easy or difficult marketing of securities and finally all details of bookkeeping, of which his thirty years of practice since he first took his place upon the high stool in his Grandfather Overholt's little counting-room at Broadford had made him a past master.

A Capitalist

April 14th, 1905, found him a director in the following railway companies:

> Chicago and Northwestern.
> Union Pacific.
> Atchison, Topeka and Santa Fé.
> Reading.

To these were added shortly:

> The Pennsylvania.
> Baltimore and Ohio.
> Norfolk and Western.

Small interests in small companies did not attract him. Those enumerated he selected as the ones preferable among the large corporations and, adding steadily to his holdings from his constantly increasing income, presently he became the largest individual railway stockholder in the world, being recorded on the various books at one time as the owner of an average exceeding $6,000,000 par value in each of his seven favorites, without taking into calculation many additional shares held by brokers and others for his account.

He never "speculated" in the common sense of the term; that is to say, he did not trade on margins; when he bought or sold, as frequently happened, the transactions were outright and deliveries were duly made. He never tried to break down a property; if he could not perceive a possibility of building one up by exercise of talent and use of exceptional resources, he let it alone. In voicing his views, he was always a bull, never a bear; but he seldom expressed an opinion.

Personal contact with strong financial institutions being

Frick the Man

considered a desirable safeguard for railway financing, he was recorded in 1905 as a director in the Union Trust Company and Mellon National Bank of Pittsburgh, the Commercial Trust Company and Franklin National Bank of Philadelphia, the Equitable Life Assurance Society with its allied banks and the National City Bank of New York.

During the summer of 1901, Mr. Frick had granted "with pleasure" a request from Mr. James H. Hyde, controlling owner, that he accept election as a trustee of the Equitable Life Assurance Society and wrote confirming his cablegram that he considered it "quite an honor to be offered the position on the Board of a company held in high esteem in Pittsburgh, as it is everywhere." The Board then comprised fifty-two of the most distinguished business men of the country but their titles were only nominal, as the actual power of direction, though vested by the company's charter in the directors, was exercised by small committees headed by President Alexander and Vice President Hyde. Mr. Frick was duly elected on August 7th, 1901, but in common with the other "outside" directors he did not attend a meeting until February 8th, 1905. Prior to that time he had shared without a shadow of doubt the universal belief that the phenomenal success of the great Society afforded convincing proof of the excellence of its management.

Then came the culmination of an unsuspected feud between the President and the Vice President over the future control of the Society and each made public charges against the other of such a character as to create a veritable

A Capitalist

sensation throughout the entire country. Public opinion, aroused by hundreds of thousands of indignant and frightened policy-holders, forced a meeting of the big Board of Directors, at which a thorough investigation by competent and disinterested members was decreed. A strong committee comprising Messrs. Cornelius N. Bliss, Henry C. Frick, Edward H. Harriman, Melville E. Ingalls and Brayton Ives, was promptly designated to make an investigation and to submit recommendations.

Mr. Frick who, it was well known, had done no business with the Society and had never profited directly or indirectly from its operations, was appointed Chairman. It was an arduous and thankless task which he would have gladly shunned but for his chagrin at his own apparent neglect, intensified by his consciousness of a public duty, and he accepted the responsibility.

Subsequent events clearly and quickly demonstrated that a majority of the Board, subservient to the two high officials whose acts were in question, would not have acquiesced in the appointment of Mr. Frick if they had estimated correctly the quality of the man.

The first meeting of the Committee was held on April 7th and no time was lost in beginning a searching inquiry into the practices primarily of the President and the Vice President, with the resultant findings (1) that both had profited materially through participation in underwriting syndicates at the expense of the Society with no risk to themselves, (2) that the Vice President had been guilty of irregular conduct in relation to the affairs of the Society, (3) that the President had not only

Frick the Man

been aware of but had encouraged such conduct and had concealed his knowledge from the Board, (4) that the two, therefore, were equally guilty and should be deposed, (5) that extravagant, loose and irregular methods permeated the entire force, owing to the pernicious examples set by the heads and (6) that a complete reorganization by an entirely new management was imperative.

This unanimous and unexpectedly inexorable report, fully sustained by indubitable proof, was submitted by the Chairman to the Board, with the accompanying drastic recommendations, on May 31st, but meanwhile Messrs. Alexander and Hyde, joining forces for this purpose, had mustered a sufficient number of directors to constitute a majority, and the Board rejected the report. The policy-holders, the newspapers and the public generally, however, upheld the Committee so overwhelmingly that the resignations of both President and Vice President were soon forthcoming and ultimately the complete reorganization advised was effected. Thus a very signal service was rendered, not merely to millions of policy-holders and beneficiaries, but to the fundamental practices of insurance management, and made for more scrupulous conduct of all corporations.

Mr. Frick, immediately upon the rejection of his recommendations, not only resigned from the Equitable Board, but severed his connection with all of its allied financial institutions, including the Mercantile and Equitable Trust Companies of New York and the Commercial Trust Company and Franklin National Bank of Philadelphia. He had had his lesson,—never again to lend his name to a

A Capitalist

concern with whose condition and operations he could not maintain full familiarity.

In point of fact, he did not, during the remaining fourteen years, join another Board and, resigning from the National City Bank of New York in 1910 and from the Union Pacific and its auxiliary railways in 1911, he restricted his directorships to his favored Pennsylvania, Reading, Atchison and Northwestern railways; to his trusted Pittsburgh banks, the Mellon National and the Union Trust Company, in each of which he was a large shareholder; and of course to the United States Steel Corporation, of whose meetings he practically never missed one except when abroad, and is said to have attended more than a thousand between 1905 and 1919.

One of the most difficult problems confronting the United States Government at the conclusion of the war pertained to the return of the railways of the country to the control and direction of their original owners. The condition of the vast properties was inevitably deplorable. Normal progress had been arrested even before the country became directly involved in strife by the virtual impossibility of obtaining either capital, labor or materials essential to adequate maintenance and, following the armistice, the Congress had undertaken to enact requisite legislation, but progress was distressingly slow.

Fortunately the Administration had, in Walker D. Hines, Esq., who had succeeded Secretary McAdoo as Director General of the Railroads on January 10th, 1919, a man who did not hesitate to face the situation squarely while there was yet time to avert widespread disaster.

Frick the Man

On October 7th, 1919, he addressed a communication to Chairmen Cummins and Esch of the Senate and House Committees depicting the situation and setting forth the urgent need of legislation to avert irreparable damage to shippers and consumers no less than to holders of securities.

This statement, presently published by the Congressmen, attracted the attention of Mr. Frick who, as the largest individual holder of railway securities, was naturally concerned most seriously. Theretofore he had taken no part in the discussion of ways and means of accomplishing the purpose, relying upon the Association of Railway Executives, of which Mr. T. De Witt Cuyler, his co-director of the Pennsylvania Railroad, was Chairman, to co-operate with the Director General, whom he knew well and held in high esteem. But the latter's open warning to the Congress gave rise in his mind to apprehension that all was not going well and he dictated the following lucid and convincing argument:

New York, October 17th, 1919.

Hon. Walker D. Hines,
Director General of Railways,
Washington, D. C.
My dear Mr. Hines:

Permit me to express the personal gratification which I feel at the convincing clearness with which you have put before the Congress and the public the exact situation of the railways of the country. I frankly cannot conceive how it could have been done more forcibly and effectively and, for that reason, I should consider that I were remiss in my duty as a citizen if I should fail to congratulate you most heartily and sincerely upon your rendering of a notable public service.

In common with many others I am deeply distressed by the

A Capitalist

appalling conditions which now confront us as a part of the aftermath of the war, and while I cannot doubt that a just and true solution will ultimately be reached, I cannot escape the conclusion that something must be done at once to avert overwhelming disaster. That you are fully appreciative of the dangers which lurk in delay in grasping the situation manfully, even boldly, you show plainly in your lucid statement which, to my mind, as I have said, could not be improved upon.

There is one phase of the existing condition, however, which I trust you will permit me to submit for your consideration without meaning to be in the slightest degree intrusive. It is the essential element of *time*. What the whole country needs now above all else is restoration of confidence, and this can be obtained only through prompt and decisive action such as would follow naturally and logically your admirable diagnosis. Everybody realizes that adequate railway service is the keystone of the entire arch of industrial progress and prosperity. Even more vital than the circulation of money is the circulation of goods. Without that the enormous demands now being made upon the manufacturers of all kinds of products cannot be met and business will continue to be at a standstill so long as the requisite facilities are not provided. As of course you are aware, the manufacturers are overwhelmed with orders which they cannot fill and they naturally refrain from making necessary enlargements of their plants while in doubt as to their ability to make deliveries.

So it all comes straight back to the railroads. They must have relief and have it quickly, not merely in justice to the great army of investors in railway securities who accepted without question the President's definite promises of fair treatment when they turned over their properties, but all for the general effect upon the public mind of reassurance in the good faith of their Government.

The United States simply cannot afford, from even a purely practical standpoint, to send the railroads further along the road to rack and ruin. And the only way in the world to prevent this is to increase the rates *immediately*, so that everybody may know to a certainty that when the properties are turned back to their owners they will be given a chance to live and to obtain readily on a fair basis the vast amount of capital whose outlay alone can prevent the choking of the great arteries of commerce.

Frick the Man

How large an increase should be allowed I do not pretend to know. You are far better qualified to judge than I because my information is necessarily general and not expert. But upon one point I do not hesitate to express a very positive opinion. This is no time for cheese-paring or niggardly treatment. Desperate diseases call for drastic remedies. Homeopathic doses in the present condition would be hardly better than none at all. Personally I am convinced that less than a 25 percent general increase would not get results. It ought, in fact, to be more, but this would probably be sufficient to tide over the crisis and give heart, encouragement and resolution to all whose earnest co-operation must be had.

We have in this country everything to do with. The only essential thing is to press the button and you are the one person in a position to do it. I appreciate fully the magnitude of your responsibility and how seriously you must regard it. But there it is upon your shoulders and there is no escape. Nor, holding as I do so high an opinion of your breadth and courage, do I believe for a moment that you would care to evade it. Consequently I do not hesitate to point out what strikes me as a superb opportunity to do the right thing at the right time and the only thing as I perceive it, that can lift the pall of depression and mistrust which is surely settling down over the country.

I am confident that I need make no apology for speaking thus frankly. I should feel hurt if I suspected for a moment that you would not welcome frank suggestion or that by any possibility you should attribute to me any unworthy motives. I only want what is best for our country and for all the people in it.

If I should seem to have written too earnestly I beg you to accept my assurance that my doing so is due simply to the fact that that is the way I feel.

With renewed appreciation of your splendid statement,
I am,
Most sincerely yours,
H. C. Frick.

This letter quickly elicited the information that a serious disagreement between the Director General and the Railway Executives had produced a dangerous deadlock

A Capitalist

which seemed unlikely to be broken. Mr. Hines gladly welcomed Mr. Frick's intervention and promptly responded from a train en route from Chicago to Washington, putting him in possession of the facts.

The crux of the entire difficulty lay in the question of rate-raising, which the Executives had demanded somewhat peremptorily and which the Director General had refused to grant on the general ground that such action by the Government, for the sole benefit of the railways, upon the eve of relinquishing control, would surely evoke strong disapprobation throughout the country, which might in turn produce a severe rebuke from the Congress. Moreover, as a matter of right, legal and moral, no less than that of the impracticability noted, he could not see his own way clear to take advantage of a technical, war-time privilege to deprive the Interstate Commerce Commission of the power of regulation which it was designed by law to possess, and the exercise of which in ordinary course it would soon resume.

All this, Mr. Hines informed Mr. Frick, he had presented to the Railway Executives in amplified communications, copies of which he inclosed for his inspection, adding simply but sturdily:

> I am glad to get the benefit of your views, and appreciate your writing me frankly on the subject, but I cannot escape the conclusion above expressed.

Thus Mr. Frick found himself in a position of grave responsibility which he had not sought but could not evade. The Director General's attitude obviously was fixed irrevocably and the resolution adopted by the

Frick the Man

Executives was unanimous, embracing the representations of all of the companies in which he was interested to a greater degree than anybody else. Clearly, he must reach a decision upon the merits of the case, to the exclusion of all other considerations. And this he did with characteristic thoroughness. After having carefully weighed the arguments of both sides, he conferred at length with members of the Railway Committee, who were in effect his own representatives.

But he did not stop there. He called into consultation a few friends who, having no personal interest in the matter, he thought might have a clearer comprehension of public opinion and its probable effect upon both the Congress and the future of the properties. His situation, indeed, was akin to that which confronted him when he was requested by the President to answer questions respecting the actual cost of steel manufacture "as a citizen, not as a director." He took a full week to decide; then, following a final conversation with one whom he knew to be wholly disinterested, he summarized decisively:

"Hines is right; I shall stand by him."

He then dictated the following letter:

New York, October 27th, 1919.

Hon. Walker D. Hines,
Director General of Railways
Washington, D. C.
My dear Mr. Hines:

I have to thank you for your valued favor of the 19th, and am inclined to the belief from the accompanying letters and what you say, that you could not well have taken any other course.

A Capitalist

I may take the liberty of writing you again in the near future. I might say, however, as it stands today, it seems to me the only thing to do is to turn the railroads back to the owners with a guaranty for several months—probably as long as a year—or until proper railroad legislation can be secured.

Sincerely yours,
H. C. Frick.

The relief borne by this crisp message to the Director General, who fully realized that the obdurate Executives were powerless against Mr. Frick's complete reversal of his own position, must have been intense. Writing of the results years afterward, in response to an inquiry, he said:

Mr. Frick's attitude was exactly in line with what you said. Although in his letter of October 17th he was most emphatic that there ought to be a large and immediate increase in freight rates, yet when he had considered the explanation which I placed before him he stated in his letter of October 27th that he was "inclined to the belief from the accompanying letters and what you say, that you could not well have taken any other course," and indicates that instead of an immediate rate increase "the only thing to do is to turn the railroads back to their owners with a guaranty for several months—probably as long as a year—or until proper railroad legislation can be secured."

The thing turned out much in line with Mr. Frick's idea as thus expressed. It had already been announced that the railroads would be turned back on December 31st, 1919, and Congress was actively engaged in shaping comprehensive railroad legislation. This legislation included a six months' guaranty, within which time the Interstate Commerce Commission made a very heavy rate increase, —substantially greater than Mr. Frick recommended and far greater than anything that would have been possible during the last days of Federal control.

As a matter of fact, in order to enable Congress to complete the legislation, the actual turning back of the railroads did not take

Frick the Man

place until March 1st, 1920, and the President signed the new railroad legislation on February 28th.

Sincerely yours,
WALKER D. HINES.

That this achievement of Mr. Hines, thus aided by Mr. Frick, counted for one of the most powerful factors in averting a deplorable renewal of hostility to rate advances seems now to be undeniable.

It is, moreover, a noteworthy circumstance, with respect to this biographical record, that this was the last and perhaps, from a public standpoint, the most helpful act of a business and financial nature in the career of Henry Clay Frick.

XXI

Public Affairs

ALTHOUGH Mr. Frick had several opportunities to enter public life, he was really tempted but once. That was in 1880 when he was offered a Republican nomination for Congress. The time was propitious and the proposal alluring. He was thirty years old, had just made his first million, was master of an established business which did not require his exclusive attention, and his inclination was to broader fields. The position which he had attained in the community had brought the proffer to him unsought and a nomination was equivalent to an election. He had been too fully occupied to take an active part in politics but, like his grandfather before him, he had felt a keen interest in all public affairs. Naturally, too, he was flattered to be thus singled out by the leaders as the one young man most likely to reflect credit upon the district.

One morning, after having transacted his business at the Mellon bank, he made casual allusion to the matter but, as he sought no advice, none was volunteered.

"He is getting ambitious," the Judge remarked to his son Andrew when he had left, "but he would be foolish to take it."

"Never fear," came the rejoinder, "he often jumps at a thing but he never decides until he has taken time to think it out and then he is pretty sure to reach the right conclusion."

The next day he announced perfunctorily that he had declined the offer and thanked his friends for their commendation of his judgment.

"It is always a mistake for a good business man to take public office," mused Mr. Andrew Mellon, recalling the incident some forty years later, while gazing meditatively at the Washington monument from the office of the Secretary of the Treasury.

Mr. Frick's closest political associate was Philander C. Knox and far-reaching consequences were attributable to their mutual fidelity. Never a seeker of office for himself, Mr. Frick was always chary of urging the candidacies of others outside of his own State but, feeling in 1896 that his notably effective support of the Republican ticket might justify the breaking of his rule, he paid his friend the following striking tribute in a letter to the President-elect:

Pittsburgh.
Dec. 16th, 1896.

Hon. William McKinley,
    Canton, Ohio.
Dear Sir:—

Knowing how great have been the demands upon your time, I have refrained from writing to extend my congratulations, but I feel that I must trespass upon your patience in regard to a matter in which I take a sincere personal interest.

The Pittsburgh papers, have, as you have doubtless seen, several times referred to P. C. Knox, Esq., as a possible appointee to the position of Attorney General under your administration. It has been my idea that a President should be free to choose his advisers without pressure or solicitations from outsiders, but as custom

Public Affairs

seems to have made it permissible to present names for your consideration, I venture to call your attention to the merits of Mr. Knox.

I have known him through both business and personal relations, I may say intimately, for twenty years past. As counsel for the Carnegie Company, and other interests with which I have been connected, I have had abundant opportunity, from a business man's standpoint, to judge of his ability as a lawyer and his character as a man. You are better qualified to judge of his legal education, but the estimation in which his brother lawyers hold him, having lately elected him President of the State Bar Association, would seem sufficient evidence upon that point.

Mr. Knox possesses certain traits which it seems to me would be especially valuable in such a position. He has well been described to me by a Pittsburgh lawyer as a crystal thinker, and his statements are always clear and to the point, but what is more important, he is an independent adviser, by which I mean that he does not trim his advice to suit the desire of his client, but if in his judgment the proposed course is unwise, or wrong, he does not hesitate to say so. He is intensely loyal, not only to the interests of his clients, but as a friend, as I can especially testify, for I have gone through some troublesome times, when he has stood faithfully beside me.

Let me venture to say that, if you are considering the desirability of giving Pennsylvania a representative in your Cabinet, that you could not find a more loyal lieutenant. I think I may say also that his appointment would be entirely satisfactory to both factions of the party in this State, and perhaps might be a step towards a very much desired harmonizing of masters in State politics.

With great respect,
Yours, &c.,
H. C. FRICK.

President McKinley made the tender, which Mr. Knox felt constrained to decline for financial reasons of a personal nature which, he ingenuously added, might not subsist four years later, at the end of which the offer was, in fact, renewed and accepted.

Frick the Man

So it came about that, but for his own disinclination, Mr. Frick would have become Senator for Pennsylvania in 1904 when, following the death of Senator Quay, Attorney General Knox and ex-Senator Donald Cameron, representing the dominant Republican oligarchy, waited upon him and offered him the ad interim appointment to be supplemented by an election for the full term in 1905. Taken completely by surprise, he demurred but by their earnest request withheld a positive refusal for a few days. Thereupon Mr. Knox appealed to President Roosevelt for aid and on May 27th wrote to Mr. Frick:

> The President was very much delighted about the matter you, Cameron and I discussed, and I sincerely hope that you will not interfere with its going through.

But in the meantime Mr. Frick had reached a decision and three days later replied:

> Regarding the other matter. I am decidedly of the opinion that I should adhere to my determination not to accept any position, however prominent, even if it could be secured without much effort. I certainly appreciate most highly the fact that I have some friends who think I might satisfactorily fill such a position.

Being assured over the telephone that this was final, Mr. Knox with characteristic frankness announced that, in that case, his own name might be considered, and Mr. Frick did not rest until he had obtained the pledges requisite to his election.

Mr. Knox resigned in 1909 to become Secretary of State under Mr. Taft and, subsequently being again returned to the Senate largely through Mr. Frick's influence, was enabled, in the year following the latter's death, to induce President-elect Harding to appoint their mutual

Public Affairs

friend, Mr. Andrew W. Mellon, Secretary of the Treasury.

Besought a second time to permit his name to be used in connection with the Senatorship, again, in a letter to ex-Senator Cameron, Mr. Frick definitely refused upon the ground that he had "no political ambition."

Mr. Frick was a staunch Republican of the type of George F. Edmunds, who held to his dying day that "the Democratic party never was, is not now and never will be fit to govern the United States." But the preponderance of voters in Pennsylvania who shared this view was so overwhelming that there arose no occasion for partisan service following the retirement of the solitary Democratic Governor, Mr. Robert E. Pattison, and his support was restricted to modest, though invariable, contributions "to maintain the organization." Disgusted at being forced into a defiance of his party's managers during the Homestead strike, he refrained thereafter from public declaration of his personal preferences as between candidates but he never hesitated to voice privately his opinions.

"I thoroughly agree with you," he wrote to Mr. John W. Gates on January 26th, 1896, "that Thomas B. Reed is the man for President. He is my first choice and has been since his name was first mentioned."

A month later, however, without changing his view, he could not resist the appeal of a friend and wrote to Mr. J. C. Morse of the Illinois Steel Company:

> It looks now as if there was going to be quite a struggle for the Republican nomination for President. On Saturday I had an interview with Senator Quay who told me he was going to try to secure

Frick the Man

the nomination, and he thought his chances were very good, although he admitted that at the present time McKinley seemed to be in the lead. Quay would make a splendid President, from what I know of him. He is a man on whose word you can absolutely rely, and has much greater ability than is generally conceded him. If he does not get the nomination for himself, I am inclined to think he will be in a position to name the successful man. In that event, it will not be McKinley, in my opinion.

But Mr. McKinley was nominated and elected after a desperate struggle with Mr. Bryan. Immediately there arose a powerful demand from manufacturers for an excessively upward revision of tariff rates and the House of Representatives responded readily. But fortunately for the Republican party its Senate leader, Mr. Nelson W. Aldrich, experienced and far-sighted, had not forgotten the disaster of 1892 generally accredited in about equal proportions to the ill-fated McKinley Bill and the Homestead warfare, and he grimly determined to avert a possible repetition.

The task was not easy. Industrialists and manufacturers, in common with capitalists and bankers, had dumped millions into Mr. Hanna's war chest to accomplish the defeat of Mr. Bryan and their calls for recompense were both insistent and extortionate. As a result of this pressure, the steel industry had been particularly and most unduly favored by the House of Representatives, and it was this circumstance, oddly, that suggested to Mr. Aldrich a move which must be reckoned among the most adroit ever conceived even by his extraordinary mind. Taking pen in hand, he wrote the following letter:

Public Affairs

United States Senate
Washington, D.C.

Dear Mr. Frick:— March 29th, 1897.

I am very anxious to talk with someone connected with your concern or otherwise, who would be willing to give me reliable information in regard to the present condition of the different branches of the iron and steel industry, and who would make suggestions as to the proper relative rates of duty upon different products. I would treat all information and suggestions as strictly confidential.

I believe that it is extremely important to the country, and to the iron and steel industry, that there should be no excessive rates levied in any portion of the new tariff bill, and I cannot help thinking that some of those suggested by the Ways and Means Committee in the metal schedule are unnecessarily high.

Very truly yours
NELSON W. ALDRICH.

Senator Aldrich's purposes, now revealed for the first time to our knowledge in this seemingly naïve communication, were manifold, concentrated into one,— to save the Republican party from the perpetration of a second blunder which to his politic mind bade fair to prove worse than a crime. To modify the claims of the tariff barons through presentation of facts proving them to be excessive and greedy; to appease capital by testimony of the man who then stood forth as the foremost champion of property rights; to confound political opponents who eagerly awaited evidences of Republican subserviency to the moneyed power which undoubtedly had restored its political supremacy; to surprise and gratify the great body of consumers who still believed that they were being

Frick the Man

mulcted in the interest of the few; to justify Protection as an economic principle operating to the advantage of the whole country and of all the people; to show from practice that tariffs "for revenue only" resulted in depression and dearth of employment while moderate, scientifically adjusted "protective" duties produced advancement and prosperity,—these were the essentials of re-establishment of the Republican party upon a sound and enduring basis.

So the sagacious leader went for aid straight to headquarters, to the head of the greatest metal manufacturing unit which had most to lose or to gain, to the operator whose facts and figures were at his finger tips and could not be confuted, whose skill had been directed to reduction of costs and corresponding increases in wages through inventive processes, resulting in lower prices for larger production to consumers, to the employer who could not be denied by capital and, by ordeal of battle, had actually won the favor of labor,—and his appeal, not to the selfishness, but to the wisdom and reason and broad vision of this man was not made in vain.

There was no delay. The minds of Mr. Carnegie and Mr. Frick, the one perhaps altruistically, the other surely practically, had met long before in realization that the high protection under which their industry had thrived had reached its peak of necessity or advantage and that gradual subsidence from artificial planes to natural bases had become the part of wisdom in striving for an impregnable position. Consultation was not requisite. Mr. Frick replied immediately:

Public Affairs

My dear Mr. Aldrich:—   March 31st, 1897.

Acknowledging receipt of your esteemed favor of the 29th:

I beg to say that we will be glad to give you any information as to the present condition of the different branches of the Iron and Steel industries we can, if you will kindly write, specifying just what information you would like.

We entirely agree with you that it is extremely important for every one that there should be no excessive rates levied in any portion of the new tariff bill.

We have had some communication with Mr. Swank, of Philadelphia, and have said to him, among other things, as follows:

"If a bill can be passed which even our opponents will consider moderate, and which keeps primarily in view increased revenue, we shall have done a great day's work for Protection. It is not in the increase of duties that our advantage lies so much as in the change from advalorem to specific duties, and the leaders of every branch of manufacturies should be required to submit schedules of specific duties as far as possible. The undervaluations going on are scandalous, and rapidly driving honest importers out of the business. Speaking broadly, we do not know anything in the Iron and Steel Schedule that requires increased duties. Of course Cotton Ties should be taken from the free list, and made to pay, say one-half of the duty imposed by the 'McKinley Bill'."

We have preferred thus far to leave this matter with Mr. Swank, after giving him our views, as he is well posted, or should be, as to what is generally needed, or wanted, by the Iron and Steel Manufacturers.

        Very respectfully yours

            H. C. FRICK.

The metal schedules presented by the House of Representatives were studied carefully anew by Mr. Frick and his associates and revised sharply but accurately downward conjointly with Senator Aldrich and his advisers, to the end that the strong leader easily won the approval of his own chamber and scored perhaps the most notable of his many triumphs in conference. To Aldrich, credit

Frick the Man

for the sagacious idea; to Frick, thanks largely for the successful performance; so the record stands; and, both being men looking always to results without exploitation, the inwardness of the achievement was never revealed.

Mr. Frick was so fully occupied trying to save his fortune that he paid slight attention to the National campaign of 1900, the result of which in any case seemed to be assured, but he took a most active interest in 1904 on behalf of President Roosevelt, with whom casual acquaintance had been ripened by mutual respect and admiration into close personal relationship.

"I feel," wrote the President in 1903 in a cordial letter asking him to serve on the Isthmian Canal Commission, "that no man's name in the country would carry more weight than yours," and Mr. Frick, while constrained to decline, added heartily, "Your administration has my warmest endorsement and where I feel I can be of service I am yours to command."

The time came during the following year when Mr. Roosevelt became so surprisingly and needlessly alarmed at what he regarded as his prospective defeat that he drew upon all available sources for aid. Mr. Frick responded promptly and generously with both time and money, consulting frequently with Chairman Cortelyou, persuading Mr. Cornelius N. Bliss to accept the treasuryship, effecting a temporary reconciliation of Mr. E. H. Harriman with the President, selecting a Pittsburgh finance committee whose initial contribution was $100,-000, personally subscribing even more than that and

Public Affairs

abandoning his customary trip to Europe in order that he might remain within call to do whatever might be asked of him. Immensely gratified by the result, he telegraphed the President on election night:

> The endorsement of yourself and your policies by your fellow citizens is magnificent and truly well deserved. Cordial congratulations!
> H. C. FRICK.

Shortly after the election, the inside struggle for control of the Equitable Assurance Society, of which Mr. Frick had become a trustee, approached a climax and he joined with other prominent Republicans in trying to effect a solution by obtaining the appointment of Mr. James H. Hyde as Ambassador to France, but the best the President could be persuaded to offer was the Ministry to Belgium, which the young man promptly declined, and the insurance investigation which brought Mr. Charles Evans Hughes into public life ensued. With this unimportant exception, the relations of Mr. Roosevelt and Mr. Frick seem to have been wholly social until the latter part of 1905, when the latter, replying to the President's request that he find a position for a friend, expressed his views on the railway strike situation in the following communication:

October 27th, 1905.
Dear Mr. President:—

Your personal note of the sixteenth regarding Mr. Loomis just received, having been wrongly addressed.

There is no opening at present suitable for Mr. Loomis. President Corey of the Steel Corporation, however, will, through Mr. Bacon invite Loomis to call on him and it is possible he can be placed in the near future. We are extremely anxious to secure

Frick the Man

orders for battleships and cruisers from Russia, and in this connection may be able to use him.

Your visit to the South has been very successful, and no doubt of great benefit; and I congratulate you.

I am pleased to note that you have not in any respect departed from your previous public announcement that you do not favor any legislation or action which will injure or retard business prosperity or interfere with private property. I am sure the members of your Cabinet and others in authority will be influenced by your conclusions. This is particularly applicable at the present time to the Department of Commerce and Labor.

Also, I believe with you that the demand for legislation relating to transportation rates is imperative and pressing. It seems to me that the idea of placing the power in a commission to originate rates is more or less impracticable, and would result in fixing them on a basis of mileage, which, in view of widely different conditions, as applied to different localities, would be unjust and unreasonable. By this I mean the commission should not have the right to fix rates generally nor except on complaint in specific cases that rates put in force by the railroad are unreasonable.

But I think the evils which now exist may be overcome without any legislation which will seriously damage property rights or the great railroad business of the country so closely identified with business prosperity. What we need is a prevention of unjust rates, and, particularly, unjust discrimination, and a prompt remedy for existing wrongs. I think there should be created a court or courts, with competent, adequate and final jurisdiction, whose duties should be confined to the disposition of rate cases; or, if additional jurisdiction is given, the rate cases should always have preference as to disposition.

Also, there should be an Interstate Commerce Commission, composed of, say, nine of the highest ability and standing, which might perhaps sit in groups of three in different parts of the country, or in a body, as circumstances might require, to whom complaints might be made. This committee should have power to secure the evidence applicable, and its decision should go into immediate effect, with heavy penalties for violation, unless an appeal should be promptly presented to the court above referred to. In case of appeal, the appellant should be required to give bond

Public Affairs

to cover damages and costs. If the decision appealed from be sustained the judgment of the court would date from the time of the decision by the commission, and the bond would protect the aggrieved party; and, in either case, the loser should pay all costs including reasonable attorneys fees. Possibly the complaining party at the outset should file a bond to cover costs in case he is finally unsuccessful. Under such a law very few appeals would be taken; and in any event both sides to a controversy would be fully protected.

Cordial congratulations. Many and happy returns of this day. (Mr. Roosevelt's birthday.)

With great respect, always,

Sincerely yours
H. C. Frick.

The position subsequently assumed by the President clearly indicated that his course was influenced by attentive consideration to these sensible suggestions,—greatly, no doubt, to the gratification of Mr. Frick,—and the cordial relationship continued.

Two years elapsed, however, before the two men were brought into contact by questions bearing upon public policy and governmental action. The autumn of 1907 found the business and financial worlds in a state of unrest and apprehension. President Roosevelt's warfare on the trusts had already produced, under the Sherman law, six important actions, of which two had been won and four were pending, and no less than thirty-four prosecutions under the Elkins act forbidding the giving or acceptance of rebates, involving large sums of money, were under way. Nobody could tell where the headsman's axe would fall next, large business was rapidly approaching paralysis and financial conditions were distinctly alarming.

Frick the Man

Although the country banks had drawn as heavily as possible upon their reserves in New York, they were unable to supply their customers and were calling all collectable loans, while in the city itself runs were beginning on many small banks and were seriously menacing two big trust companies. Large depositors had not been denied but they were well aware that they could not get their money and, for mutual protection, they refrained from asking. The fright had not yet become so widespread as to present unmistakable signs of a panic, but it was becoming more general daily and only the lighting of a match was needed to explode the magazine.

Bankers were meeting nightly in Mr. J. P. Morgan's library, often remaining till daybreak, studying reports, investigating rumors, recapitulating resources and making tentative plans to meet any contingencies that might arise, under the direction of the most courageous financier of his time. All appreciated the magnitude of the danger but none could foresee the extent of the disaster and suffering that would inevitably ensue from a general panic, once become nation-wide and irresistible.

The supreme test came in the last week of October, when the fact transpired that the key of the situation lay in a stock brokerage house. Moore and Schley, one of the largest firms in the country, were heavy borrowers of money from financial institutions, not only in New York but in Philadelphia and Chicago, with which they had deposited, along with other collateral securities, a huge number of shares of the Tennessee Coal and Iron Company which, the exigencies of the time quickly de-

Public Affairs

veloped, had no market value. If some other disposition could not be made of this large block of stock, not only would the firm be forced into bankruptcy but many of the lending banks throughout the country would also be imperilled.

Among the friends of Moore and Schley was Colonel Oliver H. Payne, who had exchanged with them millions of current securities for these useless shares, hoping to tide them over the crisis. But the effort was unavailing and, simultaneously with the failure of a Providence trust company and the issuance of clearing-house certificates, Colonel Payne put the matter before his attorney, Lewis Cass Ledyard, Esq., and directed him to place it before Mr. Morgan, with expression of his own belief that a smash was inevitable unless the United States Steel Corporation could see its way clear to purchase the Tennessee shares at a price that would relieve the brokers. Four years later, in testifying before a Congressional committee, Mr. Ledyard recounted the subsequent happenings.

Mr. Morgan was deeply concerned. "It is very serious," he said, "the most serious thing that has appeared in connection with the panic. If Moore and Schley go, there's no telling what the effect will be on Wall Street and the financial institutions or how many houses will go with them or how many banks throughout the country will go down. I will see what can be done about it at once."

Judge Gary and Mr. Frick were summoned by telephone. Both were familiar with the Tennessee property. Neither considered the stock worth more than $60 a share and neither approved buying it then at any price,

Frick the Man

fearing that its absorption might invite a government suit under the anti-trust act such as was then pending against the Standard Oil Company.

"I do not know," ejaculated Mr. Morgan, "whether the United States Steel Corporation can afford to buy this stock or not, but I will say that, in my opinion, if it does not or unless someone furnishes immediate relief, no man on earth can say what the effect will be on the financial institutions of the country under these critical conditions."

Others were called in and conference followed conference in rapid succession during the night. Mr. Frick was visibly impressed by Mr. Morgan's argument and finally admitted that, in so perilous a condition, the interests of the whole country should be regarded as paramount and that, if necessary to avert the disastrous consequences of a vast panic, the Steel Corporation should not hesitate to pay an excessive price for the stock; and yet at the last moment before definitely registering his assent, he forsook the conference and sought Mr. Ledyard, who testified as follows:

Mr. Frick came into the room where I was, and he said, "Mr. Ledyard, I want to ask you something. I have known you for years, and I know you very well, and I depend absolutely upon what you say. Have you looked into this situation yourself of Moore & Schley?" I said, "Mr. Frick, I have looked into it to the extent I have been able. I have not been personally over their books, but I have been over it with their bookkeepers, and I have been over it with Mr. Schley, and I have done what I can to familiarize myself with their affairs and the necessities of their condition." He said, "Are you of the opinion, from what you have seen and from what information you have gathered—are you frankly of the opinion that nothing less than par will pull these people out and save them?" I said, "I am, Mr. Frick. I do not think any less than par for the Tennessee stock will pull them out, and I do not know whether that will do it, but I think it will." He said, "Very good, Mr. Ledyard; if you say so, that is the end of the entire question for me."

The question of the stock purchase was thus disposed of. But the apprehension respecting governmental prosecution was still grave to the mind of Judge Gary, who gave this testimony:

I said to Mr. Morgan, "In the first place, I would not think of considering the purchase of this stock without going to Washington first and taking the matter up with the President or the Department of Justice, or both." He said,"Why? Have they any right to say whether you buy or not?" I said, "No; they have not. But here is a financial crisis, and from your standpoint the object of buying this stock would be to allay this storm, to assist in overcoming this panic, and if the Department of Justice or the President should find out we had purchased, or were about to purchase it, and should enjoin us from purchasing on the ground that it would add to our holdings and thereby raise the question of creating or adding to a monopoly, you can see at once that what we had done would be to make the financial conditions very much worse than they are now; and therefore, it seems to me, we ought to know how the President and the Department of Justice would feel about the question." He said, "Well, I think that is very forcible, and I see no objection to your going over there if you feel like it."

But Mr. Morgan was still dubious and did not make his half-hearted assent definite until, at his earnest insistence and greatly against his own inclination, Mr. Frick agreed to join with Judge Gary in presenting the case to the President. Time was a vital factor in the undertaking. It was Sunday evening and announcement of

Frick the Man

the completion of the transaction with the approval of the government was deemed essential to obviate calamitous frenzy on the Stock Exchange at its opening at 10 o'clock on the following morning.

The story of the subsequent happenings is familiar. A special train bore the two commissioners to Washington in the early morning hours; the President was induced to leave his breakfast untouched to hear them; in the absence of Attorney General Bonaparte, Secretary Root was hastily summoned and, before the gong sounded in the Stock Exchange, the glad tidings had swept through Wall Street that the menace of the Tennessee steel pool no longer existed, that United States Steel bonds would be substituted immediately for the uncurrent shares, that the big brokerage house was saved from dissolution and that President Roosevelt had personally assured Messrs. Frick and Gary, upon the legal advice of Mr. Root that, "while he could not advise them to take the action proposed, he felt it no public duty of his to interpose any objection."

This "good enough Morgan" saved the situation and the two commissioners returned from Washington the recipients of hearty congratulations and many expressions of gratitude.

But Mr. Frick, now thoroughly aroused, soon realized that only a breathing spell had been gained and that heavier clouds still hovered over the financial and industrial conditions of the country. Most threatening of these, to his mind, which turned invariably to the common advantages of consolidation and concentration, was the

Public Affairs

government suit pending for the dissolution of the Standard Oil Company. If that could be settled out of court upon terms which would effect practical compliance with the anti-trust law by ensuring full protection of the public through some form of governmental supervision and regulation, without depriving the producers of their legitimate opportunities, he became convinced that an enormous revival of business and corresponding restoration of universal prosperity would follow promptly.

Having no interest in the oil concern and being averse on principle to interference with other people's business, he hesitated to make even a gesture along the natural line but finally, after carefully studying the grounds of complaint and conferring with Judge Gary, he sought the advice of Senator Knox as to the advisability and propriety of requesting an informal interview with the President, in the hope of supplementing the successful outcome of their recent conversation.

"I think," Senator Knox replied, "that it is always a help to the President to talk with you and Judge Gary, and such a talk at this time would be helpful to the general situation irrespective of the results in the particular matter. With respect to that, nothing can be done except it meets with his approval and therefore, Mr. Kellogg consenting, it would be best in my view to take it up directly with the President if you think it possible to get him to agree to anything the other side would accept."

Whereupon Mr. Frick, still reluctant but emboldened

Frick the Man

by the President's previous reception, addressed the following communication to Mr. Roosevelt:

New York,
November 30th, 1907.

Personal

My dear Mr. President:—

    For some time Judge Gary and I have been considering the possibility of some disposition of the pending suit brought by the Government against the Standard Oil Company which would be satisfactory to the Government and to the public generally, and at the same time might be accepted by, if not entirely satisfactory to, the defender.

    I think there is no doubt this litigation materially affects the business situation and very greatly adds to the feeling of financial uncertainty which exists in this country and other countries. It is not necessary at this time to discuss its merits. No doubt you and I would agree as to where the responsibility lies. But conditions are very grave and are not improving as we could wish. The importance of the subject-matter cannot be over-estimated. My interest in the question is confined to the public welfare.

    Judge Gary and I have discussed the propriety of consulting you in regard to this matter. We have had some conversation with Mr. Kellogg upon this subject. We stated to him that we might desire to talk with you; and understand that he does not object. It is our intention to keep the matter very confidential. If you think favorably of my suggestion, it would be the effort of Judge Gary and myself from an independent standpoint and solely in the public interest to get into communication with those who control the defense and ascertain exactly what can be done, using our influence to bring about such a solution as would be satisfactory to the Administration and yet protect the properties involved.

    If in your opinion what I propose is impracticable or improper or unwelcome, of course I know you will say so frankly.

Sincerely yours,
H. C. Frick.

Three days later, probably after conference with his advisers, the President replied:

Public Affairs

The White House
Washington

December 3rd, 1907.

My dear Mr. Frick:

Your letter of the 30th ultimo was duly received. I should always be glad to see you and Judge Gary on any matter, but it seems to me that the only wise course in the case of a suit before the Department of Justice is to have the communication come from the counsel of the Standard Oil Company to the counsel of the Government. While, as I say, I should be glad to see you and Judge Gary, the only possible outcome of any talk with me would be that I should ask you to have the Standard Oil Company, thru its counsel, formulate any proposals and put them before Mr. Kellogg, who would then go over them with the Attorney General, and afterwards, if it was necessary, they would be brought before me. I hope you understand the reasons which actuate me in writing thus. I think if you will go over the matter with Judge Gary you will see that it would be inadvisable for me, from the standpoint of the Government, to take any other course; and I think Knox would tell you so if you would consult him.

With regard, believe me,
Sincerely yours,
Theodore Roosevelt.

The courteous but definite response, restricting negotiations strictly to official channels, disposed of the suggestion, and Mr. Frick, though naturally disappointed at being denied the privilege of placing the outlines of the plan which he had conceived to be a possible practical solution before Messrs. Roosevelt and Rockefeller personally, abandoned the attempt with a sense of relief rather than of resentment.

Mr. Frick supported Mr. Taft, as a "regular," from force of habit. After having contributed through various channels sums aggregating $50,000, he replied to an earnest solicitation from Mr. Charles D. Hilles for an additional subscription at the last moment:

>PRIDE'S CROSSING
>MASSACHUSETTS
>November 2nd, 1912.

My dear Mr. Hilles:

I am just in receipt of your favor of the first. I think President Taft has no show for reelection on Tuesday next. I have contributed, as you state, towards the campaign and I would contribute almost any amount to insure the success of the Republican party if I thought there was a chance. But I think I should not have been asked to contribute to this campaign.

The administration utterly failed to treat many of its warmest friends fairly. Take for instance, the case of the suit against the United States Steel Corporation, in which they charge me with misrepresenting very important matters to the President in order to enable the Steel Company to purchase a property which I was always opposed to its buying at any price. After much discussion I was prevailed on to go to Washington, as its purchase looked as if it would save the country from a very disastrous panic.

Much to my surprise Secretary Knox, when I last saw him, told me the bringing of the suit had never been brought before the cabinet. The President, I think, also told me that he did not know that such a charge in the suit was to be made against me. This shows a great lack of interest in very important matters on the part of the President and his Secretary, Mr. Knox.

I write you thus fully as I do not want my position misunderstood.

>Sincerely yours,
>H. C. FRICK.

Although Mr. Frick obviously felt aggrieved by such misrepresentation of his own position by the government and seemed quite willing that Mr. Taft and even Mr. Knox should be informed of the fact, his chief complaint was of what he regarded as a breach of faith on

Public Affairs

the part of the Attorney General, to whom Judge Gary reported to the Board he had pledged prompt correction of any practices which the Department should give notice were deemed illegal or improper, and Mr. Wickersham had tacitly acquiesced in this arrangement. Nevertheless, shortly thereafter, according to Judge Gary's biographer, without specifying a single objection, or suggesting the slightest change, Mr. Wickersham mentioned casually to Judge Gary at a dinner that the excitement over the Stanley investigation, the hostility to the Steel Corporation and the charges of its being favored by the Administration led the Administration to feel that it must bring suit for dissolution of the corporation. Mr. Gary confessed himself "overwhelmed" by this announcement and Mr. Frick was highly indignant at what he considered a contemptible admission of yielding to political exigencies, at the cost of simple right and a solemn pledge. It may be mentioned, in passing, that the suit was brought and dragged through the courts, at heavy cost, for seven years, only to fail in the end, but Mr. Frick did not forget. Writing to Secretary Knox in 1915, he said:

> I see by the press that Mr. George W. Wickersham is making himself quite prominent in calling and conferring with Mr. Hughes, and leaving the impression that he is his chief adviser. It will cool the ardor of a great many friends of the nominee if they are left under the impression that that gentleman is to be prominent in the coming administration. I wish some one would give Mr. Hughes an intimation of this. Of course, we want everyone's assistance, but I should be sorry to think that after election Mr. Hughes might feel obliged to give Mr. Wickersham a prominent place in his administration.

Frick the Man

But Mr. Hughes was defeated and presently, when the war spirit became irresistible, partisanship was buried in a vast wave of patriotism and the whole American people rallied with unprecedented vigor and determination around their eloquent leader in the White House.

XXII

The Patriot

BIG BUSINESS accepted the return of the Democratic party to power in 1913, without serious misgivings, as the inevitable consequence of a Republican row which had been universally "discounted" by Wall Street. Republican capitalists pronounced Mr. Roosevelt responsible and tranquilly reconciled themselves to the prospect of a respite in business which they hoped might not run into general depression.

They felt no animosity toward Mr. Wilson for such of his utterances as they regarded as radical and menacing to their interests. He had simply played the political game, after the manner of a candidate to whom American tradition had accorded much latitude, in his choice of methods and varied appeals to discordant elements. Many believed that at heart he was conservative, as befitted a highly intelligent student of government, and that, once confronted by the grave responsibilities of authority, he would revert to the call of his reasoning faculties. In any case he was "safer than Roosevelt"; so perhaps, after all, an interlude in control by the only party really fit to govern might serve an excellent purpose in conveying a needed lesson to the Republican politicians upon whom Big Business relied for intelligent pursuit of their trade.

Frick the Man

But while sojourning in Bermuda for rest and reflection immediately following his election Mr. Wilson derived either from some undisclosed source or from his own imagination an impression that Wall Street was conspiring to discredit his administration from the start and, upon his return, he publicly assumed a belligerent and menacing attitude. After heralding at a banquet of the Southern Society his suspicion that the moneyed power was fomenting a panic "to create the impression that the wrong thing is going to be done," he said:

> I do not believe there is any man living who dares to use that machinery to create such a panic. And if any one attempts it I promise you that I will build the gibbet for him as high as Haman's. But that is only figuratively speaking. What I will do will be to direct the attention of the people to him, and I think that they will manage to cut him to the quick. With their eyes open, the people are not going to let any man do such a thing.

What precisely this mystifying and startling declaration foreboded nobody assumed to know, since nothing whatever had transpired from Wall Street so likely to arouse panicky apprehensions as the utterance itself. Even so, somewhat oddly, manifestations of alarm and remonstrance were confined chiefly to the columns of public journals which had supported Mr. Wilson's candidacy; Capital, as represented by "the Street," remained unruffled and apparently passive. Large undertakings on the part especially of railway corporations were not abandoned; they were not even put aside; they were merely subjected to a process, so quiet as to be hardly noticeable, of masterly inactivity.

The Patriot

"It is a time to abide events," was the calm advice of Mr. Frick, who arranged accordingly to prolong his usual stay abroad in search of Old Masters.

This was the last of his many visits abroad. Disturbed by the Continental outlook in the Summer of 1914, he remained at home as a precautionary measure bearing upon his heavy responsibilities and was at Pride's when the live coals which he had been carefully watching flicker in the furnaces of Europe burst into flame.

In common with the great majority of thoughtful Americans, he simply adhered to his own admonition to his friends at the beginning of the war to "stand with the President," and he did not grieve when the responsibility continued undivided as the result of Democratic success at the Congressional elections. But his sympathies were strong with the Allies from the beginning and, while sedulously avoiding any appearance of being anything but "neutral even in his thoughts," he never missed an opportunity to extend quietly, even furtively, such aid and comfort as he considered suitable. A complete tabulation of his contributions cannot be compiled as they were made deliberately for secrecy's sake through different agencies from various funds, and in many instances no records were made. His largest subscription during this period was to the Gold Note Syndicate for the relief of the British Treasury, but this was in the form of a low-rate loan which presumably would be, and ultimately was, repaid. Outright gifts were made, in varying amounts, to the Belgian Relief Fund, the American Ambulance Hospital in France, the maimed

Frick the Man

French soldiers, the families of disabled French artists, "French sufferers," the Armored Motor Squadron, the Allies' Bazar, and to other like organizations whenever solicited by responsible persons.

Altogether, the total of gifts made during the war for humanitarian purposes by Mr. Frick personally and through generous members of his family must have exceeded one million of dollars; in truth, he never knew how much and he permitted no computation.

His initial subscription to the First Liberty Loan was made on the morning of May 22nd, 1917, when Mr. Frick was called to the telephone by Mr. George F. Baker of the First National Bank of New York, his closest financial friend, and the following conversation ensued:

MR. BAKER—Washington is about to ask for subscriptions to the First Liberty Loan and of course we want to give it a good start.
MR. FRICK—Of course.
MR. BAKER—How many shall I put you down for?
MR. FRICK—The same as you take yourself.
MR. BAKER—I thought a million.
MR. FRICK—All right. If you should want any more, don't bother to ring. Put me down.

Subsequently, Mr. McEldowney's records show, Mr. Frick bought $4,545,000 of the various issues through the Union Trust Company. How many additional he purchased through other channels cannot be ascertained. But he never failed to respond to a call,—not even when later the stock of a company, with whose affairs he was fully conversant, was purchasable on a 15 per cent earn-

The Patriot

ing basis, as contrasted with a yield of 4 per cent from government bonds.

Characteristically, in sending his final subscription of $1,500,000 to the Fourth Liberty Loan on September 28th, 1918, he requested Mr. McEldowney to see that it receive no special mention at the big public meeting but "be treated as you treat all other subscriptions," but the amount was too large to be ignored and was heralded by the Pittsburgh newspapers as "the largest ever subscribed by one person to any war activity."

Mr. Frick's only son was accepted for air service and his only daughter sailed for Red Cross service in France in November.

A joint resolution declaring a state of war against Germany was introduced in the Senate by Senator Martin of Virginia and referred to the Committee on Foreign Relations on April 2nd. Being found unsatisfactory in form, a substitute resolution pronounced by many Senators "a model," was reported back on April 3rd and adopted by the votes of all Senators except Messrs. La Follette, Gronna, Lane, Stone, Vardaman and Norris.

"I was glad to hear through Mr. Schoonmaker," Mr. Frick wrote to Senator Knox, "that you were the author of the Declaration of War; it struck me as a very good paper; and I rejoice that we have you in the Senate to continue doing many fine things that you will get no credit for."

"Of course," he added in reply to a query, "I thoroughly believe that those of us who stay at home and take our ease should willingly pay any taxes that may

Frick the Man

be assessed to carry on the war, although I have to confess that the present disposition seems to be to impose unfairly upon those who are supposed to have large incomes."

In common with a vast number of Americans of like energizing disposition, Mr. Frick chafed at the laggardliness of the government during the Summer, but he was so thrilled by the splendor of President Wilson's address to Congress at its reopening in December that he could not refrain from voicing his approbation in these enthusiastic terms:

New York,
December 7th, 1917.

Dear Mr. President:

May I be permitted to congratulate you and the country on your admirable address to Congress—only one of many. You have stated the situation just as any true American or citizen of any country should view it, and every one should be willing to make any necessary sacrifice to bring about what you have stated should be done.

It is a great satisfaction to feel that we have in you a leader in whom we should be proud: and, while I differ from you in politics, I subscribe without reservation to all you are contending for.

It is my fervent wish that you may be spared to see the trouble ended satisfactorily, as I firmly feel you are devoted to this great work and will carry it forward fairly and honestly.

Cordially yours,
HENRY C. FRICK.

Hon. Woodrow Wilson.

To which the President responded expressing his gratification and his feeling that the sentiment of the country was more and more uniting for a great demonstration of the nation's power as well as its high purpose.

From that day forward Mr. Frick held himself at the

The Patriot

call of the Administration and engaged, both in New York and at Pride's, in frequent consultations with its representatives. One notable instance afforded an interesting test of relative loyalties.

Responding one morning to a summons to the White House, Mr. Bernard M. Baruch, the New York financier who subsequently became a member of the Commission in charge of all purchases for the Allies, Chairman of the War Industries Board and economic adviser of the American Peace Commission, found the President greatly disturbed by complaints that the prices of steel—particularly ship plates—as offered by the manufacturers were in excess of fair prices.

Mr. Baruch suggested that a meeting with the heads of the various steel companies be arranged and the President, acquiescing, authorized him to take the necessary steps and to act by official authority as his personal representative.

The conference with the heads of the various companies was held in the office of the United States Steel Corporation and proved most unsatisfactory to Mr. Baruch. Judge Gary did the talking. Yes, it was true, as alleged, that the manufacturers desired to charge the United States four and one-fourth cents per pound for steel plates; and Judge Gary considered this a fair price, especially in view of the President's insistence that no higher price be charged the Allies,—a matter seriously affecting the profits of the manufacturers. Mr. Baruch urged that Big Business was missing an opportunity in failing to show that in time of war its representatives placed the welfare of their

Frick the Man

government ahead of their own and insisted that Judge Gary call up the White House and get the President's views. Judge Gary refused to do this and declared the conference ended.

The discomfiture of Mr. Baruch is easily imagined. His mission was an abject failure and he must report accordingly; his pride was shaken; his vanity, hurt; and the fault was his, and his alone. He had not insisted upon presenting his entire case; he had not depicted the gruesomeness of the situation as it appeared to the Chief Magistrate, keenly sensitive to his personal responsibility for the keeping of his official engagements, whether written or understood, and to the safeguarding of his country's honor to the smallest detail. His mission must be fulfilled. He could not, he would not, return to Washington humiliated.

Diligent inquiry elicited the information that Judge Gary, then out of reach, was to dine that evening at his club where, at an hour which he deemed suitable for calling, Mr. Baruch was informed that Mr. Gary was in conference and could not see him. Very well, he replied, he would wait; the matter was important. At the expiration of half an hour, he sent up a card upon which he had written:

My message is from the President and I must return tonight.

There was no answer. An hour passed. Finally Judge Gary appeared and, saying simply that he thought the Government would accept his judgment that the price fixed was fair, he left the club.

The Patriot

On the following morning Mr. Baruch, perturbed and indignant, called upon Mr. Frick at his house and told his story from start to finish. Mr. Frick listened attentively.

"Of course," he remarked when his visitor had finished, "you are aware that I am a director of the Steel Corporation."

"Certainly," Mr. Baruch replied, "but I am not here to see you in that capacity. This country is at war and I have come here by the President's direction to obtain from you as a patriotic citizen certain information for his guidance in the performance of his duties."

"What precisely does the President wish to know?"

"I have already told you that the manufacturers are charging the Allies four and one-quarter cents per pound for ship plates."

Mr. Frick nodded assent.

"The President would like to learn from you, if you can tell, what the production cost of ship plates is."

Mr. Frick medidated for a moment and then said:

"Mr. Baruch, I have nothing to do with selling operations of the Corporation. I know nothing of the arrangements between the manufacturers and the various governments to which you refer. I do not interfere with business which does not fall within my province. But if the President, for purposes of his own, in the proper and honorable conduct of the war, has authorized you to ask me as a citizen to state the production cost of ship plates I can answer his question. It is two and one-half cents a pound."

"Including a profit?"

Frick the Man

"Only sufficient to safeguard the manufacturer against loss,—which is only fair and proper. Mind you, that is the cost to the United States Steel Corporation. I have no information respecting costs to other companies."

Mr. Baruch was profuse in his thanks and assured him that the information which he had given the President would be held in strictest confidence.

"Naturally," Mr. Frick replied simply, "I should prefer that it be kept that way. I should be criticized no doubt, and perhaps rightly. But if I had wished to dodge, I should not have answered at all. I am always responsible for what I say and you may tell the President that, if the accuracy of my figures should be questioned in any such way as might embarrass him, he need not hesitate to ask me to prove them openly."

The President's order to the Commission to stand firm, was so convincing of his knowledge of the facts that Mr. Frick's testimony was not required and, after much haggling over the evidence that costs to the smaller concerns, whose products were essential, were materially higher, a compromise, generally considered fair, was effected upon the basis of three and forty-one-hundredths cents per pound. Thereafter, by the President's explicit direction, Mr. Baruch kept in constant touch with Mr. Frick respecting all perplexing problems of the War Industry Board, "and," in Mr. Baruch's own words "he never failed to keep an appointment whenever and wherever suggested."

Mr. Frick's attitude toward personal profiteering during the war was disclosed incidentally. A luncheon guest

The Patriot

just returned from Washington reported remarks heard at the capital somewhat critical of the methods of a certain Syndicate engaged in financing a huge shipbuilding project with the approval and prospective support of the Government from which, it was anticipated, construction contracts would be obtained on a cost-plus basis. Questions were being asked, not with respect to the percentages to be allowed for profits, which were published and appeared moderate, but as to the need of forming subsidiary companies for manufacturing and other purposes whose costs might easily be enhanced in various ways without being so readily ascertained.

Although, in the confusion attendant upon the making of many other like arrangements upon a large scale, this particular operation had escaped public attention, vague suspicions of the devious workings of High Finance were becoming rife, and observant persons were manifesting concern lest unpleasant disclosures impair the navy's fighting capacity at a critical time.

Mr. Frick listened attentively but said nothing. Following the luncheon, however, he excused himself for a moment to send a telephone message before rejoining his guest in the drawing room. Presently he was summoned to his office and, upon returning, remarked quietly:

"I had an interest in that Syndicate. I took it up to help the Government by relieving it of a part of its heavy financing and with the understanding that subscribers would receive no more than a moderate rate of interest on their payments to be fixed openly by the Government. The thought of making a profit never crossed my mind.

Frick the Man

I find, however, upon inquiry, that my money is no longer needed by the Syndicate, as the subscriptions are selling at a premium, which seems to indicate some ground for the rumor you heard. I gave orders to sell my interest when I went to the telephone and have just now been notified that it has been sold. I don't know whether there is a profit in the transaction or not. I hope not, but my report will show in the morning, and if there is, it will go into the United War Work treasury before night.

"It is difficult for a man of means to know what to do in all instances," he added. "Some of my shareholdings will increase in value during the war, no doubt to my ultimate advantage; others may decrease for one reason or another; nobody can tell; I cannot keep shifting my investments in any case and it would do no good if I could; so the best I can do is to stand pat."

In point of fact, the appraisal of Mr. Frick's estate following his death showed that his fortune shrank many millions between the beginning and the ending of the war of the United States against the Central Powers of Europe.

It is an interesting fact, not generally known, that the only two multi-millionaires who supported quietly, but effectively, the successful organized effort to prevent the inclusion of the United States in the League of Nations were Messrs. Henry Clay Frick and Andrew W. Mellon. This endeavor, it may be recalled, was initiated and directed by a small group comprising a dozen resolute United States Senators and a few publicists. The contest quickly resolved into a bitter struggle against heavy odds. Ani-

The Patriot

mated by a natural revulsion against warfare, following the world's greatest devastation, a powerful sentiment sprang up throughout the entire country in favor of any movement designed to perpetuate peace. Republicans and Democrats alike fell into line behind President Wilson and Former President Taft and of all classes none was so zealous, so determined and so active as the moneyed element of New York. Bankers noticeably and capitalists, though less aggressively, seemed to be literally unanimous in their advocacy of the most far-reaching and most appealing experiment ever adventured by the Republic. To oppose its undertaking was to invite personal ignominy.

Such was the atmosphere in which Henry Clay Frick lived when, one evening in May, 1919, the group opposed to joining the League, assembled at their accustomed meeting place in Senator Brandegee's residence in Washington, were apprized that their whole plan of campaign was seriously endangered. Their strategy had consisted of disseminating propaganda chiefly throughout the middle West at mass meetings and by distribution of quantities of "campaign literature" for the purpose of starting "back fires" upon wavering Senators. Thus far, with the powerful aid of a few public journals headed in the West by the CHICAGO TRIBUNE and the KANSAS CITY STAR, in the East by the NEW YORK SUN, BOSTON EVENING TRANSCRIPT and WASHINGTON POST, and nationally by the aggregation of public journals owned by William Randolph Hearst and, incidentally, by a small but energetic weekly paper printed in New York,

Frick the Man

the campaign had progressed favorably, but the time had come when essential travelling and mailing expenditures required considerable sums, and the modest funds which the committee had been able to supply were completely exhausted. The problem of ways and means, to oppose successfully skilful antagonists suffering from no such handicap was poignant. The finding of a deeper reservoir upon which to draw for financial aid had become a paramount necessity.

Various plans were proposed only to be rejected as impracticable and the outlook was lamentably gloomy when late in the evening the resourceful Senator Knox suggested as a last resort an appeal to Mr. Frick and Mr. Mellon, who he said were accustomed to act together in such matters and both of whom, he thought—with no reason for his surmise—might be impressed with the merits of the cause, if it could be placed before them effectively. He felt confident, in any case, that if either could be won over, the other would join. The suggestion had crossed his mind in consequence of a chance remark by the New York representative present that he would be obliged to leave on the following morning to attend a complimentary dinner which Mr. Frick was to give to General Wood on the following evening. This might afford him an opportunity, Senator Knox suggested, to broach the subject and, if the response should by chance be favorable, he himself would follow it up immediately with Mr. Mellon.

The proposal was accepted and the dinner, attended by forty of New York's most distinguished men, was so

The Patriot

successful that afterwards the host pronounced it perhaps the most satisfactory he had ever given. Fortunately for his design, the delegated conspirator was requested by his host to remain after the party had dissolved and, yet more happily for his purpose, he was informed presently that enlightenment respecting the contest over joining the League of Nations was desired.

"Those whom I come into contact with," said Mr. Frick, "seem to feel that this country ought to join and I am being constantly urged to support the movement. But the fact is that I have been so busy of late that I haven't followed the discussion as closely probably as I ought. I went to the opera house and listened to the President and Mr. Taft and I must confess that, while Mr. Taft's speech seemed to me very good, Mr. Wilson's was not convincing. I should like to hear the other side if there is one, and I judge from the little I have read about it that there is."

Marvelling at this auspicious fortuity, the eager propagandist set forth the stock arguments of the group of Irreconcilables with whom he was aligned as succinctly as he was capable of doing, although at considerable length. Mr. Frick followed the statement closely, asking many questions, and finally said:

"As I understand it, then, the proposition is to pledge the United States, now the richest and most powerful nation in the world, to pool its issues with other countries, which are largely its debtors, and to agree in advance to abide by the policies and practices adopted by a majority or two-thirds of its associates; that is, to sur-

Frick the Man

render its present right of independence of action upon any specific question whenever such a question may arise."

"That is substantially it."

"Well, I am opposed to that. Of course I am. I don't see how any experienced business man could fail to be. Why, it seems to me a crazy thing to do."

"That is what Senator Knox and the rest of us think. Now the question is, Will you help us to beat it?"

"What do you want me to do?"

The visitor then recounted the happening of the previous evening in Washington as the simplest way of presenting the full situation.

"So," remarked Mr. Frick, smiling, "you were going to fetch up the matter anyway?"

"If I could get a chance, yes."

"That's rather odd; but" he added quizzically, "I understood you to say that Knox was going to see Mr. Mellon; why didn't he?"

"Well, as it happens, Mr. Mellon was here tonight; also, for some reason or other, the Senator seemed to think it might be well for me to pull your leg first."

"Come now, do you consider that a compliment or a reflection?"

"Oh, a compliment surely. In fact, my only objection to his programme was that Mr. Mellon might feel aggrieved."

This was too much for one possessed of humor in Mr. Frick's gay mood.

"I don't think you needed to worry about that," he chuckled; then sobering quickly, he added:

The Patriot

"Well, I'll go along. How much do you want?"

A sum was mentioned.

"That won't go far."

"Only for a starter of course; to Senator Pepper, to-morrow; time is important."

"It will be sent in the morning."

The highly gratified guest had said good-night and was on the threshold when a quick step was heard down the long corridor and Mr. Frick, his eyes gleaming with the joyous light of battle, appeared pointing a finger admonitorily and with seriousness, partly mock and partly real, he said:

"Be sure you put up a good fight. Now that we are in, we must win, you know. Keep me posted. Good luck and good-night."

Three days later the New York member of the cabal received the following note from the Senate Chamber:

> Thanks for your note. I had already received a letter from Mr. Frick announcing what he had done and I wrote to Pittsburgh and obtained the same amount from Mr. Mellon. I told Medill [Senator McCormick] today and he says he can now go to Chicago and raise about twenty [thousand].
> Very sincerely yours,
> P. C. Knox.

The desired reservoir had been found and it was both deep and full. All anxiety respecting sinews of war was dispelled. Rejoicing pervaded the camp of the Irreconcilables, efforts were redoubled all along the line and the redoubtable little band pushed on to the victory which, whether desirable or not, presently was won in the Senate and ultimately was ratified by the people.

Frick the Man

Mr. Frick's interest became intense and never flagged for a moment during the seven months left to him of earthly existence. After listening, three days before he died, to an encouraging report of progress in what proved to be his last fight, he smiled contentedly and pronounced it "GOOD."

XXIII

An Art Collector

THAT MR. FRICK's love of art was innate there can be no question. While yet in his teens, as already noted, the walls of his living room were covered with such "prints and sketches" as were obtainable in a remote country village for the meager remnants of small earnings at his disposal. Whether he actually essayed the use of pencil and brush, as vaguely recalled by one or two of his contemporaries, is perhaps a question, although a surmise to that effect is not improbable. But testimony to his inherent interest is abundant and evidences of a steadily increasing bent and a signal refinement of taste are manifest at least from the time of furnishing his home in Pittsburgh.

He was attracted first to the French School, and beginning while abroad in 1895 he bought a number of paintings of varying merits, many of which, as his taste became more catholic, he subsequently disposed of. Although he undertook his new avocation with characteristic caution and only after studies as thorough and as painstaking as he ever applied to a business venture, he quickly developed a rare power of discrimination which he applied unhesitatingly whenever an opportunity arose to substitute an example of an artist's genius superior to one which he had acquired, thus pursuing his unwavering policy of

Frick the Man

always getting the best obtainable. Even while proceeding by this winnowing process, at the end of three years he had gathered into his mansion in Pittsburgh no less than seventy-one pictures fairly representative of Rembrandt, Nattier, Hoppner, Reynolds, Watts, Dagnan Bouveret, Corot, Daubigny, Troyon, Millet, Jacque, Rousseau, Alma Tadema, Jules Breton, Fritz Thaulow, Mauve, Greuze, Van Marcke, Monet, Cazin, Bouguereau, Gérôme, his particular friend Chartran and others, constituting altogether an admirable nucleus for the superb collection ultimately achieved.

This much he did solely for the gratification of himself, his family and his friends. It was not until after he had resided in New York that he was inspired by an inspection of the famous Wallace collection in London to make his own as complete and as nearly perfect as possible for ultimate exhibition, suitably housed and amply endowed for acquirement of meritorious additions through all years to come, to the people of his own country.

To compare with other collections, that left by Mr. Frick in fulfilment of his noble aspiration might seem invidious and could serve no useful purpose, but there can hardly be dissent from the expert judgment of Mr. Cortissoz that "this excels any single gift ever made to the public in the past." It comprises more than a hundred paintings, and every one is a masterpiece representing the best work of fifty or more of the world's greatest artists.

In addition to paintings, Mr. Frick acquired exquisite examples in sculpture, Renaissance bronzes, Limoges

An Art Collector

enamels, and Chinese porcelains. The bust of a Neapolitan Princess by Laurana and the Portrait of Madame Cayla by Houdon, are masterpieces in marble, and among the bronzes, are the works of Giovanni da Bologna, Benvenuto Cellini, Verrocchio and Michelangelo.

Both Limousin and Pénicaud, those rare masters in the art of "Limoges," are represented, and thus the enamels rival in quality the finest in the museums of Europe.

The collection of so-called black hawthorn vases of the K'ang and Hsi period is one of the most choice in existence, and the beauty of these objets d'art is greatly enhanced by the dignity and harmony of the setting afforded by the paintings themselves.

"A Noble Landmark in our Art History," was the title given by Mr. Cortissoz to his appreciative and discriminating tribute, published simultaneously with Mr. Frick's Will.

"Comment upon Mr. Frick's gift of his collection to the public," he wrote, "is naturally enough concentrated just now upon the mere magnitude of his bequest. He leaves to the city, or to the state as the exact terms of his will may determine, a prodigious body of artistic treasures. It is said that it cost him from $30,000,000 to $40,000,000 and the estimate seems reasonable. Yet it is in the particular disposition of his works of art that he has done most to place his countrymen in his debt. For a number of years, when our great private collections have not gone to the auction room, they have gravitated to public museums. Nothing could be more commendable—save the newer policy which has given a Johnson

Frick the Man

Museum to Philadelphia, a Freer Museum to Washington, and now a Frick Museum to New York.

"The independent gathering of masterpieces, isolated in a building of their own, is a boon for which we are always bound to be grateful, and it takes on a particularly rare atmosphere when it reduces to a minimum the institutional character inseparable from the public museums. The Frick collection will inevitably be compared with the Wallace Collection in London. But when the reader is making comparisons of this sort let him think of another, smaller shrine of art; instead of Hertford House, let him think of the Poldi-pezzoli, at Milan. There is the ideal precedent which Mr. Frick has followed.

"In giving his house along with his pictures and other beautiful possessions he has done all that a collector could do to send Velasquez or a Rembrandt or a Gainsborough down to posterity, not as a 'museum specimen' but as a human thing, a work made truly for the delight of mankind. We would be lost without museums, but we are trebly enriched when the museum idea is camouflaged, so to say, by the atmosphere of an individual's home. It is an interesting coincidence that, at the time when the historic interiors of Europe and Great Britain are being broken up as never before, the announcement of the Frick bequest should be made. The old order changeth, giving place to the new. Is the ancient tradition to be revived in the United States, ancestral collections being scattered abroad only to enter upon a more permanent form of existence on this side of the Atlantic?

An Art Collector

"It requires no great stretching of the imagination to recognize in Mr. Frick's gift the establishment of something like a landmark in our art history."

Mr. Frick did not merely admire and enjoy his beautiful pictures; he loved them with a passion as tender as he felt for little children. They rested him, refreshed his mind, soothed his spirit. Often late at night, at the end of a trying day, when perfect stillness reigned, he would slip noiselessly, almost furtively, into the darkened gallery, turn on the lights and sit for an hour or more, first on one divan then on another, absorbing solace and happiness through the mirrors of his heart before seeking the mental and physical relaxation of dreamless sleep. And nothing gave him so much pleasure as quietly witnessing, himself unseen, the delights of enraptured visitors, and listening to their comments.

In his later years, he personally superintended and directed the unwrapping and hanging of every fresh acquisition and made careful notation, in a diary deplorably casual in other respects, of dates of arrival and the like, but with no superfluous word, as for example:

1919
    March 12.—Purchased Stuart "Geo. Washington."
       "   23.—Re the Vermeer.
    May 24.—Purchased paintings from Bacon Estate.
    Aug. 13.—Vermeer arrived. Taken to Pride's.
    Sept. 7.—Brought the Vermeer from Pride's.

The first Old Master purchased was Rembrandt's "Portrait of a Painter."

The Vermeer referred to, "Lady with a Letter," was the last painting bought by Mr. Frick, and this, with

Frick the Man

Rembrandt's "Self Portrait," Velasquez's "Philip the Fourth," Holbein's "Sir Thomas More," and Bellini's "St. Francis," comprised his favorites. But he never wavered in allegiance to his first choice among artists. Asked late in life what man's gift he would have preferred to inherit if he had possessed the privilege of selection, he replied unhesitatingly:

"Rembrandt's."

His first announcement of his purpose, after viewing the Wallace collection was made confidentially to a friend.

"The American people," he said, "are fond—and properly so—of going to Europe, chiefly to see the famous paintings and other works of art there. I am going to try to bring some of them here where all Americans may have the opportunity of seeing them without crossing the ocean."

And toward the last, while showing the last Vermeer purchased to another friend, he looked down the long gallery and remarked quietly:

"I can only hope that the public will get one-half the pleasure that has been afforded me in enjoyment of these masterpieces in proper surroundings. I want this collection to be my monument."

An Art Collector

PAINTINGS, DRAWINGS, AND ETCHINGS SELECTED AND PURCHASED BY
MR. FRICK PERSONALLY BETWEEN 1881 AND 1919

DATE OF PURCHASE	ARTIST	TITLE
1881	Luis Jiminez	In the Louvre
1887	Tito Lessi	The Reader
	Meyer von Bremen	The Darlings
1895	Martin Rico	Fishermen's Houses, Venice
	J. B. Robie	Flower Piece
	Bouguereau	Espièglerie
	Breton	Last Gleanings
	Cazin	Sunday Evening in a Miners' Village
	Cazin	The Pool—Gray Night
	C. E. Jacque	Minding the Flock
	A. B. Wale	Sheep
	J. G. Jacquet	Manon
	Harnett	Still Life
	J. R. Woodwell	Landscape
	Rosa Bonheur	Horse Fair
	J. W. Beatty	Harvest Scene
	Monet	Argenteuil
	Thaulow	Village Night Scene
1896	Picknell	Among the Polls
	Van Os	Fruit
	Mauve	A Quiet Hour
	Chartran	Portrait of H. C. Frick
	Rosenboom	Five Water Colors
	Harpignies	Lake at Briare
	Harpignies	Sunset Pool
	Daubigny	Les Laveuses
	Ziem	French Gardens in Venice
	Diaz	A Pond of Vipers
	Rosenboom	Yellow Roses
	Mauve	Early Morning Ploughing
	Rousseau	Edge of Woods
1897	Diaz	Love's Caresses
	L'Hermite	The Haymakers
	Alma Tadema	Watching
	Millet	The Farmer's Wife A drawing

Frick the Man

DATE OF PURCHASE	ARTIST	TITLE
1897	J. Dupré	*La Rivière
	Linnell	Evening: Hampstead Heath
1898	Romney	*Mary Finch Hatton
	Cazin	The Dipper
	Raffaelli	La Toilette
	Corot	*Ville d'Avray
	Troyon	Landscape
	Swan	Tigers Drinking
	Millet	The Knitting Lesson A drawing
	Cuvillon	Le Lever
	Wm. A. Coffin	A Rainy Day
	Thaulow	Hoar Frost
	Dagnan-Bouveret	Disciples at Emmaus
	Millet	Shepherd Minding Sheep A drawing
1899	Chelminski	Moonlight Drive
	Thaulow	Winter in Norway
	Millet	The Sower A drawing
	Troyon	Road near the Woods
	Chartran	Portrait of P. C. Knox
	Hoppner	*Miss Byng
	Thaulow	The Smoky City
	Friant	Chagrin d'Enfant
	Leroy	Cats the Burglars
	Millet	Puy-de-Dôme A drawing
	Millet	Cow Herder "
	Rembrandt	*A Young Painter
	Nattier	*The Honorable Elizabeth Hamilton
	Dagnan-Bouveret	Head of Christ
	Corot	*L'Etang
	Morland	Horse in Stable
	Troyon	Pâturage en Normandie
	Daubigny	Le Village de Glaton
1900	Vollon	Still Life
1901	Monet	Bords de la Seine
	Turner	*Antwerp: Van Goyen Looking for a Subject
	Dagnan-Bouveret	Consoling the Afflicted

*In the Frick Collection

An Art Collector

DATE OF PURCHASE	ARTIST	TITLE
1901	Jacob Ruisdael	A Waterfall
	Jacob Maris	Amsterdam
	Israels	Mother and Children
	Vermeer	*The Music Lesson
	Wouverman	*Cavalry Camp
	Diaz	La Plaine
	Diaz	Les Baigneuses
	Israels	Near the Cradle
	Jacob Maris	Mussel Gatherers
	Mauve	Hauling Logs
1902	Hobbema	*A Woody Country
	Thomas Lawrence	Marquise de Blaisel
	Rousseau	*Village de Becquigny
	Cuyp	*Herdsman and Cows
	Reynolds	Lady Beaumont
	Reynolds	Sir George Beaumont
1903	Corot	*Le Matin: Lac de Garde
	Romney	*The Honorable Miss Harford
	Gainsborough	*Mrs. Hatchett
	Gerald Terburg	*Portrait of Lady in Black
	Constable	Agitated Sea
1904	Daubigny	*Dieppe
	Murillo	Portrait of the Artist
	Thomas Lawrence	*Lady Peel
	Romney	*Lady Hamilton
	Turner	*Boats Entering Calais Harbor
1905	Raeburn	*Mrs. Cruikshank
	El Greco	*Portrait of a Cardinal
	Van Dyck	*Portrait of Canevari
	Cuyp	*Sunrise on the Maas or Dort
	Metsu	*Lady in Blue Negligé
	Titian	*Pietro Aretino
	Teniers	Family Party
	Solomon Ruysdael	*Landscape
	Vlieger	Sea Shore
1906	Franz Hals	*Portrait of an Artist
	Le Quesne	Settlement of St. Louis

*In the Frick Collection

339

Frick the Man

DATE OF PURCHASE	ARTIST	TITLE
1906	VAN DE CAPELLE	*View of Dort
	MILLET	*La Femme à la Lampe
	COROT	*Le Lac
	REYNOLDS	*Mrs. Harcourt
	REYNOLDS	*Lady Skipworth
	REMBRANDT	*Self Portrait
1907	VAN DYCK	*Marchesa Giovanna Cattaneo
	VAN OSTADE	*Halt at the Inn
	SCHOOL OF AVIGNON	*Pietà
1908	C. HASSAM	The June Idyl
	ROMNEY	*Lady Warwick and Children
	MILLET	La Sortie A drawing
	CONSTABLE	*Salisbury Cathedral
	VELASQUEZ	Marianna of Austria
1909	GAINSBOROUGH	The Honorable Mrs. Watson
	TURNER	*Mortlake Terrace
	EL GRECO	*Purification of Temple
	ZIEM	La Galère
	VAN DYCK	*Mrs. Snyders
	VAN DYCK	*Franz Snyders
	TARBELL	Scene in the Berkshire Hills
	CUYP	*River Scene
1910	BROUWER	Landscape
	REYNOLDS	*Lady Elizabeth Taylor
	REMBRANDT	*Polish Rider
	FRANZ HALS	*Portrait of a Woman
	JACOB RUISDAEL	*The Quay at Amsterdam
	FRANZ HALS	*A Burgomaster
	RUBENS	Italian Prince in Armor
	REMBRANDT	Man in Broad-brimmed Hat and Ruff
	REMBRANDT	Woman in White Cap and Ruff
1911	GOYA	Tirana
	VELASQUEZ	*Philip IV
	VERMEER	*Soldier and Laughing Girl
	HOBBEMA	*Landscape
	RAEBURN	*James Cruikshank
	GAINSBOROUGH	*The Honorable Frances Duncombe

*In the Frick Collection

An Art Collector

DATE OF PURCHASE	ARTIST	TITLE	
1911	ROMNEY	*Lady Milnes	
1912	HOLBEIN	*Sir Thomas More	
	VERONESE	*Wisdom and Strength	
	VERONESE	*Virtue and Vice	
1913	VAN DYCK	*James Stanley, Earl of Derby, his Wife and Child	
	EL GRECO	*Knight of Malta	
	GUARDI	Canal Scene	
	GUARDI	Canal Scene	
	GAINSBOROUGH	*Study of a Lady Seated	A drawing
	GAINSBOROUGH	*Study of a Lady Seated	″
	GAINSBOROUGH	*Landscape	″
	REMBRANDT	*Landscape with Cottage	″
	REMBRANDT	*Houses around Courtyard	″
	REMBRANDT	*Isaac Blessing Jacob	″
1914	VAN DYCK	*Paola Adorno	
	JACOB MARIS	*The Bridge	
	HOGARTH	*The Honorable Mary Edwards	
	GOYA	*Señora Dona Maria Martinez da Puga	
	GOYA	*Count Teba	
	GAINSBOROUGH	*Lady Innes	
	WHISTLER	*Rosa Corder	
	WHISTLER	*Comte de Montesquieu	
	WHISTLER	*The Ocean (Nocturne)	
	TURNER	*Cologne: Arrival of the Packet Boat	
	TURNER	*Dieppe: Moving Day	
1915	GERHARDT DAVID	*Descent from the Cross	
	GIOVANNI BELLINI	*St. Francis in the Desert	
	HOLBEIN	*Sir Thomas Cromwell	
	HOPPNER	*The Misses Bligh	
	RUBENS	*Ambrose Spinola	
	FRAGONARD	*Romance of Love and Youth	
1916	GAINSBOROUGH	*The Mall in St. James Park	
	VAN DER PLUYM	*Old Woman with a Bible	
	WHISTLER	*Lady Meux	
	WHISTLER	*Mrs. Leyland	
	TITIAN	*Man with a Red Cap	

*In the Frick Collection

Frick the Man

DATE OF PURCHASE	ARTIST	TITLE	
1916	Goya	*The Forge	
1917	Franz Hals	*Admiral de Ruyter	
	Van Dyck	*Countess of Clanbrassil	
	Gainsborough	*Mrs. Wm. Peter Baker	
1918	Peter de Hoogh	*Interior with Figures	
	Van Dyck	*Sir John Suckling	
	Boucher	*La Musique	
	Boucher	*Le Dessin	
	Boucher	*Jeune Fille Tenant Fleurs	
	Whistler	*The Ferry, Venice	An etching
	Whistler	*Nocturne, Venice	,,
	Whistler	*La Cimetiere, Venice	,,
	Dürer	*Adam and Eve	,,
	Rembrandt	*The Three Trees	,,
	Rembrandt	*The Goldweigher's Field	,,
	Van Dyck	*Pierre Breughel, Younger	,,
	Van Dyck	*Franz Snyders	,,
	Dürer	*Knight, Death and the Devil	,,
	Dürer	*Coat of Arms with the Scull	,,
	Rembrandt	*Cottage with White Palings	,,
	Rembrandt	*Landscape	,,
	Rembrandt	*Landscape	,,
	Rembrandt	*Clement de Jonghe	,,
	Rembrandt	*St. Francis Beneath a Tree	,,
	Meryon	*Le Pont au Change	,,
	Meryon	*L'Arche du Pont Notre Dame	,,
	Meryon	*Fourteen Etchings	
	Tiepolo	*Perseus and Andromeda	
	Rénoir	*Mother and Children	
	Bellows	Docks in Winter	
	R. Kent	Seiners	
	Gilbert Stuart	*George Washington	
	Lemordant	Sketch	
	Goya	*Portrait of a Man	
	Raeburn	Portrait of a Man	
	Hogarth	Portrait of a Man	
	Hoppner	Princess Sophia	

*In the Frick Collection

An Art Collector

DATE OF PURCHASE	ARTIST	TITLE
1918	JACOB RUISDAEL	Waterfall
	ROMNEY	Mrs. Thomas Raikes and Child
	DIRK HALS	Dutch Interior
	REYNOLDS	Portrait of Lady Cecil Rice
	GAINSBOROUGH	R. B. Sheridan
	GUARDI	Venetian Scene
	PATER	*L'Orchestre du Village
	PATER	*Marche Comique
	BOUCHER	Four Engravings after Boucher
1919	VERMEER	*Reading a Letter

*In the Frick Collection

343

XXIV

Benefactions and Bequests

THAT Princeton University stood first among educational institutions in the estimation of Mr. Frick was made clear to the public when announcement was made that he had bequeathed to it thirty out of a total of one hundred shares in the residue of his estate, but the fact is not generally known that this splendid donation, though the greatest, was but the last of many gifts that had preceded it. His first contributions of $20,500, subsequently increased to $36,314, for the purchase of land for the Colonial Club and $20,000 for the gymnasium were made during the first year of President Woodrow Wilson's administration in 1903.

Others followed chronologically as follows:

1906—To endow a bed in the infirmary, $3,000; 1914—for erection of Freshman and Sophomore dining halls, $10,000; 1915—to deficit and library book fund, $10,000; land for campus $23,500; 1916—sketches for chemical laboratory, $2,200; organ, $46,000; endowment for upkeep of organ, $100,000; land for campus, $92,-000; 1918—additional compensation for organist, $5,000; Princeton Bureau, Paris, for service to men overseas, $1000; 1919—alterations to chemical laboratory, $9,500; total, $358,514.

The University also profited handsomely from Mr. Frick's possession of ready money in 1916. It held in its treasury at that time one thousand shares of the Chase National Bank, whose capital was about to be doubled,

Benefactions and Bequests

affording stockholders an opportunity to subscribe for their respective allotments at par. The privilege was valuable but the University was unable to exercise it, owing to lack of funds and inability to get a bid for its holdings. Even the "insiders" had "enough of the stock," reported Mr. Moses Taylor Pyne, when he sought advice from Mr. Frick, who promptly loaned the University $100,-000 at 4 per cent for such time as might be required to protect its rights, with the result that at the end of six months the treasurer was able to sell three hundred shares for enough to pay off the loan, leaving seven hundred shares free and clear and realizing for the University a net profit of $225,000.

But Mr. Frick's interest in educational advancement was not confined to universities and colleges. It was even keener in common schools. This was but natural. To those humble institutions he was indebted chiefly for such intellectual training as he was able to acquire in his youth, and subsequent experience undoubtedly impressed upon his mind a sense of their deficiencies. It is quite probable, too, that he took pride in his Grandfather Overholt's successful endeavors to raise the system in Pennsylvania to a higher plane. What better service could he render than to supplement the work of his most revered progenitor? That such an aspiration crossed his mind when, in 1909, he directed his attention to the needs of his native community may well be believed. The only question was how to render real service in a practical way, and this he answered from a close study of conditions which convinced him that the first requisite of improvement was

Frick the Man

teaching of the teachers. To carry out his purpose he summoned to Pride's his old friend, John A. Brashear, the humble millwright and idealist who had become famous for his invention of astronomical instruments which had widened the boundaries of science, simply because he "loved the stars," and confided to him his design.

"Briefly," says Mr. Brashear in his naïve Memoirs, "he made me custodian of a fund of $250,000 for the betterment of our grade schools, with especial reference to assisting to improve their methods of teaching. Mr. Frick wished that the name of the donor of the fund remain unknown, and it was so for seven years. With his help and consent I appointed a committee of enthusiastic men to assist in this important work, but I remained the spokesman of the unannounced donor. The Educational Fund Commission contained two judges, two experienced members of local boards of education (now the Board of Public Education of Pittsburgh), and two manufacturing engineers interested in educational work. At the first meeting of the Commission, October 2nd, 1909, I was elected President. We all entered upon our duties with enthusiasm and a deep sense of responsibility which had devolved upon us in such an unexpected and unusual manner."

Seven years later Judge Joseph Buffington, an original member of the Commission, made public the following report:

> The desire of the donor to now make the fund permanent has necessitated the disclosure of his identity; and at a recent confer-

Benefactions and Bequests

ence with him at which he made the fund of $250,000 permanent, he added an annual income of $12,500 for a term of five years, the donor has at our urgent request permitted us to lift the veil of modest retirement which has hitherto characterized this splendid anonymous gift.

There have been, of course, instances here and there of small gifts to the public schools, but this gift is, historically speaking, I believe, the first and only instance of an endowment by an individual, on a large scale, of an American public-school system.

In starting out on this new field the Commission sought the views of the best educators over the country, but after they had been heard from, the Commission finally, as in most cases of responsibility, had to evolve its own plan. In substance that plan was to create, stimulate, and develop the ambition, field, and vision of the two thousand teachers who were moulding the eighty thousand school children of the city. They determined that in the public school the individual teacher was, in the final analysis, the power behind the gun; and if that teacher could be led from the sphere of humdrum routine into an atmosphere of progressive self-improvement, that the child, the schools, and the community would be benefited.

With that specific end in view—the energizing, vitalizing, and inspiring the individual teacher—the Commission turned to the summer schools of pedagogy which were being established in different parts of the country. These schools were beginning to draw to their sessions the most ambitious and progressive teachers, and the Commission determined as an experiment to select about seventy Pittsburgh teachers and send them to these schools with the distinct idea of coupling vocational and vacational work, and enable these teachers to bring back to Pittsburgh the best ideas they could from the best teachers from other American cities who attended these summer schools.

It will thus be seen that the basic feature of the Commission was teaching the child by teaching the teacher, and in doing that to get the best ideas of the best school work of other cities and bring that best to the schools of Pittsburgh . . .

The keynote had been struck, the problem solved. Henceforth it was a mere question of going ahead on the lines mapped. By the time three years had passed, the teachers grasped the idea of the

Frick the Man

need of mobilizing the forces and powers which had been called into being in their summer studies, and the result was the formation of the Phoebe Brashear Club, a tribute to the memory of a good woman who had made much of the life-work of the administrator of this fund possible.

This great club has now, 1917, grown into some seven hundred members. It is the Tenth Legion of the educational forces of Pittsburgh. It is the dynamic force that inspires the whole teaching force of the city and reaches the home of every school child.

"I feel free to say," Mr. Brashear declared, "that the splendid gift of Henry Clay Frick for the betterment of the public schools of Pittsburgh has done more good, more effective work than any endowment ever given for education, be it in college, university, or public schools."

Mr. Frick was so deeply impressed by the progress made as early as 1915 that he bequeathed to the Educational Commission, in addition to the original donation, one-tenth of his entire residuary estate. On May 3rd, 1927, the Superintendent of Schools, Dr. William M. Davidson recounted the results to date in these words:

> Since and before that bequest, Mr. Frick's beneficence has made it possible for the Educational Commission to award free scholarships to more than three thousand teachers connected with the Pittsburgh Public Schools. On these free scholarships teachers have been able to attend summer vacation schools conducted by the leading colleges and universities of the land.
>
> The Commission has not only awarded scholarships to teachers, but it has paid either part or all of their expenses incurred while attending these summer schools. In the year 1927 the Commission awarded 639 scholarships to members of the Pittsburgh Teaching Staff at a total cost to the Commission of $96,000.
>
> The Commission has likewise brought from the fields of Art and Literature some of the most eminent and successful men and women in America to inspire the twenty thousand boys and girls enrolled in the High Schools of the city.

Benefactions and Bequests

The Commission has generously encouraged the routine professional work being carried on with the teachers throughout the school year by making an appropriation to pay for the services of outside school experts who may be brought to the city to assist in the development of such work.

"This gift of Henry Clay Frick," Dr. Davidson concluded, "is unique in the annals of America. I venture to say that no bequest has ever been made to an educational institution in this country that has accomplished so much in a given space of time as has been accomplished by the magnificent bequest of Henry Clay Frick to the uses of the public school teachers of Pittsburgh. Due to this beneficence this city is today among the foremost cities of America and of the world in all matters pertaining to the professional growth and the professional improvement of its teachers."

The old observatory of the Western University had become useless in 1894 and Mr. Brashear was made Chairman of a committee to raise funds for construction of a new one. At the expiration of four years enough money had been subscribed to prepare plans and lay a corner stone but that was about all. Seven additional years rolled by and the undertaking was still lagging in the Spring of 1905 when, one evening while visiting Pittsburgh, Mr. Frick invited his old friend to dinner.

"Brashear," he asked, "how is the observatory coming on?"

The depressed scientist shook his head. Mr. William Thaw had contributed handsomely, but a second standstill had been reached.

"Well," rejoined Mr. Frick, "go and find out what it

Frick the Man

will cost to finish and equip it and if you can raise half of the amount by October 15th, I will pay the other half."

So the beautiful observatory was completed and in the crypt was placed a tablet in memory of the two best-beloved of all residents of Pittsburgh, before or since:

> PHOEBE · S · BRASHEAR
> 1843–1910
> We have loved the stars too fondly
> To be fearful of the night.
>
> JOHN · A · BRASHEAR
> 1840–1920

Responding in 1900 to a request for a contribution to a fund for the construction of a library for the College of Wooster in Ohio, the home of his parents, Mr. Frick decided to bear the entire cost of the building, but declined to have it called the "Frick Library," although finally he consented to the placing of a tablet reciting that it was erected in memory of his parents.

No records of his many miscellaneous gifts, prior to 1914, can be found, but a partial list of contributions for educational and humanitarian purposes, exclusive of those mentioned elsewhere, comprises the following:

EDUCATIONAL:—Harvard University; American Academy in Rome; Pennsylvania College for Women; General Education; Beverly High School; Pittsburgh Civic Commission; Metropolitan Museum of Arts; Boston Museum; Young Women's Association.

HUMANITARIAN:—Pittsburgh Newsboys' Home; Home for the Friendless; Home for Crippled Children; Beverly Hospital; Asso-

Benefactions and Bequests

ciation for Improving Condition of the Poor; Children's Aid Society; Pittsburgh Tuberculosis Hospital; Homestead Hospital; Gloucester Fishermen; Beverly Playgrounds; Seamen's Church; New York Dispensary and Hospital; Association for the Blind; Homestead Park; Kingsley House Association; Lakeside Hospital, Cleveland; Children's Hospital; Mercy Hospital; Presbyterian Aged Women's Home; Home for Incurables; Eye, Ear, and Throat Hospital; Public Baths, Pittsburgh; Martinique Sufferers; Allegheny General Hospital; Actors' Hospital; Soho Bath House; Russian Jews; San Francisco Sufferers; San Bois Coal Mine Sufferers; Infants' Hospital, and Mt. Pleasant Park.

The year 1914 brought a contribution for the Salem sufferers followed by donations of various sums to the Lying-In-Hospital, the Women's Service League, the Horticulture Society, the New York Militia, the Masonic Homes, the Memorial to Mrs. Schenley, the Railroad Fund, the New York Police Relief Fund, the New York Charity Organization, the Museum of Natural History, Dorchester House Hospital, for the Unemployed of Pittsburgh and New York, the Valley Forge Memorial, the Roanoke Auditorium, the American School in Rome, the Scottdale Temperance Campaign, the Actors Fund and many others, notably for anything helpful to children,— Boy Scouts, Girls' Camp Outings, Home for Deficient Children and nurseries. Nearly all of such gifts were made anonymously and frequently in cash to avoid publicity. Probably no man ever gave more freely and constantly or strove more earnestly to prevent his left hand from knowing what his right hand was doing.

Mr. Frick's final disposition of his great accumulations was made in 1915, in a Will pronounced by Lewis Cass Ledyard, Esq., leader of the American Bar, the most ad-

Frick the Man

mirable and the easiest to put into form of the many involving large bequests he had drawn.

"Mr. Frick," he once said, "not only knew precisely what he wanted to do but precisely how he wanted to do it. His own detailed conception called for no more than certain legal phrasing to become as nearly perfect as any testament I have ever read."

After allotting about one-sixth of his estate to members of his family, he made the following public bequests:

To THE FRICK COLLECTION (Incorporated):—Real estate bounded by Fifth Avenue, Seventieth Street, Madison Avenue and Seventy-first Street, dwelling house thereon with contents thereof, comprising paintings and other works of art, furnishings and organ, subject to occupancy by Mrs. Frick during her lifetime, "for the purpose of establishing and maintaining a gallery of art in and at the said house and premises above described, and encouraging and developing the study of the fine arts, and of advancing the general knowledge of kindred subjects; such gallery of art to be for the use and benefit of all persons whomsoever, to the end that the same shall be a public gallery of art to which the entire public shall forever have access, subject only to reasonable regulations to be from time to time established by the said corporation."

To THE TRUSTEES OF THE FRICK COLLECTION (Mrs. Frick, Miss Frick, Mr. Childs Frick and Messrs. George F. Baker, Jr., J. Horace Harding, Walker D. Hines, Lewis Cass Ledyard, John D. Rockefeller, Jr., and Horace Havemeyer and their successors)—$15,000,000 in trust to collect the income therefrom and use the same for maintenance of, and additions to, the said Collection.

"SECTION 6. I am conscious that, in asking their acceptance of these trusts for carrying out my wishes for the formation and organization of THE FRICK COLLECTION, I am imposing upon these gentlemen a duty which may prove very burdensome, and my only justification for asking this advice at their hands is found in my belief that they will undertake it because it is a public service.

"SECTION 7. It is my desire and purpose through the provisions of this Article of my will to found an institution which shall be

Benefactions and Bequests

permanent in character and which shall encourage and develop the study of the fine arts and which shall promote the general knowledge of kindred subjects among the public at large.

"The devise and gifts made by this Article to the said corporation herein directed to be formed and to be known as THE FRICK COLLECTION are subject only to the condition that the said gallery of art shall at all times subsequent to the termination of the estate in my said dwelling house devised to my wife in and by the first section of this Article of my will, be maintained under the name which I have directed to be given to said corporation, and in and upon the premises mentioned in this Article, and it is my will that such of my paintings and other works of art as are herein bequeathed to it shall at all times be there preserved and maintained."

TO THE CITY OF PITTSBURGH—One hundred and fifty-one acres of land (described) as a public park, free to the people, and in trust the income of $2,000,000 for its maintenance.

The public institutions which shared in the residuary estate were the following:

Educational Fund Commission, Children's Hospital, Allegheny General Hospital, Home for the Friendless, Kingsley House Association, Mercy Hospital, Pittsburgh Free Dispensary, Pittsburgh Newsboys Home, Western Pennsylvania Hospital, Central Young Women's Christian Association, Uniontown Hospital, Cottage State Hospital, Westmoreland Hospital, Mount Pleasant Memorial Hospital, Braddock General Hospital, Homestead Hospital, Trustees of Princeton University, President and Fellows of Harvard College, Massachusetts Institute of Technology, and the Society of the Lying-In-Hospital of the City of New York.

Although circumstances required Mr. Frick to reside elsewhere much of the time, he retained his citizenship of Pittsburgh and never lost interest in the community which had contributed much to, and had profited no less from, his success. Not even his splendid donations to educative and humanitarian services will live longer in the grateful recollection of his former neighbors than a relatively trifling but very fine act done by him in 1915,

Frick the Man

when the Pittsburgh Bank for Savings closed its doors and he promptly telegraphed to his bank to advance hundreds of thousands of dollars to pay depositors in full, "so that the children shall not be deprived of their Christmas funds."

"He was always on the look-out for a chance to help anyone in distress without being detected," writes his private secretary as of that time, who still recalls a few of innumerable instances in these words:

To go back to the days of horse cars: One day, in coming to the city, he found himself without the necessary carfare and accepted the loan of a nickel proffered by a workingman who was sitting beside him, asking him to stop in the office, and when he came, he received a five dollar bill, not by way of charity, but as an expression of appreciation. Perhaps in referring to this side of Mr. Frick's nature, I should have first mentioned the long list of persons to whom he sent monthly checks in such a way as not to make them feel they were under any obligations to him for the money.

Another thing that impressed me was his sympathy for the sick and afflicted.

In coming from the club one day, he saw the Mercy Hospital ambulance pulling off the tracks, with iron tires on the wheels. When he reached the office, he immediately asked his bookkeeper to telephone the hospital to have rubber tires substituted, and send the bill to him, which was done.

Another time, in walking along the street, he found a poor family being forced from their home, and their belongings piled on the sidewalk. Upon making inquiry into the cause of the trouble, he learned that their rent had not been paid. A check for the amount was promptly sent to the landlord, and the furniture was replaced in the house, which continued to be a home.

A blind man, living in McKeesport, wrote Mr. Frick about a broom machine (giving him the name of the manufacturer) the possession of which would enable him to make a comfortable living. Mr. Frick, finding the man was what he represented himself to be, took the greatest pains to look into the merits of the machine

Benefactions and Bequests

and receiving a satisfactory report, he had one sent to this man and later had a most satisfactory letter from him, telling how he was providing for his family,—not charity, but a chance.

At a time before the Salvation Army came into its own, and when it was not receiving much sympathy and financial support, one of its workers came into the office for a contribution which was not only cheerfully given, but the amount of the check was so large as to almost stagger the recipient. Mr. Frick always appreciated the work done by the Salvation Army.

Two elderly women, who would have spurned the idea of charity, but who were obliged to make a living, appealed to him to take some of their fancy work, which was the only thing they were able to do. This he did, paying a good price for something for which he had no use, as it was not suitable for his own home, and at times was put to it to know what to do with it as he soon found he had become a regular customer, but he never failed to make a purchase.

I regret not being able to recall more of the kind and generous acts of Mr. Frick, for they were many, but what always impressed me most was the spirit in which everything was given.

Proud of his thriving city, Mr. Frick could always be counted upon to aid any movement to make it appear as prosperous as it really was. The William Penn hotel was built largely with his money, but his most impressive contribution to the material splendor of Pittsburgh was the great "FRICK BUILDING" and the "Union Arcade," two of the most striking and artistic structures of their kind in the world. The site which he deemed most suitable for the building bearing his name was occupied by the big St. Peter's Episcopal church, but by paying a handsome sum for the land and moving the edifice, stone by stone, and re-erecting it in a superior location, he accomplished his purpose, as someone remarked at the time, "to the glory of God and the satisfaction of all concerned."

XXV

Personality

Mr. Frick's most splendid inheritance from a long line of outdoor-bred ancestors was an exceptionally rugged constitution and, when he had mastered for the time the congenital infirmities of his youth, he grew to be a powerful man physically. His shoulders were broad for his medium height, his chest was very deep and the lines of his torso were hardly less classical than those drawn of Hercules by a student of the master Lycippus in the famous marble statue in the Vatican. But one may well doubt that the great god matched him in nimbleness of movement; he was quick as lightning.

The physical attractiveness of his boyhood ripened into a highly distinguished appearance in his later years, never failing, greatly to his annoyance, to draw the attention of onlookers when he passed along a street or through a railway station. Not that he was shy; he was fully composed under all conditions; he was simply, innately, modest. But his squarely moulded head and finely chiseled features, illumed by a pair of twinkling, though scrutinizing eyes, combined to make of him a notably handsome man. And he always dressed the part, usually in dark blue cloth with a hairline stripe and without a suspicion of jewelry showing.

Personality

His voice was low, soft and melodious and was never raised. Whatever annoyance or resentment he ever felt appeared in the expression of those eyes, which could become "very steely" very quickly. Invariably courteous to a degree, his minor manners were, as the discerning and somewhat critical Professor Sargent of Harvard remarked once upon a time, "literally exquisite, without a trace of affectation"; that is to say, in familiar proverbial phrase, he was, beyond compare—

"*suaviter in modo, fortiter in re.*"

His habits were methodical, punctuated by frequent manifestations of impatience at unnecessary interruption of routine; and he was never idle for a moment, nor even still except at such times as when, having finished the morning's dictation, he would thrust his hands into his trousers' pockets, lean far back in his chair, half close his eyes and engage in the silent meditation allotted for the day; only to flash into action at its close in putting the determination reached summarily into effect. Even while holding this favorite posture of apparent repose, he personified power—under restraint.

Paradoxically, his notably quick mind did not respond readily to wit; he hardly ever laughed; his real delight lay in humor, the subtler the better, which never failed to elicit that "slow, understanding smile," for which the equally reticent General Grant became noted, and was beloved by his friends.

The two men were much alike.

When finally the opportunity came to heed rare Ben Jonson's advice to "Recreate yourself; go, sport!" Mr.

Frick the Man

Frick experienced much difficulty in learning how to play. Asked once upon a time what was the secret of his success, he replied sententiously:

"Work and sleep. My alarm clock is always set eight hours ahead of the time I go to bed and I have trained both body and mind to relax. But hard work is the thing. During my first six years with the Steel company I reached my office every weekday morning between seven and eight and never left till six. I walked enough to keep fit and became actually robust. In fact, if I hadn't been pretty husky when assaulted I probably shouldn't have got off as well as I did. Carnegie often remarked to me, 'You certainly do get work out of those fellows.' I did, too. It was the force of example. When they saw what their Chairman was doing they all followed suit gladly and enthusiastically. So we got on very well."

"Follow suit," a term used in playing certain games at cards, was familiar to him. Beginning with dominoes when a boy, he stepped up to Authors when at school, then to high-low-jack, euchre, penny ante and finally short whist from which, following the trend of the time, he passed on to Bridge and Auction, which became and remained his favorite indoor sport, although when "a fourth" was not available he seemed quite content with Solitaire, which he would play by the hour.

The necessity of obtaining outdoor exercise when he dropped desk work in New York presented a problem. Coming from inland, he first tried yachting and liked it so well that he had plans drawn for a novel creation of his own designing but, before beginning to build, his

Personality

restless spirit revolted at enforced confinement, and boredom did the rest.

His real hobby was speed, terrific speed, which came as a reaction from years of patient drudgery and as a revival of the impatience of an inherently eager disposition. Motoring he found delightfully exhilarating unless hampered by road regulations, to which ultimately, after securing the most expertly daring chauffeur to be found in France, he paid little heed. Nevertheless, with the multiplication of cars, came more and more "jams" and greater necessity for hateful "crawling along" until finally automobiling, as a pastime, was perforce abandoned.

Paradoxically, the need was supplied by the outdoor sport which calls for more pensive deliberation than any other ever devised. Golf held no appeal whatever to Mr. Frick; it was "too slow" and must be "very tedious" and seemed, in Mr. Roosevelt's phrase, rather "namby pamby for live men"; but he had always walked for exercise, and one afternoon, following luncheon at a club, he was tempted to follow a match, chiefly from a sense of duty. Like many another, amused at first, presently he became sufficiently interested to "try a shot," with the result that invariably attends a successful effort. He tried another and a third, which he missed entirely, but he persisted doggedly until, with his fifth stroke he luckily dropped a long putt and won the hole.

That settled it. From the moment the ball struck the tin, he was a golfer, and his interest never after flagged. A very few lessons sufficed. He watched others closely, developed his own methods, practiced assiduously and

Frick the Man

became a very fair player, especially in foursomes, which he preferred for their wider opportunities in both competition and betting. He was always eager to play, rain or shine, would accept or give any odds proposed and was never satisfied without "double or quits" on the last hole. Wherever he played, he "joined the Club" and at the last was "at home," on five links about New York, three near Pittsburgh, two adjacent to Pride's, at Sunningdale, England, and La Boulie and St. Cloud in France.

His play was characterized by the same concentration that he applied to business, hardly exceeded by a Travis, and in quickness of stroke he was like a Duncan, although by stern determination he finally schooled himself to a certain deliberateness on the greens. Elsewhere, do his best, he could not overcome the urge of his temperament; he fairly raced around a course, uphill and downdale, particularly at his favorite Myopia, where he enjoyed special privileges, and where all stood aside when the good-natured warning was passed forward, "Look out, Mr. Frick's coming!" But he never broke a rule, flouted "etiquette" or failed in courtesy. His indignation could be aroused only by a suspicion that his antagonist was "letting up" on him. Once he hinted as much, only to hear the grave response:

"I am playing badly today, I know, but I don't let up; I never did."

"Neither do I," he rejoined quickly, "and I don't like others to do so. It was my mistake. I am sure you didn't. I'm sorry I spoke,"—and stepping across the tee, he held out his hand.

Personality

Writing to Mr. Frick from Murray Bay in 1914, to thank him on behalf of the trustees for a "generous gift" to Hampton Institute, ex-President Taft added slyly:

> I hope that Myopia Links still give you the pleasure you used to derive from them when I was at Beverly. These links at Murray Bay are by no means so difficult as you may judge from the fact that I have been around once in 82 and once in 83. But I get much enjoyment out of them nevertheless.

Mr. Frick read that portion of the note aloud at luncheon.

"Eighty-two and eighty-three!" Pretty good, I should say. And I used to wonder why I couldn't beat him. I ought to. I am eight years older than he is. I wonder if he would have mentioned the scores if they had been a hundred and two and a hundred and three. I guess he would. There's nothing small about Taft. I must get a game with Mr. Rockefeller. He is ten years older than I am and I may have a chance."

And he got his game some time later,—at the same country place at Pocantico where he had induced Mr. Rockefeller to sell his ore properties to the Steel Corporation in 1901. Asked when he returned how the match came out, he replied:

"Oh, Mr. Rockefeller was most polite; he always is. He said he felt sure I wasn't quite 'on my game' today, and asked if he was not right?"

"And what did you say?"

"I said 'Yes' and added 'I never was.' That brought a good laugh but he was not to be outdone.

"'Oh, Mr. Frick,' he said, 'I shouldn't say that, at least of any other game I have ever known you to play.'

Frick the Man

"So we were both pleased and satisfied, even though he did pull a funny little alphabetical game on me, played on the table after luncheon, that I couldn't make head nor tail of."

The outbreak of war, involving cessation of his annual trips abroad, prolonged Mr. Frick's stays at Pride's and multiplied his opportunities to engage in his favorite pastime.

"Golf in the morning," was frequently recorded as many as six times a week in his daily memoranda, which also were enlivened by specific entries indicating his boyish zestfulness, such as, for example:

> Played with Helen at Tombstone Tournament with Miss Eleanor Sears and Harold Vanderbilt and came in third best.
> Played eighteen holes with Helen against Bryce Allan and Miss Holmes and won, four up.
> Played Mr. Parker and was beaten.
> Played Charles Winslow even and won two up and one to play.
> Played Judge Moore six up and five to play. Went out in 49. Bogie beat me coming in.

So pages were filled in Summer and, less profusely, in Winter year in and year out, from Dixville Notch to Palm Beach, with "Auction in the afternoon" a frequent accompaniment.

And yet beginning with 1914, the first Winter in his new mansion at No. 1 East 70th Street, to which he had transferred his office from downtown, the number of calls received was amazing,—marked, however, more by frequency than by diversity, as he had few close friends.

He loved to give small luncheons, with attractive women included, and large dinners to "interesting" men

Personality

rather than exclusively to business associates. An admirable host, he attended to every detail, arranging the placing of guests and personally distributing their cards to avert possibility of error.

Always in his box if he liked the opera and never if he did not care for it, he was almost equally fond of amusing plays and hardly ever missed one that had been recommended by a person of like taste. A few of his favorite organ selections were "Largo," "The Pilgrims' Chorus," "William Tell," "The Rosary" and Gounod's "Ave Maria."

Odd items appear in the memoranda, jotted usually by his secretary but occasionally by his daughter:

At Sherry's (in 1912) Mr. Grier bet (me?) $50,000 to $400 that if Roosevelt gets both Republican and Progressive nominations, he will be elected.

In Pittsburgh (1916) attended Chamber of Commerce dinner, met Senator Warren Harding of Ohio; he looks like fine Presidential timber.

Movies taken of Mr. F. playing cards. Very lifelike.

Had ten young farmers from Montana on their way to the war at Thanksgiving Dinner. Splendid chaps.

Hereafter when I purchase anything from (naming a certain picture dealer) it will be entered in this diary on the day I buy it. If no memo is entered it is understood that everything left is on approval.

Dr. Pritchett lunched with others and showed up Wilson's character. Mr. F. drew out others but did not express opinion.

Stopped at Baltimore and saw the Walters Collection.

Will Hays called. Contribution.

Mr. F. left Pride's for New York with Mr. Grier. He had refused to take an overcoat but found one in the car and threw it out of the window to tease his daughter.

Although a "great reader" in his youth, Mr. Frick seldom opened a modern novel in his late years, but took

Frick the Man

pleasure from such books as the "Sayings of Marcus Aurelius," the "Memoirs of Cellini," the "Autobiography of Benjamin Franklin," biographies and quotations which he made freely from the Bible and Shakespeare, much to the edification of his surprised hearers, but when he happened upon a volume typified by William George Jordan's "Self Control: Its Kinship and Majesty," he would buy many copies and send them to his friends.

He had all of the daily newspapers brought to him but only glanced through them, noting the conspicuous headlines and the topics of editorials, but paying scant attention to financial pages whose information he regarded as based upon gossip and untrustworthy. But two widely diverse public journals he was never without: Mr. Barron's NEWS BUREAU, containing market reports, and oddly the NEW YORK WORLD, his most savage critic during the Homestead struggle and continuously an advocate of distasteful public policies, "in order," he remarked, "to get the other side." He was greatly annoyed once by the appearance of a cartoon in the PITTSBURGH LEADER portraying himself.

"This won't do," he ejaculated, "this won't do at all; go find who owns this paper and buy it."

But realizing quickly that he had spoken impulsively, he was relieved when the secretary returned and reported that Mr. William Flinn, the Republican leader, whose feelings also had been hurt, was arranging to purchase the paper.

"That's much better," he said, "let Flinn do the worrying, it is no business for me to get into anyway."

Personality

And this reflection fixed his policy. Replying to a suggestion from President Ripley of the Atchison railway in 1916, he wrote:

> I carefully note your valued favor of the 25th. I have made it a rule never to make an investment in a newspaper. It is a great detriment to the newspaper itself to have a man who is supposed to be worth considerable money to have an interest in it.

But he proved himself to be a competent editor at that. Abhorring notoriety, he never gave interviews for publication, but once while in Pittsburgh he broke his rule and spoke freely to a reporter, with the understanding that he should have the privilege of editing the copy. The reporter wrote painstakingly a full column and sent it to his office. Presently it came back, without a word of comment, reduced to exactly ten lines.

At another time, when the stock market was distinctly bearish and Mr. Frick was conferring with the equally uncommunicative Mr. James Stillman in the National City Bank, a financial writer whom both respected persisted in seeking their opinion of the situation and, after waiting an hour, he received this card:

> The U. S. A. is a great and growing country.
> (Signed) JAMES STILLMAN
> HENRY C. FRICK
> This is confidential and not for publication unless names are omitted.

He wrote but two letters in his whole life for publication. One was addressed to the representative of Mayor Hylan, who had asked him to serve on a committee appointed to erect in France a monument in memory of the soldiers from New York City who had served in the war.

Frick the Man

Mr. Frick felt that he would do himself injustice if he should decline such a request without presenting his reasons for doing so, and these he set forth with such clarity and restraint in a communication, which not only breathed his intense nationalism but outlined his broad conception of America's "one great compensation" for its sacrifices and voiced his earnest hope for great good to come out of it for his country, that a better illustration of his soundness of thought could hardly be found.

From a sense of duty, hoping that his views might bear some influence in the direction which he considered both right and patriotic, he sent his letter to the TRIBUNE, which published it as follows:

New York, Dec. 5, 1918.

My dear Mr. Whalen:

I beg that you will express to His Honor the Mayor my sincere appreciation of his courtesy in asking me to serve as a member of the committee to superintend the erection of a monument on a battlefield of France to commemorate the valorous deeds of the soldiers from New York City. I need hardly say that I am in full accord and sympathy with the admirable impulse which actuates His Honor in this matter, and it is for that reason I wish you to assure him that most reluctantly I feel obliged to decline the commission which he has so graciously proffered me.

There occur to my mind two general objections, not, of course, to the laudable spirit of the undertaking, but to the carrying out of the project itself. The first is one of practicability. An example such as this, set by the foremost municipality of the Union, would be followed inevitably by hundreds of other cities and towns. It is altogether probable, moreover, that the citizens of Great Britain and her colonies, Italy and Portugal, would take similar action in recognition of their brave sons who no less splendidly fought and died in the great common cause.

Might not such happenings, arising from the requests from thousands of segregated communities for suitable sites, prove a

Personality

source of infinite embarrassment to the authorities of France, who naturally would be desirous of pleasing all and treating all alike? Then, too, in our own country, would not the natural rivalry between towns as to which should furnish the best monument and obtain the best site be likely to engender bitterness unbecoming a great nation which put forth its best efforts as a unified force? And would it be fair to smaller and poorer communities, which may have suffered greater sacrifices proportionately, to overshadow their modest shafts with great monuments such as opulent cities like New York, Chicago, Philadelphia and Pittsburgh would surely erect?

All of our soldiers in this great war fought, as I understand it, as a national army for their common country. New York fought for Wyoming and Wyoming for New York; Texas for Wisconsin and Wisconsin for Texas—one for all and all for one—a mighty Union, solid as a rock in defence of national freedom. Ought we who remained at home, even in praiseworthy endeavor to prove our undying gratitude, do anything that might tend in history to apportion the credit between even states, to say nothing of innumerable towns and villages?

I cannot think so. Indeed, I do not hesitate to say that, grateful as I am to the brave men from New York or from my home city, Pittsburgh, I am no less, and perhaps ought to be more, grateful to those equally courageous who went from far-off Kansas and Utah to safeguard the lives and properties of those of us who live on the seaboard.

My second point in what I am confident His Honor will accept as a most friendly remonstrance is this: The one great compensation of this war for America has been the unifying of our country at the very moment when we were drifting dangerously apart, both racially and sectionally, and segregating ourselves unconsciously into classes. The common peril brought us together, until now I, for one, really feel that we are more nearly 'one and inseparable' than ever before.

Let us hold to that, and, above all, do nothing that might by any possibility revive the prejudices which formerly prevailed to no small degree against the people of this imperial city, who now, all must admit, have proved their patriotism.

I most heartily approve a movement to commemorate upon the battlefields of France the splendid deeds of the splendid sons of

Frick the Man

America, and I am only too glad to accord to Mayor Hylan the highest credit for having originated the thought, but my conviction is so strong that it should be a national movement for our own sake, and conducted through a national agency in consideration of both France and our other allies, that I find myself unable to accept the honor conferred upon me.

Again begging you to extend to His Honor assurances of my deep appreciation, and with hearty good wishes, I remain, my dear Mr. Whan, faithfully yours,

H. C. Frick.

The effect of this communication, couched in terms, characteristic of the writer, so gracious that the Mayor could by no possibility take offense, was instantaneous. Many who had received like invitations politely declined, several who had already assented withdrew their acceptances and the project was abandoned, to the great elation of Mr. Frick who, while disclaiming more than a modest part of credit for the result, exclaimed gleefully, "Now doesn't that just show that, if I had been thoroughly educated, I might have accomplished something with my pen?"

It was this sense of regret, almost of resentment, of which, in common with most men in like circumstances, he was conscious,—unduly so, because in his early years he had trained his mind for all practical purposes so thoroughly that his letters reveal exceptional proficiency in clear, concise and well-defined expression. Nevertheless there can be no doubt that the educational advantages conferred by his bounty upon thousands of boys, girls and young teachers was attributable in large measure to cognizance of his own early handicap.

Personality

"Don't tell the little girls fairy tales, teach them real things," was a constant admonition.

His well-considered judgment of relative values of methods appeared in the following striking response to a query from Princeton:

New York. February 19th, 1916.

The Daily Princetonian,
Princeton, N. J.
Gentlemen:

In reply to your Mr. Robert Cresswell's letter of the 10th inst., as to my opinion on "whether a man is benefited or handicapped for a business career by a college education," I would say that it depends largely upon the man. Some men are spoiled by college; others pass through college with gain. Whether, in the latter case, the gain outweighs that which they might have obtained by spending the same time and effort in business is an open question; my opinion again is that it depends upon the man.

Looking at the matter broadly, it seems to me that the chief gain of a college education, is not the education itself, but the friendships made. On the other hand, to weak natures, this is its greatest danger, and in individual cases explains the prejudice which you concede exists against colleges.

The fact that the college system is being called into question is an indication of some inherent weakness in it; and I have long felt myself in agreement with William George Jordan, the author of Mental Training, a Remedy for Education, who, in this and other writings, holds that the weakness of our whole system of education, including that given in colleges, is that it is based on information, not inspiration. He claims that it stuffs the mind with undigested facts, but does not develop power. And it is beyond question that our schools and colleges rarely produce men with minds trained, clear, efficient, with power to concentrate, ready on the instant to be applied to any problem.

What our colleges give, few men either remember or use in business or in life; it is, as Jordan says, constant mental feeding without developing the basic mental powers all men need in their daily living. They need trained senses, keen observation, clear thinking,

Frick the Man

rapid reasoning, active, alert memories, trained imagination, expression in language, mental efficiency of every phase, so that the mind is as ready as the hand for every motion of which it is capable. In business life men gain these powers somewhat and somehow, and the measure of their attainment is the measure of their individual success.

If Jordan is right, no school, or college has for its ideal the direct practical development of these mental powers, as physical exercises develop the muscles of the body. If the schools and colleges did give this, as they should, and as, in the future, under some better system, they will, the world would be transformed.

Yours very truly,
H. C. Frick.

Many offers to confer upon him an honorary degree came to Mr. Frick from universities and colleges but he declined invariably upon the ground that he did not feel that he had done anything to justify acceptance of the honor. He recognized the propriety, however, of being chosen a Fellow in Perpetuity of the Metropolitan Museum of Art and greatly appreciated a unanimous tender of a Life Trusteeship of Princeton in response to the plea that his business experience would be of value to the university, but he took care to seek confirmation of the Board's stated reason by writing to President Hibben:

> Will you kindly send me a complete financial statement of Princeton University, as I think I should become aware of its financial condition before I qualify as Trustee.

At the time of his death Mr. Frick held life membership in sixty-seven clubs and associations, with those prefixed "National" and "American" predominating. As early as 1872 he joined the King Solomon Lodge of Free and Accepted Masons of Connellsville and won the

Personality

prescribed Scottish Rite and Commandery degrees before 1880, when he became a life member of the Order of the Knights of the Red Cross, of the Knights Templars and of the Knights of Malta.

Although he became a communicant of the Baptist Church at the age of eighteen, he was never a strict sectarian, later in life attending the Protestant Episcopal Church, whose form of service appealed more strongly to his sense of dignity, harmony and beauty, and contributing generously to the support of both, as well as to the Lutheran Church of his parents. He was devout rather than pious—apparently agreeing with Southwell that—

> Bare communion with a good church can never make a good man; if it could, we should have had no bad ones.

Hence his gifts to the two undenominational Young Men's and Young Women's Christian Associations and uncounted sums to the Salvation Army.

Mr. Frick's deep tenderness for children was revealed constantly in his daily life. His attitude towards them was more than kind, more than affectionate; it was, in the words of a gentle lady who had been watching the expression of his eyes and the lightness of his touch when at rest with his grandchildren, "positively reverential."

Not that he was averse to play! Far from it! He was always ready for a frolic and never hesitated, upon call, to "leap frog" or even to swish down the sliding board and land, amid gales of delight, with "an awful bump." But when all had tired and clambered upon his knees and snuggled close to his breast, there was something

Frick the Man

akin to awe in his loving observance of their tousled heads, and he would sit moveless so long as they could keep their eyes closed in pretense of sleep.

This arousal of the unsuspected emotional side of his nature undoubtedly sprang from the first grievous tragedy that entered his life. He could never wholly appease the intense sorrow which nearly overwhelmed him at the passing of his little daughter Martha at the age of six in 1891. Asked timidly twenty years later if the report published at the time that her apparently living image dazzled his vision while he lay in his office dazed by the anarchist's assault upon him, was true, he simply nodded affirmatively and bowed his head, and unfailingly, on the morning of August 5th of each year thereafter, he remarked quietly to his family, "If Martha had lived, she would have been (so many) years old today." And when he paid in advance the full amount of the deposits of thousands of children in the bankrupt savings bank in Pittsburgh, an engraved portrait of Martha appeared upon every check.

That his firstborn girl baby held to the end first place in the shrine of his heart there can be no question, but ample room was left for those who followed and to them also, notably his grandchildren, Adelaide, Martha and Frances, he was passionately devoted. And when word came on October 18th, 1919, that Henry Clay Frick, 2nd, was born, he lost not a minute in writing and dispatching to the mother this pretty and gleeful letter:

Personality

Saturday 6 P.M.
Oct. 18th, 1919
One East Seventieth Street

Well done, Dear Frances!

Heartiest congratulations! You have your wish, and I have mine, for now that the youngster has come and proved a boy, I will confess that I, too, am especially gratified and pleased. Not that a granddaughter would not have been welcomed as heartily as before—for we should have felt that you were multiplying our happiness by four instead of three—but as Burns says "A man's a man for a' that!" and a mother of three girls is justified in her wish for a son.

I send a cordial welcome to the boy, who has thus early shown great discrimination in the selection of his parents—to say nothing of his grand parents.

Best wishes for your early convalescence.

Affectionately
Your Devoted
Father

The next day but one, before going to inspect the new arrival, he remarked to his wife, according to the Diary:

You were saying how pretty the baby is; I want to know if he has a good head? Does he have it all back of his ears or is it above his ears? She replied: "When I come to think of it, his head is just like yours"! He laughed and, upon returning from the hospital, assured Mrs. F. that she hadn't said a word too much about the baby, that he was a fine little chap and really had "a splendid head."

Returning from a business meeting in Pittsburgh, where he told an inquisitive reporter that the only "new business enterprise" he had on hand, or should undertake, was on Long Island, and on November 2nd he brought the four children together in their home, promising to pay another visit in a few days. But on the 4th, following a luncheon which he gave in honor of Senator James A. Reed, the Missouri "Irreconcilable," he became ill

Frick the Man

of ptomaine poisoning and a cold, which brought on an attack of his lifelong malady, inflammatory rheumatism threatening his heart, and on the 7th, after participating in his last meeting of the Steel Company's directors in his house, he was put to bed, where he remained until the 19th, when he was permitted to come downstairs and "sit with my pictures."

This proved to be a fatal error. His pledge to visit his grandson was uppermost in his mind and he determined to keep it, regardless of the stern injunction of his physician that under no circumstances, should he leave the house.

On the next day but one he ordered his car to go to Long Island. The horrified nurse quickly informed his wife and daughter and the three united in pleading endeavor to dissuade him from undertaking the trip, but he would not listen. Off he started, followed furtively by his distracted daughter and nurse. The trip required an hour or more but he reached his son's house in happy mood and good condition, remained for half an hour petting and playing with his grandchildren, and returned home proud and satisfied.

But complete exhaustion soon followed and an urgent summons quickly brought the doctor, who prescribed restoratives but notified the family upon leaving that he would no longer attend a patient who had disobeyed his orders. Another physician was called in but he could not gain the confidence of the sick man, and wife and daughter renewed their fervid appeals to his predecessor to resume charge of the case, but in vain.

Personality

Mr. Frick showed signs of a gradual though slight improvement during the succeeding eleven days and gave no cause for apprehension when, at five o'clock on the morning of December 2nd, as had frequently happened in the night, he summoned his nurse and said quietly:

"Please give me a glass of water."

The response was prompt and, taking and holding the glass without effort, Mr. Frick drank the water and, thanking the nurse, resumed an easy position and said:

"That will be all; now I think I'll go to sleep."

A few moments later, the nurse tiptoed into the room and, hearing no sound, stepped noiselessly to the bedside and looked down upon a pallid but wholly tranquil countenance. Thus quietly and peacefully the spirit of Henry Clay Frick passed into the haven of intrepid souls.

Index

ABBOTT, WILLIAM L., 103, 106-8, 253-4.
ALDRICH, SEN. NELSON W., 294-8.
ALEXANDER, JAMES W., 278-80.
ALLIES' Bazar, 316.
AMALGAMATED ASSOCIATION OF IRON & STEEL WORKERS, 106, 108-29, 133-4, 140, 148-54, 164, 172, 177.
AMERICAN AMBULANCE HOSPITAL IN FRANCE, 315.
AMERICAN FEDERATION OF LABOR, 176.
AMERICAN REVOLUTION, 5.
ANCESTRY, 1-11.
ARBUCKLE, MR., 180.
ARMORED MOTOR SQUADRON, 315.
ARNOLD, BENEDICT, 3
ART COLLECTOR, H. C. Frick as an, 331-43.
ATCHISON, TOPEKA & SANTA FÉ, 277, 281, 365.
ATTEMPTED ASSASSINATION, 136-45.
ATWOOD, ALBERT W., 274.

BACHMAN, SIMON, see Alexander Berkman.
BAKER, GEORGE F., 209, 274, 316.
BALTIMORE & OHIO RAILWAY, 52, 277.
BARRON, CHARLES W., 275.
BARUCH, BERNARD M., 319-22.
BEAL, MR., 244.
BEITLER, ANNA, (Wife of Henry Overholt), 5-6.
BENEFACTIONS AND BEQUESTS, 343-55.
BELGIAN RELIEF FUND, 315.
BERKMAN, ALEXANDER, 135-9, 142, 144-5, 176, 188.
BESSEMER ORE, 187-8.
BIRTH OF H. C. FRICK, 11.
BISPHAM, GEORGE T., 243.
BLACKBURN, WILLIAM W., 103.
BLAINE, JAMES G., 97, 146.
BLAIR, WILLIAM G., 25.
BLISS, CORNELIUS N., 279, 298.
BOARD OF PARDONS, 176.
BONAPARTE, C. J., Attorney General, 306, 311.
BOPE, HENRY B., 103.
BORNTRAEGER, HENRY W., 103.
BOSWORTH, MR., 233.
BOYHOOD OF H. C. FRICK, 12-28.
BRADDOCK FIELD, National Guards at, 133.
BRANDEGEE, SEN. F. B., 325.
BRASHEAR, JOHN A., 346-50.

BRASHEAR, MRS. JOHN A., 350.
BRIDGE, JAMES H., quoted, 77-8, 122-3, 230.
BRYAN, WILLIAM JENNINGS, 294.
BUCKS COUNTY MILITIA, 5.
BUFFINGTON, JUDGE JOSEPH, 346.
BURLEIGH, CLARENCE, 243.
BYERS, A. M., 191.
BYERS, J. FREDERICK, 191.

CAMERON, SEN. DONALD, 292-3.
C. G. C. Co. & HUTCHINSON, 80.
CAPITAL AND LABOR, 147, 161-2.
CAPITALIST, H. C. FRICK, a, 269-88.
CARNEGIE, ANDREW, 74-108, 127, 139, 148-268, 271, 273, 296, 358.
CARNEGIE, MRS. ANDREW, 88, 89.
CARNEGIE BROTHERS & CO., LTD., 77-8, 87, 93, 97, 100-2, 240.
CARNEGIE COMPANY, THE, 257-9.
CARNEGIE PHIPPS & CO., 97-8, 101-2, 106, 219.
CARNEGIE STEEL CO., History of — by J. H. Bridge, 77-8, 122-3, 230.
CARNEGIE STEEL CO., LTD., 102-5, 124, 133-4, 140-1, 151, 155, 173, 175-210, 218-57, 291.
CARNEGIE, THOMAS, 76-9, 83.
CARNEGIE, MRS. WILLIAM, 74-5.
CARTER, SEN. THOMAS H., 157.
CHASE NATIONAL BANK, 344.
CHICAGO & NORTHWESTERN RAILWAY, 277, 281.
CHILDS, MISS ADELAIDE, see Mrs. H. C. Frick.
CHILDS, ASA P., 73.
CHILDS, MRS. ASA P., 88.
CHILDS, MISS MARTHA H., 88.
CHILDS, OTIS H., 103, 125.
CLARK, E. L., 100.
CLARKSON, JAMES S., 157.
CLAY, HENRY, 11.
CLEMSON, MR., 216, 221, 233, 255.
CLEVELAND, PRESIDENT GROVER, 146, 157, 178.
CLEWS & CO., HENRY, 46.
COKE, Beginning Business in, 29-43.
COLEMAN, WILLIAM, 77.
COMMERCIAL TRUST COMPANY OF PHILADELPHIA, 278, 280.
CONGRESSIONAL INVESTIGATING COMMITTEE, 107, 205-7, 243-5.

377

Index

CONNELLSVILLE COKE, 50-1, 53, 62, 65, 72.
CONTINENTAL CONGRESS, 2.
COOKE & CO., Failure of Jay, 46-7.
COREY, JAMES B., 42-3, 66.
COREY, W. E., 275, 299.
CORTELYOU, GEORGE B., 298.
CORTISSOZ, ROYAL, 332-5.
CUMMINS, SENATOR, 282.
CURRY, HENRY M., 103, 105, 171, 216, 248.
CUYLER, T. DE WITT, 282.
CYCLOPS MILL, 213.

DALE, RICHARD C., 243.
DALZELL, SCOTT & GORDON, 243.
DAVIDSON, DANIEL, 63-4.
DAVIDSON, DR. WILLIAM M., 348-9.
DEATH OF H. C. FRICK, 375.
DEMPSEY, HUGH, 175.
DICK, SAMUEL B., 198.
DILLON, PATRICK R., 103.
DIXON, DR., 58-9.
DOLAN, THOMAS, 157.
DUQUESNE STEEL COMPANY, 100.
DUQUESNE WORKS, 110, 165, 172, 175.

EARL, E. T., 275.
EDGAR THOMSON WORKS, 77, 110, 165, 172, 177.
EDMUNDS, GEORGE F., 293.
EDUCATIONAL FUND COMMISSION, 345-9.
EDUCATIONAL INSTITUTIONS, Gifts to, 344-5, 350.
EIGHTH PENNSYLVANIA REGIMENT, 2-3.
ELKINS ACT, 301.
ELKINS, STEPHEN B., 149, 153-7.
EQUITABLE LIFE ASSURANCE SOCIETY, 278-80, 299.
EQUITABLE TRUST COMPANY OF NEW YORK, 280.
EQUITY SUIT against the C. S. Co., Ltd., by H. C. Frick, 243.
ESCH, JOHN J., 282.

FERGUSON, E. M., 64, 78-9, 87.
FERGUSON, WALTON, 78-9, 87.
FIFTH AVENUE RESIDENCE, 362.
FIRST NATIONAL BANK OF NEW YORK, 316.
FISK & HATCH, 46.
FINAL DRAMATIC BREAK between H. C. Frick and Andrew Carnegie, 227-36.
FLEMING, JOHN C., 103.
FLOWER, GOVERNOR ROSWELL P., 209.

FLINN, WILLIAM, 364.
FOREIGN RELATIONS, Committee on, 317.
FOSTER, JOHN W., 148.
FRANKLIN NATIONAL BANK OF PHILADELPHIA, 278, 280.
FREE TRADE, 146-7.
FREER MUSEUM, 334.
FRENCH ARTISTS, Families of Disabled, 316.
FRICK AND COMPANY, 36-7, 40-3, 48-51, 56-66.
FRICK BUILDING, PITTSBURGH, 270, 355.
FRICK, MRS. CHILDS, 373.
FRICK COKE COMPANY, THE H. C., 78-92, 102, 180, 185, 199, 203-4, 212, 221-9, 233-7, 246, 256.
FRICK COLLECTION, 331-43.
FRICK, CONRAD, 1-2.
FRICK, DANIEL, 4, 12.
FRICK, GEORGE, 4.
FRICK, MISS HELEN C., 202.
FRICK, HENRY CLAY, Ancestry, 1-11; Birth, 11; Boyhood, 12-28; Schooldays, 13-19; Starts to work, 19; Interest in reading, 21, 70, 364; Games played, 22; Attends Otterbein College, 14-15, 23; Goes to work in Pittsburgh, 24; Typhoid Fever, 27; Enters Overholt Distillery as bookkeeper, 27; Beginning Business in Coke, 29-43; Frick & Co. organized, 36; Rechristened "H. C. Frick & Co.", 64; Reorganized as "The H. C. Frick Coke Co.", 78; First loans from T. Mellon & Sons, 35, 38-43; A Triumph of Faith and Courage, 44-64; Death of Grandmother, 58; Inflammatory Rheumatism, 58-64; Panic of 1873, 44-66; Interlude, 67-75; First holiday in Europe, 71-2; Meets Miss Adelaide Childs, 73; Marriage, 74; First meeting with Andrew Carnegie, 74; Enter the Carnegies, 76-92; Coke Strike of 1887, 83-6; Resigns as Pres. of Coke Co., 85; Offers to sell his interest in Coke Co., 87; Takes his family to Europe (1887), 88-9; Visits Andrew Carnegie in Scotland, 89; Reelected President of Coke Co., 89; Coke strikes of 1889 and 1890, 90-2; "The Man" in Steel, 93-105; Chairman of Carnegie Bros. & Co., 93; Acquisition of Duquesne Steel Co., 100;

378

Index

Steel Company reorganized as Carnegie Steel Co., Ltd., 102; Increases his interest in steel, 103-5; Chairman of Carnegie Steel Co., Ltd., 105; Homestead Strike, 106-86; Birth of Son, Henry Clay, Jr., 129; Attempted Assassination, 136-45; Death of infant son, 141; Politics, 146-59; "The Laird" and "the Man," 160-74; Victory's Cost and Gain, 175-86; Visits Cluny Castle, 183; Mr. & Mrs. Carnegie visit Frick Home, 183; Oliver and Frick, 187-99; Moore Syndicate, 200-17; Receives his Resignation, 218-26; Sale of Peter's Creek land, 218-20; Mr. Carnegie must apologize, 219-20; Final Dramatic Break, 227-36; Wins the Fight, 237-57; Iron-clad agreement, 238-57; Brings Equity Suit against Carnegie Steel Co., Ltd., 243; U.S. Steel Corporation, 258-68; Moves to New York, 269; A Capitalist, 269-88; Public Affairs, 289-312; Union Steel Company, 273; Director in various Railway Cos., 277, 281; Equitable Life Assurance Soc., 278-80, 299; The Patriot, 313-30; An Art Collector, 331-43; Paintings purchased, 337-43; Benefactions and Bequests, 344-55; Personality, 356-75; Music and the Theatre, 363; Choice of books and newspapers, 364; Declines Honorary Degrees, 370; Made Fellow in Perpetuity of Metropolitan Museum, 370; Life Trusteeship of Princeton, 370; Masonic Lodges, 370-1; Religion, 371; Last Illness, 374-5; Death, 375.
FRICK, MRS. HENRY CLAY, (Miss Adelaide Childs), 73-4, 88, 140, 143, 169.
FRICK, HENRY CLAY, JR., Birth, 129, Death, 141.
FRICK, HENRY CLAY, 2ND, 372-3.
FRICK, JOHANN NICHOLAS, 1, 3, 6.
FRICK, JOHN, 2.
FRICK, JOHN W., 4, 10, 23, 32-5, 40.
FRICK, MRS. JOHN W., 4, 10-13, 35, 38, 40.
FRICK, MISS MARIA O., 11, 27, 30-1.
FRICK, Swiss family of, 1.
FULLER, DR., 58-9.

GARDNER, CONGRESSMAN, 207.
GARY, ELBERT H., 245, 260-8, 273-4, 303-9, 311, 319.
GATES, JOHN W., 293.
GAYLEY, MR., 216, 221, 233, 255.
GLADSTONE, MR. & MRS. LINCOLN, 96.
GOLD NOTE SYNDICATE, 315.
GOLDMAN, EMMA, 136, 145.
GOLF, Interest in, 359-62.
GOMPERS, SAMUEL, 132, 176.
GOOD TEMPLARS, INDEPENDENT ORDER OF, 21.
GRANDCHILDREN, 372-3.
GRANT, PRESIDENT ULYSSES S., 44, 46, 357.
GRAY, COL. JOSEPH H., 117-20.
GRONNA, SEN. ASLE J., 317.

HARDING, PRESIDENT WARREN G., 292.
HARRIMAN, EDWARD H., 279, 298.
HARRISON, PRESIDENT BENJAMIN, 146, 149, 151, 156-59.
HEINDE, CAPT., 117, 119-20.
HIGH, REV. J. C., 21.
HILLES, CHARLES D., 310.
HINES, WALKER D., 281-8.
HOFFMAN, J. OGDEN, 103.
HOMESTEAD, 106-86, 188, 294.
HOWES & MACY, 46.
HUGHES, CHARLES EVANS, 299, 311-12.
HYDE, JAMES H., 278-80, 299.
HYLAN, MAYOR JOHN F., 365.

ILLINOIS STEEL COMPANY, 184, 202, 293.
INGALLS, MELVILLE E., 279.
INSTITUTE OF MINING & METALLURGICAL ENGINEERS, 196.
INTERLUDE, 67-75.
INTERSTATE COMMERCE COMMISSION, 300-1.
IRON-CLAD AGREEMENT, 238-57.
ISTHMIAN CANAL COMMISSION, 298.
IVES, BRAYTON, 279.

JACKSON, PRESIDENT ANDREW, 8.
JEFFERSON, PRESIDENT THOMAS, 162.
JOHNSON, JOHN G., 243, 249.
JOHNSON MUSEUM, 333-4.
JONES, MR., 96.
JONSON, BEN, 357.

KEENE, JAMES R., 271.
KELLOGG, FRANK B., 307-9.
KLINE, CAPT., 117.
KLOMAN BROTHERS, 213.
KNIGHTS OF LABOR, 83, 108, 175-6.
KNOX, PHILANDER C., 290-2, 307, 310-11, 317, 326, 328-9.

Index

Knox & Reed, Messrs., 117, 233, 243, 249.

Labor and Capital, 147.
Labor, Knights of, 83, 108, 175-6.
La Follette, Sen. Robert M., 317.
"Laird" and the "Man," The, 160-74.
Lane, Sen. Harry, 317.
Lauder, George, 103, 105, 152, 158, 165, 169-72, 203, 205, 212, 221-3, 231, 233, 241.
League of Nations, 324, 327-30.
Ledyard, Lewis Cass, 303-5, 351.
Leishman, John G. A., 103, 105, 137-8, 142, 171, 185.
Lenox Library, 270.
Liberty Loans, 316-17.
Lincoln, Abraham, 9.
Literature, H. C. Frick's interest in, 21, 70, 364.
Lovejoy, Francis T. F., 103, 105, 203, 216-17, 221, 241, 247-9, 255.
Lynch, Mr., 233-4.

McAdoo, William G., 281.
McCleary, Sheriff, 117, 123, 129-31.
McCook, Willis F., 243.
McCormick, Sen. J. Medill, 329.
McEldowney, Mr., 316, 317.
Mackay, Col. Aeneas, 2.
McKinley Bill, 147, 294, 297.
McKinley, President William, 290-1, 294.
Macrum & Carlisle, 25.
"Man" in Steel, The, 93-105.
Markle, Capt. C. C., 52, 59, 62.
Markle, Cornelia, (Mrs. Abraham Tinstman), 60.
Martin, Matilda, J., (2nd wife of Daniel Frick), 4.
Martin, Sen. Thomas S., 317.
Masonic Lodges, 370-1.
Mellon, Andrew, 38.
Mellon, Andrew W., 69-73, 180, 186, 256, 265, 269-70, 273, 289-90, 293, 324, 326-29.
Mellon National Bank of Pittsburgh, 278, 281.
Mellon, Richard, 71.
Mellon & Sons, Thomas, 35, 48, 54.
Mellon, Judge Thomas, 38-43, 47, 54, 66, 69-70, 289.

Mennonites, 5, 9.
Mercantile Company of New York, 280.
Metropolitan Museum of Art, 370.
Milholland, John E., 150-3, 156.
Miller, Catherine, (1st wife of Daniel Frick), 4.
Moore Brothers, 207.
Moore & Schley, 302-6.
Moore, Judge W. H., 204-15.
Moore Syndicate, 204-15.
Moreland, Mr., 233, 255.
Morgan, Col. A. S. M., 29, 60.
Morgan & Co., A. S. M., 43, 59-60.
Morgan, J. P., 261-8, 271-5, 302-6.
Morgan & Co., J. P., 258.
Morgan Syndicate, 95.
Morrison, Thomas, 99, 101, 195, 216 221, 233, 255.
Morse, J. C., 135, 293.
Morton, Levi P., 148.
Most, John, 136.
Mount Pleasant Water Co., 87.
Myers, Joseph, 33-4.

Nash, Augnis, (Widow of Martin Overholt), 5.
Nash, William, 5.
National Bank of the Commonwealth, 46.
National City Bank of New York, 278, 281.
National Guards of Pennsylvania, 131-2.
National Tube Company, 258-9.
New, John C., Consul General, 149-56.
Newspapers, Selection of, 364.
New York Central Railway, 46.
Nordrum, Capt., 120.
Norfolk and Western Railway, 277.
Norrie Options, 194.
Norris, Senator, 317.
North Chicago Rolling Mill Co., 87.
Northern Pacific Railway, 46.

Oates, Chairman, 113.
Observatory at Western University, 349.
O'Donnell, Hugh, 111-12, 118, 122, 148-56.
Oliver and Frick, 187-99.
Oliver, Henry W., 188-99.

Index

OLIVER IRON MINING CO., 188, 193, 197, 199.
O'MARA, SUPERINTENDENT, 143.
OTTERBEIN COLLEGE, 14, 23.
OVERHOLT, ABRAHAM, 4, 6-9, 13, 16, 27-8, 35, 38, 40, 276, 345.
OVERHOLT & CO., ABRAHAM, 2, 7, 36, 48.
OVERHOLT, ANNA, 27.
OVERHOLT, ANNA BEITLER, (Wife of Henry Overholt), 5-6.
OVERHOLT, AUGNIS, (Widow of Martin Overholt), 5.
OVERHOLT, BENJAMIN, 34.
OVERHOLT, CHRISTIAN, 6-8.
OVERHOLT, CHRISTIAN S., 19, 23-4, 31, 35, 58-9.
OVERHOLT, ELIZABETH, (Mrs. John W. Frick), 4, 10-13, 35, 38, 40.
OVERHOLT, ELIZABETH S., (Wife of Christian Overholt), 7.
OVERHOLT ESTATE, 35.
OVERHOLT, HENRY, (Son of Martin), 5-7.
OVERHOLT, HENRY, (Son of Henry and Anna), 6-7.
OVERHOLT, HENRY S., 27.
OVERHOLT, ISAAC, 13.
OVERHOLT, JOHN S. R., 30-1, 36-7, 40.
OVERHOLT, KATHERINE, (Wife of Christian S. Overholt), 23.
OVERHOLT, MARIA O. FRICK, (Mrs. John S. R. Overholt), 11, 27, 30-1.
OVERHOLT, MARIA S., (Wife of Abraham Overholt), 7, 9-11, 24, 27, 57-8.
OVERHOLT, MARTIN, 1, 4, 5.
OVERHOLT, MARTIN S., 19, 23, 31, 35.
OVERHOLT, SARAH, 6.
OVERHOLT, SUSANNA, 5-6.

PAINTINGS PURCHASED BY H. C. FRICK, 337-43.
PALMER, WILLIAM P., 103.
PANIC OF 1873, 44-66.
PARDONS, BOARD OF, 176.
PARK, D. E., 100.
PARK, WILLIAM G., 100.
PATTERSON, ALFRED, 64.
PATTISON, GOV. ROBERT E., 129-33.
PAXSON, CHIEF JUSTICE, 125.
PAYNE, COL. OLIVER H., 303.
PEACOCK, ALEXANDER R., 103, 203, 216, 221.
PEARSON, REV. DR., 27.

PENKERT NIHILISTS, 136.
PENN, WILLIAM, 1.
PENN HOTEL, WILLIAM, 355.
PENNSYLVANIA RAILROAD, 50, 76, 95, 97, 197, 277, 281-2.
PEPPER, SENATOR, 329.
PERSONALITY OF H. C. FRICK, 356-75.
PHILLIPS, DR., 5, 8-9.
PHIPPS, HENRY, JR., 76, 78, 84-6, 89, 93-5, 98, 103-5, 152, 158, 165, 170-1, 203, 205-17, 221, 231-2, 240-2, 247-57.
PHIPPS, LAWRENCE C., 103, 105, 216, 218, 221, 255.
PHOEBE BRASHEAR CLUB, 348.
PINKERTON GUARDS, 114-16, 118-23.
PINKERTON, ROBERT A., 114-15.
PITTSBURGH, BESSEMER & LAKE ERIE RAILROAD, 198.
PITTSBURGH, SHENANGO & LAKE ERIE RAILROAD, 198.
PITTSBURGH STEAMSHIP CO., 199.
POLDI-PEZZOLI, 334.
POLITICS, 146-59.
POTTER, JOHN A., 109-10, 117, 119-20, 125, 134.
POWDERLY, T. V., 176.
PRIDE'S CROSSING, 269, 319, 346.
PRINCE, FREDERICK H., 198.
PRINCETON UNIVERSITY, 344-5, 369-70.
PRINCETONIAN, THE DAILY, 369-70.
PROTECTION, 146-7, 296-7.
PUBLIC AFFAIRS, 289-312.
PYNE, MOSES T., 345.

QUAKERS, 5.
QUAY, SEN. M. S., 157, 292-4.

READING RAILROAD CO., 277, 281.
RED CROSS, 317.
REDMOND, GEORGE F., 273.
REED, SEN. JAMES A., 373.
REED, JUDGE JAMES H., 207, 243-4.
REID, E. H., 63.
REID, WHITELAW, 148-56, 158-9.
RELIGION, 371.
RESIGNATION, H. C. FRICK receives his, 218-26.
RIPLEY, E. P., 365.
RIST, JOSEPH, 29-31, 36-7, 40, 48, 60.
ROBERTS, MR., 95.
ROCKEFELLER, JOHN D., 188-99, 261-68, 309, 361.

381

Index

Rockefeller, John D., Jr., 263.
Rodgers, Capt., 117, 120.
Roosevelt, President Theodore, 292, 298-301, 305-10, 313, 359.
Root, Elihu, 306.

St. Peter's Episcopal Church, Pittsburgh, 355.
Salvation Army, 355, 371.
Sargent, Prof., 357.
Schallenberger, Lloyd, 23.
Schoonmaker, Sylvanus O., 150, 270, 317.
Schwab, Charles M., 99, 177, 181, 195-6, 203, 216, 218, 221-2, 231-2, 235, 241-2, 247, 249, 251, 255-7, 259-61.
Scotch and Irish Settlers, 2, 38.
Scott, Thomas A., 50.
Sherman Law, 301.
Simpson, James H., 103.
Singer, William H., 103, 105, 216, 221.
Snowden, Maj.-Gen. George R., 131.
Spring House, The Little, 10-11.
Standard Mines Property, 87.
Standard Oil Company, 304, 307-9.
Stanley, Chairman, 205-6, 311.
Stauffer, Rev. Abraham, 7.
Stauffer, Elizabeth, (Wife of Christian Overholt), 7.
Stauffer, Rev. John, 7.
Stauffer, Maria, (Wife of Abraham Overholt), 7, 9-11, 24, 27, 57-8.
Stillman, James, 365.
Stone, Senator, 317.
Strikes (1887) 83-6; (1889 & 1890) 90-2; (Homestead) 106-86.
Swank, Mr., 297.

Taft, President William H., 292, 309-10, 325, 327, 361.
Tariff Bill, New, 296-7.
Tennessee Coal & Iron Co., 302-6.
Thaw, William, 349.
Thornton, Arthur, 133-4.
Tinstman, Abraham O., 27, 29-31, 34, 36-7, 40, 48, 57, 60, 63.
Tinstman, Mrs. Abraham O., 60, 63.
Tinstman, Jacob O., 32, 35, 57.
Triumph of Faith and Courage, 44-64
Trusts, Warfare on, 302-4.

Union Arcade Building, Pittsburgh, 355.
Union Iron Mills Co., 213.
Union Pacific Railroad, 44, 277, 281.
Union Steel Company, 273.
Union Trust Co. of Pittsburgh, 278, 281, 316.
United Coal & Coke Co., 87.
United States Steel Corporation, 196, 214, 238, 258-68, 271, 273, 281, 303-4, 306, 310-11, 319-22.
United War Work, 324.

Van Buren, President Martin, 9.
Vanderbilt, George W., 270.
Vandevort, John W., 103, 247.
Vardaman, Sen. J. K., 317.
Voight, Schoolmaster, 13-14.

Walker, John, 84-6, 89, 180, 196, 219, 230-1, 233-4, 236, 246.
Wallace Collection, 332, 334.
Walter, J. Bernard, 196.
Wanamaker, John, 149, 153-7.
War against Germany, Declaration of, 317.
War Industries Board, 319-22.
Washington, George, 2, 231.
Watson, D. T., 243.
Wayne, General, 3.
Western Union, 46.
Western University, 349.
Weihe, President, 123.
Whalen, Grover A., 366-8.
Whig Party, 9, 11.
Whitney, Mr., 47.
Whitney, A. R., 227, 230, 241, 256.
Wickersham, George W., 311.
Will and Bequests, 352-3.
Wilson, Andrew Carnegie, 234, 246.
Wilson Tariff, 182.
Wilson, President Woodrow, 313-14, 318-22, 325, 327.
Wood, General Leonard, 326.
Wooster, College of, 350.
Wrigley, Superintendent, 134.

Young Men's Christian Assn., 371.
Young Women's Christian Assn., 371.